LEGISLATIVE THEATRE

Legislative Theatre is the latest and most remarkable stage in the unique Augusto Boal project. It is an attempt to use theatre within a political system to create a truer form of democracy. It is an extraordinary experiment in the potential of theatre to affect social change.

At the heart of Boal's method of Forum Theatre is the dual meaning of the verb 'to act': to perform, and to take action. In this book Boal creates new, theatrical, and truly revolutionary ways of involving everyone in the democratic process.

This book includes:

- a full explanation of the genesis and principles of *Legislative Theatre*

- a description of the process in operation in Rio

- Boal's essays, speeches and lectures on popular theatre, Paulo Freire, cultural activism, the point of playwriting, and much else besides.

Augusto Boal is a theatre director, dramatist, theorist, writer and teacher. He is the founder of the international movement 'Theatre of the Oppressed' and was Vereador (Member of the Legislative Chamber) for Rio de Janeiro from 1993 to 1996. He is the author of *Theatre of the Oppressed, Games for Actors and Non-Actors*, and *Rainbow of Desire*. He lives in Rio de Janeiro.

Adrian Jackson is Associate Director of the London Bubble Theatre Company, Artistic Director of Cardboard Citizens, and a freelance director and teacher.

LEGISLATIVE THEATRE

Using performance to make politics

Augusto Boal

TRANSLATED BY ADRIAN JACKSON

CORAGEM DE SER FELIZ

'Have the courage to be happy'

ROUTLEDGE

London and New York

First published 1998 by Routledge
11 New Fetter Lane, London EC4P 4EE

Simultaneously published in the USA and Canada
by Routledge
29 West 35th Street, New York, NY 10001

© 1998 Augusto Boal; translation © 1998 Adrian Jackson

Typeset in Janson by
J&L Composition Ltd, Filey, North Yorkshire
Printed and bound in Great Britain by
TJ International Ltd, Padstow, Cornwall

British Library Cataloguing in Publication Data
A catalogue record for this book is available from the British Library

Library of Congress Cataloging in Publication Data
A catalogue record for this book has been requested

ISBN 0–415–18240–9 (hbk)
     0–415–18241–7 (pbk)

Contents

THE 'NO-ONE HERE IS AN ASS!' BOOK

Preface

This is a BETA version . . . an interactive book . . . It
relates the first five years of an unfinished experiment . . .
this is a work in the making . . . and it is
still growing . . .

BUT . . . WHAT IS A BETA version?

When a new computer software program is released while still in an
experimental stage, it is known as a Beta version. The objective is to
collect opinions, information and suggestions from experienced
practitioners with a view to preparing a first definitive edition of
the same program. Since at the time of writing we are still in the
middle of the Legislative Theatre experiment, in the thick of it,
everything presented or posited here remains at a stage of development and is open to correction. Collaborate with us!

How to read this book*

This book is very easy to read, but you need to be acquainted with its *Instructions for Use*. This is not a book like any other: it is a work in progress, and that progress depends on you.

It is a kaleidoscopic book, covering many contradictory fields, written at different moments in my life, in different countries, in different languages, in different mental and emotional states, in different states of hope. Hope and despair, and then hope again!

I believe that it should not be read from start to finish, like a fascinating novel – which it isn't! – but that each reader should invent their own path through it.

Find your own way according to your particular personal needs, preferences, curiosities or desires. Here are some clues:

IF YOU WANT TO KNOW . . . how I was elected legislator when I really did not want to be, go to page 6 and read 1 'History: The Theatre of the Oppressed returns to its roots – Brazil and politics', in which I tell the story of my several unsuccessful attempts not to become an exile in my own country, after so many exiles abroad!

OR, if you want to know how I was not elected legislator when I really wanted to go on being one, then go to page 113 and read the last pages of my letter to Richard Schechner, which is a sort of postscript to this period.

* *Translator's note*: This user's guide was written in English by Boal. In order to give a flavour of the man, I have merely tidied it up.

ix

OR, if you want to know what's next, what I have in mind right now (along with the many others who are involved with me and with this project), what we are trying to invent, our dream, go to page 118 and read iii 'Symbolism in Munich', including the embryonic experiences of Munich and Paris and London, still just sparks which have yet to catch fire, hints of future possibilities. And remember the words of the wise old lady: 'This is symbolic, yes, but symbolic of something that may happen!' For my part, I always keep that in mind. I know very well that theatre cannot be much more than that: and I want it to be ALL THAT!

IF YOU WANT TO KNOW . . . what our propositions were, what we were up to when we started to work at the Chamber, go to page 19 and read 2 'The Proposition: Theatre as politics and transitive democracy as theatre'.

OR, if you want to know more about the city of Rio de Janeiro than you would find in a tourist guidebook – about its social make-up, about real wild lions used as guard dogs and drug-dealers engaging in open warfare in Rio's slums; about rehearsing a play to the accompaniment of the sound of machine-guns, about the kidnapping of humans and pets, racehorses and stolen cars, etc.; if you want to know where the Legislative Theatre experiment was initiated, go to page 24 and read 3 'The Context: 'How and where is this experiment being carried out?'

OR, if you want to get a general idea of the atmosphere in the Chamber of *Vereadors* (the legislative power of Rio de Janeiro, also known as 'The Gilded Cage'), if you want to know about the conflict that sometime exists between sound morals and pragmatic politics, go first to page 97 and then go directly to the section of the book which is appropriately entitled 'No-one here is an ass' and read from page 125, where I tell true stories (I swear they are true!) about my interventions at the Chamber. The original form of these stories was speeches I made at the rostrum; for this book, I have made readable versions of some of them, ridding the text of all the pomp of the chamber, all the 'Your Excellencies', 'Noble Colleagues' etc., and also of any asides or incidental remarks. They now look more like chronicles.

IF YOU WANT TO READ . . . about who our partners were, and the relations between our aims and theirs,

where theatre and society *really* met, go to page 39 and read
4 'The Structure'.

OR, if you want to know more about the way we
work read The Formation of the Nucleus, page 45 (a description
of our workshops, rehearsals and shows!).

AND, if you want to know more about the effect that this experiment
has had on its participants, about their emotions and thoughts, go to
page 86 and read 6 'The Show and the Community'.

IF YOU WANT TO KNOW . . .

about our tools, the instruments of our work, of necessity simple and
efficacious, for instance the kind of simple systematic dramaturgy
used by the popular theatre groups, including such considerations as
whether there are certain laws of playwriting which should be
obeyed or simply rules to be applied to the user's best advantage,
or, if you want to know what would be a standard structure for a
Forum-Theatre play, consult 'Dramaturgy', page 53, but don't let
these suggestions act as limitations to your own desires – create your
own style at your own risk! And be aware that this chapter explains
how to start writing for the theatre in a very simple style, which was
adequate for our partners at the time – the presentation may come
across as schematic, but it is nonetheless useful for its original
purposes.

Or, if you want to read one of the plays that were written for
that purpose, go to page 195 and read 15 *'Family.* A playscript'.

OR, if you are interested in our approach to acting,
turn to page 65 and read 'Playing a part';

. . . if you are wondering how our shows look, turn to page 73 and
read 'The image of the scene'.

. . . if you want to know about the problems of doing theatre in the
streets, scaring dogs away etc., turn to page 76 and read 'The
staging';

... if you want to know about the problems related to the voice (when actors lack a few teeth in front) and sound (when buses are louder than lungs), turn to page 84 and read 'Sound and voice'.

IF YOU ARE LOOKING FOR RESULTS ... if you want to know right away whether or not there was any kind of happy ending to this saga, and what sort of laws were approved by the Legislative Theatre process, skip to the Appendices on page 106.

IF YOU WANT A WARNING ... about the possible violent consequences of doing this kind of work in a country like Brazil, go to page 34.

IF YOU WANT TO READ ... an essay I wrote more than 35 years ago about categories of popular theatre, during those wild years of the Vietnam war, hippy movements, 'make love not war', lysergic acid, sexual revolution, flowers, handicraft, patchwork pants and perfumes, the guerrilla movement in Brazil, the Cuban Missile Crisis, Khruschev's shoes at the United Nations, then go bravely straight to page 211 and remember when it was written - the language goes with those, let's say, 'energetic' times.

IF YOU WANT TO KNOW WHAT I THINK ABOUT:

TV	go to page 79
Paulo Freire	go to page 126
streetchildren	go to page 153
chicken thieves	go to page 133
globalisation	go to page 250
Romeo and Juliet	go to page 164

But, above all, let us know what you think about this book and the experiment it describes, about the possibilities of developing it in other countries, about what you yourself might be able to do !

This book talks about a very specific reality, in the southern hemisphere. Geographically, politically and economically the *southern hemisphere*! Maybe it will differ greatly from its readers' realities, maybe it will not seem different at all. Anyway, it may be useful to you, if you are also involved with aesthetic politics in an artistic and ethical way, or simply curious about it.

DO AS YOU WISH . . . you can even read the book from end to end, I don't mind. The important thing, however, is that this is an interactive book: after your first reading, send your impressions, comments, suggestions, additions, propositions, desires to: Augusto Boal, Rua Francisco Otaviano, 185/41, CEP 22080–040, Ipanema-Arpoador, Rio de Janeiro RJ, Brazil.

This book is dedicated to those people who made this experience possible, especially Barbara Santos, Claudette Felix, Helen Sarapeck, Geo Britto, Olivar Bendelak, Sonia Cristina Costa and Luiz Mario Bheneken.

A.B.
Rio de Janeiro, 1998

The
Legislative
Theatre
Book

DOING IS THE BEST WAY OF SAYING
José Martí, poet

Prologue
Monologue and dialogue

The scene takes place in a psychiatric hospital, in England. My friend Tim Wheeler was the *Joker* – the title we use for a cultural animator in the Theatre of the Oppressed. He was about to start a series of workshops with a new group made up of patients from the hospital as well as some of their nurses and doctors. He wanted to start with a short description of the origins of the Greek theatre, whose traditions we are heir to. And he explained that, in the beginning, the people sang and danced, all together in the street, in the open air: this was the time of the famous Dithyrambic Songs – it was not yet theatre. One day, along came a man called Thespis, and he created the Protagonist. The latter stood apart from the chorus and spoke alone. Some of the time the chorus would speak, in unison, and at other times the Protagonist would speak, on his own.

'When Thespis invented the Protagonist, he invented the monologue', said Tim, the Joker. 'Prior to this, everyone sang and danced – they were the chorus. With Thespis, the monologue came into being: one person talking on his own. When a person is speaking on their own in the theatre, or anywhere else for that matter, we call it monologue. Does everyone understand?'

Everyone had understood this clear, simple explanation. The Joker continued the first lesson, encouraged by the response: 'Then Aeschylus comes along, the first Greek tragedian, and he invents the Deuteragonist, the second actor. And when he added this second actor, he invented dialogue. So then, what is dialogue?'

Silence. Tim wanted to encourage participation from the group in this new workshop – interactivity – and he asked the question again, in greater detail: 'When one person is speaking on their own, that is a monologue, they are doing a monologue. So what is a dialogue?'

More silence. The Joker resorted to visual aids: 'A monologue is when one person, a single person, is talking on his or her own . . .', and he held up the index finger of his right hand. 'One person only!

So dialogue is . . .? So what is a dialogue . . .? A dialogue is when . . .?' And this time he held up two fingers.

'I know, I know!' answered one of the patients eagerly.

'So, tell us. What is dialogue?'

'It's when there are two people talking on their own . . .'

This very simple story has stayed with me, imprinted on my mind. I always ask myself whether the patient had misunderstood or whether with his own particular brand of lucidity, he actually put his finger on a greater truth?

In reality, does dialogue exist, ever? Or is the contrary the case – that what we think is dialogue never actually goes beyond parallel or overlapping monologues? Monologues between countries, social classes, races, multiple monologues in the home or in school, conjugal monologues, sexual monologues, all the possible forms of interpersonal monologue – how often do they attain the supreme status of genuine dialogue? Could it be that we merely speak and cease speaking, intermittently, rather than speaking and listening? We know the word we speak, but we do not know what will be heard. What we say is never what is heard.

This theme has preoccupied me ever since – the idea of dialogue . . . or its absence. The Theatre of the Oppressed, in all its various modalities, is a constant search for dialogical forms, forms of theatre through which it is possible to converse, both about and as part of social activity, pedagogy, psychotherapy, politics.

This book relates, in quasi-report form, the most recent experiment of the Theatre of the Oppressed: the Legislative Theatre. The book, like the experiment itself, which is still under way, is unfinished. To finish the book, I need my readers to read it, to analyse, to interact . . . and to write to us with suggestions, critiques, arguments, ideas – all contributions are welcome. And necessary. Without this participation, it will not be possible to make a first full edition of this book, which appears here in a deliberately embryonic form. As a Beta version!

The Theatre of the Oppressed started its development during the cruellest phase of the Brazilian dictatorship; its first manifestation was the Newspaper Theatre. It continued through various dictatorial

Latin American regimes, during which time some of its other forms emerged – Forum Theatre, Invisible Theatre, Image Theatre (1971–1976).

In Europe, from 1976 to 1986, the introspective techniques developed, under the generic title *Rainbow of Desire* (Routledge, 1994), incorporating ways of theatricalising subjectivity.

Now we are back in Brazil: none of our major social and political problems has been solved. It is up to us to try new ways of tackling them. I am a man of the theatre: now that I am directly involved in politics, I use the means at my disposal – the stage! The Legislative Theatre is a new system, a more complex form, since it includes all the previous forms of Theatre of the Oppressed plus others which have a specifically parliamentary application.

I hope that this experiment may be of service, over and above its application to our own mandate – beyond our party, beyond our city, far beyond. I hope it will be useful.

We have already done some experiments in other Brazilian cities (Santo André) and in other countries (Germany and France). These are only in their beginnings.

1 History

The Theatre of the Oppressed returns to its roots – Brazil and politics

For the first time in the history of the theatre, and the history of politics, an entire theatre company enters the Legislature. How did this miracle come about? Coincidence as a category of luck. We must persevere. Our desire, our goal: to go further!

IN 1982, less than a year after coming to power, the French government invited 200 intellectuals from all over the world to a large seminar at the Sorbonne to discuss the nature of the relations between culture and the modern world. Was socialism being instituted in France and, if so, how was this happening?

They were not asking our advice; they wanted us to debate the subject. Among the invitees were various Nobel prize winners, a number of famous artists of the cinema, along with more humble folk, including Darci Ribeiro and myself.

Darci had just been elected Vice Governor of Rio de Janeiro. He was fascinated by the idea of creating Integrated Centres for Popular Education (CIEPS), a project which was, at that time, only at the planning stage. The idea was simple: to enrol as pupils the maximum possible number of children (every child, if it could be done), to keep them in school for as long as possible (the whole day, including breakfast, lunch and supper, if this was achievable), lending them support in every area of their lives: medicine, dentistry, sport and – thank God – cultural animation, including theatre.

That was where I came in, or might have come in, since I had told Darci about the work the Centre of the Theatre of the Oppressed (CTO) was doing – and is still doing, 19 years after its inception – in Paris, working right across France and in various other countries.

The CTO is engaged in the application and development of the methods of the Theatre of the Oppressed, which is founded on the conviction that theatre is the human language *par excellence.* The being becomes human when it discovers theatre. The difference between humans and other animals resides in the fact that we are capable of being theatre. Some of us 'make' theatre – all of us 'are' theatre.

What kind of theatre? The theatre which is, in its most archaic sense, our capacity to observe ourselves in action. We are able to see ourselves seeing! This possibility of our being simultaneously Protagonist and principal spectator of our actions, affords us the further possibility of thinking virtualities, of imagining possibilities, of combining memory and imagination – two indissociable psychic processes – to reinvent the past and to invent the future. Therein resides the immense power with which theatre is endowed. This is the theatre which fascinates me, and the method which I have developed and elaborated over the past 25 years, the Theatre of the Oppressed, tries to systematise these potentialities and render them accessible to and useable by anyone and everyone.

I founded the Paris CTO in 1978, when I was living there and lecturing in the self-same University of the Sorbonne at which we were to participate in the seminar three years later. Since then, this centre has organised numerous courses, seminars, interventions, shows and festivals with community groups. Darci wanted me to do the same thing in the CIEPS, throughout Rio de Janeiro. He extended an invitation to us, to myself and Cecilia Thumim, my wife, and urged us to move back to Brazil.

It was a dream. I had always wanted to go back and live in Brazil, but without abandoning the work I had been doing abroad through so many years of forced exile: five in Buenos Aires (then along came Videla . . .), two in Lisbon (till the Revolution of Carnations withered away . . .) and, finally, in Paris, which is still my second home. I felt welcome in Paris, and the minimum material conditions obtained for me to be able to work in a systematic way.

Had we been able to, we would have said 'yes' and returned to Brazil in time to be present at Darci's official investiture as Vice Governor. However, so many times in the past circumstances had obliged us to pack our bags in a hurry, leaving even essentials behind, that my family and I preferred to do things at a more measured pace.

When we did arrive back in Brazil, with only the bare necessities, it was in the middle of 1986, the end of the mandate, and the next elections were about to take place: Darci was standing for Governor. He kept his promise: he contracted us for six months, so that we could try and see if it would be possible to set up a project in Rio similar to the one which was working so well in France. At that point we did not want a longer contract, since this was only an experiment. In the event of a positive outcome, then of course we would want a long-term contract.

It worked like a dream: we assembled 35 cultural animators from the CIEPS, people who, for the most part, had never done theatre – some had never even been to a play – and did an intensive workshop, demonstrating our exercises, games and techniques of Image Theatre, Forum Theatre and Invisible Theatre. Rosa Luiza Marquez, a professor at the University of San Juan in Puerto Rico, who had worked at the CTO in Paris, came over from the Caribbean to take part in this adventure.

By the end of six weeks we already had a repertoire of five short shows around the issues of most concern to the cultural animators (and their families and neighbours in all the areas we were working in): unemployment, health, housing, sexual violence, incest, the oppression of women, of young people, mental health, drugs etc.

With this repertoire, we initiated a series of presentations in the CIEPS. As the venues for these performances were usually standard municipal school buildings, we soon learnt to construct a 'functional theatre' in the dining rooms, using whatever was to hand: two rows of audience sat on the ground, with the next two rows on seats, one row on tables and, finally, one row perched on chairs on top of tables – when there was a real crowd, another row of audience stood on tables at the back. We arranged a white tarpaulin on the ground, with a sheet by way of cyclorama.

Between 200 and 300 people came to each show; sometimes there were over 400 – students, teachers, students' parents, friends of the teachers, cleaners and kitchen staff, people who lived near the schools. The performance used to open with a brief explanation by the 'Jokers' of the show (myself and Cecilia – Rosa Luisa accompanied us on percussion) – of the uses of theatre and the function of the Theatre of the Oppressed; afterwards, we would do exercises with actors and audience not only as a 'warm-up' but also to establish a degree of theatrical communion – and then we would present the five short scenes which had been created during the workshop. This was the first part of the show.

In the second part we would ask the audience which two or three subjects had most interested them, and this led to the 'foruming' of the relevant two or three scenes: i.e., the theatrical debate which constitutes Forum Theatre, with the improvisation of possible solutions, the intervention of members of the audience, the search for alternatives for an oppressive, unjust, intolerable situation. The audience members would come on stage one at a time, to act out their own ideas on the subject, voicing their thoughts and acting out their opinions theatrically. And, still within the theatrical frame, there would be discussion about what it was possible to do, and these possibilities would be rehearsed. Theatre helping to bring about social transformation.

The Forum shows – apart from the artistic activity which they represented in themselves, the aesthetic pleasure which they offered *per se* – helped the citizens to develop their taste for political discussion (democracy) and their desire to develop their own artistic abilities (popular art). The shows contained precious moments of dialogue, of exchange, of learning, of teaching, of pleasure. These theatrical gatherings came to an end only when we were completely exhausted. But the audience, the spectators, our 'spect-actors' – those who observe (*spectare*, in Latin – to see) in order then to act – they never seemed to tire. They always wanted more.

It was at this time that I began to feel the desire to invent some form of theatre which could channel all the creative energy awakened by Forum Theatre in these men, women and children eager to change the world – their world, perhaps only their small world, their part of the big world – and to use this energy beyond the immediate duration of the show. One could not help feeling that ideas as good as those thrown up in the Forum could usefully be applied in other settings.

Forum Theatre is a reflection on reality and a rehearsal for future action. In the present, we re-live the past to create the future. The spect-actor comes on stage and rehearses what it might be possible to do in real life. Sometimes the solution to the spect-actors' problems depends on themselves, on their own individual desire, their own efforts – but, equally, sometimes the oppression is actually rooted within the law. In the latter case, to bring about the desired change would require a transformation or redrafting of the law: legislation. How could that be done? There ends the power of the theatre. We did not have an answer.

Hamlet says in his famous speech to the actors that theatre is a mirror in which may be seen the true image of nature, of reality.[1] I wanted to penetrate this mirror, to transform the image I saw in it and to bring that transformed image back to reality: to realise the

1. 'Playing, whose end, both at first and now, was and is, to hold as 'twere the mirror up to nature: to show virtue her feature, scorn her own image, and the very age and body of the time his form and pressure.' *Hamlet*, III.2.20–24.

image of my desire. I wanted it to be possible for the spect-actors in Forum Theatre to transgress, to break the conventions, to enter into the mirror of a theatrical fiction, rehearse forms of struggle and then return to reality with the images of their desires. This discontent was the genesis of the Legislative Theatre, in which the citizen makes the law through the legislator. The legislator should not be the person who makes the law, but the person through whom the law is made (by the citizens, of course!).

Seldom have I felt so happy in the theatre. I took enormous pleasure in working with the citizens of Rio, in the suburbs and the nearby towns, São João de Meriti, Duque de Caixas, Nilopolis, Angra dos Reis, and many more, spurring them to go on stage and exercise their theatrical citizenship: stimulating them to discover theatre, and the theatre within themselves, to discover that they were theatre.

We did more than 30 shows, and then the year came to an end. Darci lost the elections. In Rio de Janeiro, the policies adopted by an incoming government tend to destroy everything the previous government was doing. Everything good, that is. The bad things they leave in place. The good things they ruin.

The following year, we still tried to carry on, without the slightest help from the new government, which did not even bother to honour signed contracts. We launched into a second workshop which stopped in the middle. Our last show was dispiriting: we merely showed our pieces to each other. Some actors dropped out because they did not have the money to pay their bus fares . . . it was a disaster.

We tried for private patronage. The big businesses were beginning to use a new law, the so-called 'Incentive for Culture'; in place of part of their tax liabilities they could subsidise theatre, dance or music companies. We went to see them, almost all of them. One company suggested we do some work in their personnel department, using our techniques to help in their staff recruitment. Obviously, we turned the offer down; not for this did we develop the Theatre of the Oppressed. Others made no bones about their lack of enthusiasm for sponsoring a theatre company whose audiences were not part of 'the market'. An oil company has nothing to gain from an audience of passengers of the Central Railway. And then there was the question of image: a silk manufacturer would not want to associate its image with a bunch of scruffy actors. A manufacturer of Italian pasta would feel sadistic offering art to malnourished spectators.

We tried. In vain.

Seeds grow.

Even in arid ground, in dry barren soil. And many Theatre of the Oppressed groups had grown up in every place we had been to, organised by the people who had been the cultural animators.

In 1989, a small group of obstinate survivors of the CIEPS experiment sought me out to propose the creation of a CTO in Rio. An informal body, working from time to time, with internal meetings to study the 'arsenal' (the collection of techniques, games and exercises) and external work when a contract could be obtained.

Informally, we began a new phase – ever-hopeful of better days, believing in promises. The next elections came around and Darci was returned to power but – for reasons which it would be inappropriate to analyse here – his plans no longer coincided with our proposals.

By 1992, having lost the link with the Department of Education and the CIEPs, the CTO was living a pinched existence – a few contracts with the Bank Workers Union, a couple with the small cities of Ipatinga or São Caetano, events like 'Land and Democracy', organised by Betinho,[2] some workshops for the general public and some for people from abroad. Groups came over from Germany and from New York University to study in Rio. After the workshop with the Germans was over – I tell this story to give an idea of the climate we work in – they were on their way back to Rio one night, returning from a visit to the mining towns in the hills, when their bus was ambushed by marauding outlaws and bombarded with stones: a medieval ambush! Fortunately, the driver was an old hand and he put his foot down and everyone got away safely.

Even so, we lived in great hope, which is, as the saying goes, the last thing to die.

It died.

One day we decided to put an end to the Centre, to carry out compassionate euthanasia on our moribund dream. How best might we lay this dream to rest, after its death? We didn't want a sad, tearful burial; we preferred something in the New Orleans style. A musical funeral, a funeral which would have a joyful aspect – a bang not a whimper. We wanted a flamboyant funeral with lots of rhythm and colours and people – and people of all colours, dancing in all rhythms.

By coincidence, 1992 was an election year and elections in Brazil – in marked contrast to many European and North American countries – are an erotic moment in the national life. Elections here always

2. A charismatic HIV/AIDS and human rights activist: he and his two brothers, all haemophilliacs, became HIV positive after having had blood transfusions. He died in August 1997.

have something of carnival about them – carnival is a form of eroticism which transgresses all ideologies. And the electoral campaign here is politicised eroticism, or politics eroticised. The people dance and sing and parade and shout – and do everything under the sun, literally and metaphorically.

We wanted to lay to rest the dream of the CTO by helping either a party or a coalition to realise a larger dream: to change the country. And we went to see the Workers Party, the PT, to offer our collaboration. We were given an attentive hearing. We wanted to take part in the campaign on the streets and in the squares, singing our songs, doing forum theatre on the events of the day, using masks, aestheticising the streets. We wanted to theatricalise the campaign.

Our offer was accepted without reservation, but with one additional element: to make our participation more effective, it would be advantageous if one of us were to present him or herself as a candidate for *vereador* (legislator).

This was unexpected, but we accepted the challenge: we would go away and consider which of us would be most suitable to play the part of candidate. And we returned to our base, happily confident of our new role.

We sat round in a circle talking, trying to choose the best candidate – I sat there, looking carefully at each member of the group, trying to make my own choice. And as I looked at everybody I realised that everybody was looking at me. I was caught completely unawares.

'No, not me! No way can I be the candidate!', I protested. 'I wouldn't be able to do the campaign, I'm always travelling, my schedule is already overloaded, I have agreed commitments, I'd be an absentee candidate. I would never win these elections. It's impossible: there are 1,200 candidates from 22 parties for only 42 seats. No, not me: it would be better if it was someone else.'

They continued to look at me and I continued to resist with bravura, in a mixture of indecision, desire and fear. Till eventually someone asked:

'Who said that we were running to win? The idea is just to take part in the elections, to give the CTO a festive send-off. No-one is asking you to give up your travelling, because no-one has the least expectation of your winning . . .'

I breathed more easily.

'Fine, well, if it's like that . . . if we are not going for a win . . . then I am willing to be the candidate.'

And we relayed our decision to the leadership of the party: I would be our candidate . . . seeing as I did not have the slightest chance of being elected.

We dived head-first into the campaign. Inspired by the task at hand, the small initial group grew. We did various plays, with a new song every day. Every day fresh script was added. We took an active role in the popular movement against the President of the Republic, a champion of corruption whom we helped to remove; we assisted in the campaign of our candidate for mayor, and every day we went out into the streets. When I say 'we' went into the streets, I mean 'they' went into the streets, because more often than not at that time I was on my way to or from the airport.

Our campaign was developing and becoming better known. Photographers and cameramen love images. And so do newspapers – they have an enormous appetite for pictures. One good photo is worth a lot. And our campaign was a source of good photos. For example: in a musical piece we did against the raising of fees for students at the University of Santa Ursula, on the beach at Ipanema, 10 women were dressed as nuns – and they got dressed in their religious habits in the middle of the beach, with bikinis and black garters underneath, showing their legs, in front of the bathers and the photographers. Then a lecturer held a class on the sand, complete with blackboard, school chairs and desks all unusual, theatrical, 'photo opportunities'. Not surprisingly, we began to take up space in the papers. And with this came publicity for my candidature.

Another example: a group of women (mostly teachers), dressed in pinafores with scarves on their heads and carrying pots and pans, paraded through the streets and along the beaches singing a song they had written called: 'Maria Sem Vergonha . . . de ser feliz': 'Agora com Boal, Maria esta total/na rua afinal/em cena teatral./Agora com Bene/Maria e mais mulher/com todo o nosso axe/pro que der e vier.'[3]

As the campaign gathered steam, a few individuals left because they did not want to take part in a party political campaign, but this was offset by the many more who joined us: people who had never given any thought to the idea of making theatre – their considerations were political, they had political goals, either they were already involved in politics or they were simply fed up with the situation in

3. Which translates, with a few liberties, as: 'Maria unashamed . . . of being happy': 'Now with Boal, Maria feels whole, in the street at last, in a theatrical cast. And now with Bene, with our positive energy, she's twice the woman, and ready for anything.'

13

the country – people who welcomed with open arms the opportunity to try this new way of engaging in politics. Or simply believed in me.

Though impoverished, our campaign grew. To give an idea of our poverty and our creativity, our campaign badges were painted by hand, one by one, on beer bottle tops. Papier-mâché hats, with my caricature in harlequin form, were also painted by hand, one by one. Our colours, girl and boy, blue and pink, came ready-dyed on the material we made our banners with – we economised on dye . . . but not on ideas: our campaign sashes were loud, literally and meta-phorically, with bells hanging from ribbons accompanying the demonstrators' voices. We had to be faithful to our slogan: 'Have the courage to be happy'.[4]

4. 'Coragem de ser feliz'.

Our campaign grew much larger than we expected. So much so that one day some leading members of the party called and spoke to me in grave tones:

'Boal, you are running a risk, a serious risk . . .'

So grave was the tone that I took fright. My mind was filled with thoughts of assassination and the like . . . after all we were in Rio de Janeiro . . . that sort of thing is a mere trifle here.

'Risk of what?'

'You run the risk of being elected . . .'

Stupefaction. Me, a *vereador*?! Never! Not because I place a low value on that function – quite the contrary – but because I could not, at my time of life, change professions, habits, direction, methods, everything – I mean to say! I had a whole programme ahead of me – theatre plans – I was not about to suddenly change direction and take up the career of *vereador*, when I was sure that I did not have the right qualities – or the experience – to be a good *vereador*. The party was full of better candidates. Why me of all people?

'No way! If I run the risk of winning, then I am standing down!'

I was categorical! Absolutely categorical!

And I went back to the CTO, related my conversation and communicated my decision: I would stand down. General consterna-tion. It was all going so well. Every day, we were appearing more in the papers, on the television, we were talking on the radio stations. Every day, more people were coming into our campaign, more people wanted to participate, to practise the Theatre of the Oppressed. What a pity . . .

Then someone had an idea: 'Listen Augusto, if you ask me, you are in no danger of winning. But, suppose you did win? Wouldn't that be a good solution?'

'Who for?' I asked angrily, 'Not me!'

We reflected: we had wanted to bury the CTO in a joyful and useful way, but, actually, a burial was not what we really wanted – we wanted the CTO to live, but we did not have the right material conditions for this to be possible. If I was elected as a *vereador*, I would be entitled to contract advisers. As the CTO we needed job security, but our interlocutors, our public, did not have enough money for themselves, let alone enough to pay professional rates for 'Jokers'. Once elected, I would be able to contract all the cultural animators of the CTO and realise our experiment: to go beyond Forum Theatre and invent Legislative Theatre! As the function of *vereadors* is to create laws and to ensure the proper enactment of those that already exist, the people's participation in this process could be achieved by means of theatre: transitive democracy.

Chance and intention had collided: by chance, yes, but more than anything by virtue of our desire, our intense desire, we were now facing the possibility of going further with the Theatre of the Oppressed, of moving beyond simple reflection on reality and rehearsal of the transformation of reality: we were facing the palpable possibility of creating and transforming laws.

For the first time in the history of the theatre and the history of politics, there opened up the possibility of a whole theatre company being elected to a parliament.

Many artists before me had been elected to legislative office (Glenda Jackson, for example, a marvellous actress who became an MP in England), or to executive office, such as Ronald Reagan in the USA (not a good actor, but the holder of an American Equity card – a union card – therefore, *ipso facto*, an actor) or the playwright, Vaclav Havel, who went from prison to occupy the presidency of his country, the Czech Republic. Without forgetting the Italian politician La Cicciolina, star of a form of show business . . . at least she was better at striptease than Erroll Flynn was at duelling: respect!

For all that, I was clear that my case was different: I would not have to give up my previous theatrical activity to start a new life as a parliamentarian. The one would be the extension of the other: anyone who voted for me would know what they were doing – theatre and politics!

And I was also clear that, if elected, I would be able to realise something we had sought from the beginning: ways of making a Forum Theatre performance have practical and visible effects beyond those contained in the show itself. Not merely to rehearse for the future, but to begin to realise it. To try something beyond reflection and rehearsal.

Throughout my life I have been engaged in politics (though not party politics) and I have always been engaged in theatre. This was what seduced me in the proposition: to make 'theatre as politics', instead of simply making 'political theatre', as I had done before.

In reality, I think that I first contemplated the idea of one day becoming a legislator, for a certain length of time, when, in 1991, I received the title of 'Benemeritus Citizen of the State of Rio De Janeiro', at the Assembly of Deputies (MPs). Instead of a normal session, we organised a popular reception at the Chamber, entitled 'Be an MP for Three Minutes', during which representatives of Rio's society had the right to three minutes each in which to propose laws to be enacted: street cleaners, trade union workers, prostitutes, domestic employees, black students, slum dwellers, peasants, intellectuals, doctors, lawyers, journalists, everybody was allowed to take the floor – the session lasted five hours, instead of the usual one and a half!

So seduced was I by the idea of winning that I returned to the lists, back to the hard fight – I went back to the streets, the demonstrations, the shows, the rallies. Back to politics ! We all threw ourselves back into it with renewed courage, with more determination and greater desire to win.

Now I wanted to win and this changed the way I behaved. I felt like Shakespeare's Coriolanus, somewhat ashamed to ask for votes for myself. Sometimes, I couldn't bring myself to mount my own platform. Or, by contrast, I sometimes had an urge to accuse part of the population of stupidity in voting for certain candidates, of basing their choice on looks. It was very difficult to say 'Vote for me!' It seemed like egoism: with so many good candidates . . . I felt as if I was taking someone else's place.

5. A *favela* (shanty town) on the edge of Rio, whose name translates roughly as 'The Hill of Longing'.

One day, a boy from Morro de Saudade[5] asked me for a set of 11 shirts for his football team. I explained that my candidature was honest, that it had a project, that it was different from others he knew of, and he answered me: 'If you give nothing to the people, how do expect people to vote for you? You must have something to give . . .'

It was difficult to explain that whenever the elector accepts a *presentinho*,[6] a bribe, from the candidate, s/he has to pay later. For instance, amongst those sitting in parliament there are the lobbyists for the bus companies, to give only one example, who will always vote in favour of fare increases. The elector ends up paying dearly for presents from politicians!

6. A little present.

Another voter, a woman, wanted me not only to preside over, but to sponsor, a launch of candle-bearing balloons, which are traditionally used in the festival of São João (24 June): call the fire brigade! And all the while offering in return to deliver tens of *favelas* as 'electoral corrals' (the virtually feudal delivery of whole areas into the hands of one candidate, with the effect that no other candidate will be welcome there).

For many people like those we work with today in our community nuclei, it seems only natural for candidates to give tangible gifts, rather than make abstract promises, because it is only in the period leading up to the elections that the people and the politicians get to meet on a daily basis; afterwards they don't meet again till the next elections. There are completely shameless candidates who go as far as giving out sets of false teeth – the upper set before the election, the lower set after, subject to a favourable outcome; in many cases the people who want the dentures still have a few teeth of their own, and as these dentures come in a more or less standard model, the candidate offers the services of a dentist to extract any healthy teeth which are in the way of the false teeth. Others offer wooden legs for amputees and glass eyes for the blind, or sacks of cement and tiles for house-building. One is even in the habit of offering unsigned cheques with the sum filled out; 'I will only sign them if I am elected'. Or half a 100-dollar bill – the other half after the elections. Or, even worse, they give each half to different people living in different parts of the city, people who will never meet after the election.

For many people it is difficult to believe that anyone might want to be *vereador* for a genuine political, aesthetic, social reason. As far as a good part of the population is concerned, politicians are all the same.

Even with these problems, my campaign was creating theatre groups: ecologists, women, university students, black people, all explaining our ethos and our theatrical-political proposition.

Until finally election day came. From early in the morning my campaign officers were already at the entrances to the polling stations, trying for last-minute conversions.

17

We won. Ours was not among the candidatures which got the most votes, but the votes it got were spread right across the whole of Rio de Janeiro: people who knew me only by way of our theatre, our shows. People who believed in us. People who believed in the Theatre of the Oppressed.

On 1 January 1993, I took my seat as one of six PT *vereadors*. That was how our Legislative Theatre experiment began. An experiment which, I hope, will never end.

2 The proposition

Theatre as politics and transitive democracy as theatre

The similarity between the Theatre of the Oppressed (in which spectator is transformed into actor) and the Legislative Theatre (in which citizen is transformed into legislator). The proposition advanced by the *vereador*'s mandate, the fallacy of Greek direct democracy, and of representative democracy, and the idea of a 'transitive', or 'participatory', 'interactive' democracy.

THEATRE cannot be imprisoned inside theatrical buildings, just as religion cannot be inprisoned inside churches; the language of theatre and its forms of expression cannot be the private property of actors, just as religious practice cannot be appropriated by priests as theirs alone!

Paulo Freire talks about the transitivity of true teaching: the teacher is not a person who unloads knowledge, like you unload a lorry, and heaps it up in the head of another person – the bank vault where the money-knowledge is kept: the teacher is a person who has a particular area of knowledge, transmits it to the pupil and, at the same time, receives other knowledge in return, since the pupil also has his or her own area of knowledge. The least a teacher has to learn from his pupil is how his pupil learns. Pupils are different from one another; they learn differently. Teaching is transitivity. Democracy. Dialogue. An Argentinian teacher from Cordova relates: 'I taught a peasant how to write the word "plough": and he taught me how to use it'.

Conventional theatre is governed by an intransitive relationship, in that everything travels from stage to auditorium, everything is transported, transferred in that direction – emotions, ideas, morality! – and nothing goes the other way. The tiniest noise, the smallest exclamation, the least sign of life the spectator displays, is the

1. I am not against any kind of theatre: I love them all. I am a playwright myself, and a director, and I would not like to hear any member of the audience shout 'Stop!' and come up on stage to take Hamlet's place and shoot Claudius. But the world of theatre is large enough to accommodate all theatrical forms, including Theatre of the Oppressed. In any case, all forms of theatre can interact: I was extremely happy when the Royal Shakespeare Company, in July 1997, invited me to train 26 of their actors how to use the introspective techniques of *The Rainbow of Desire* to create characters from Shakespeare's plays. It was a wonderful experience for all of us. *AB*.

equivalent of driving the wrong way down a one-way street: danger! Lest the magic of the stage be shattered, silence is required.[1] In the Theatre of the Oppressed, by contrast, dialogue is created; transitivity is not merely tolerated, it is actively sought – this theatre asks its audience questions and expects answers. Sincerely.

Legislative Theatre is trying to do the same thing. We do not accept that the elector should be a mere spectator to the actions of the parliamentarian, even when these actions are right: we want the electors to give their opinions, to discuss the issues, to put counter-arguments, we want them to share the responsibility for what their parliamentarian does.

Our mandate's project is to bring theatre back into the centre of political action – the centre of decisions – by making theatre as politics rather than merely making political theatre. In the latter case, the theatre makes comments on politics; in the former, the theatre is, in itself, one of the ways in which political activity can be conducted.

In Greek tragedy the action led to catastrophe for its Protagonists and produced catharsis in its spectators, after a phase of euphoric, transgressive violence. At the same time as the 'tragic flaw' (*harmatia*) of the Protagonist was extirpated by death (Antigone) or by terrible punishment (Oedipus), the same transgressive desire which had been vicariously stimulated in the spectators was now eliminated. In the Legislative Theatre the aim is to bring the theatre back to the heart of the city, to produce not catharsis, but dynamisation. Its objective is not to pacify its audiences, to tranquillise them, to return them to a state of equilibrium and acceptance of society as it is, but, again contrarily, to develop their desire for change. The Theatre of the Oppressed seeks not only to develop this desire but to create a space in which it can be stimulated and experienced, and where future actions arising from it can be rehearsed. The Legislative Theatre seeks to go further and to transform that desire into law. (We must be aware that law is always someone's desire – it is always the desire of the powerful: let's democratise this desire, let's make our desire become law too!)

Curious, the origin of the word 'politics'. In Ancient Greece (before 500 BC) *polis* comprised the entirety of people who had no power at their disposal – the powerless. A farmer, for example, was obliged to give to the landlord of the fields he cultivated five-sixths of what he produced; he himself was left with only a bare sixth. He had no political power; or rather, his only power consisted of joining with those who, like him, had no power. *Polis* came to be the power of the powerless, strength in unity, 'the people united will never be defeated . . .', etc.

In the countryside, given the distances and the difficulties of travel, the *polis*es were difficult to expand: whereas the maritime *polis*es (incoporating those who rowed, sailed, loaded the ships, etc.) organised themselves more easily. In these ports, the *polis*es were larger, more numerous and stronger. For that reason we have tended to forget about the rural *polis* and the word *polis* has come to be synonymous with city. *Polis* = city. How is it to be governed? Enter politics – the art of managing the polis.

Democracy was also invented in Greece: *demos* = people, *cracia* = rule. In those days the public square, the *agora*, was a public place, a place to which people came to meet and talk, rather than a mere transit point. 'The square is to the people as the sky is to the condor', said the poet Castro Alves. The square was where everyone opined, where politics was discussed and enacted.

People talk about Athenian 'direct democracy'. Was this democracy even democratic? In the first place, women didn't vote; which means that half the population of the city didn't vote, because they were women. Secondly, only free men voted and, at that time, the majority of the population was made up of slaves, individuals taken prisoner in wars or acts of maritime piracy; these semi-citizens didn't vote because they were slaves. Even amongst the Greeks themselves, there were also a number who, because they could not pay their debts, handed themselves over to their creditors as slaves – this fact being scarcely mentioned in histories of the time, but now generally accepted. This left the few who were actually free men. Democracy of the few, the *fasces*, the small bundle of sticks. Thirdly, linear arithmetic, in which two and two make four, was not the method used in the counting of votes: while there may not have been fraud in the modern sense, nor buying of votes, there was voting by calling out, by shouting, by thumping fists on the table. The louder the voice of the speaker, the more his vote was worth, as Homer recounts in *The Odyssey*; being blessed with the voice of an agile tenor, Ulysses always won.

In spite of this, in theory, an abstract model of direct democracy existed: everyone gave their opinion, in the *agora*, in the square, they all voted. Would this be possible today? In Rio de Janeiro, would it be possible to bring together the people every Tuesday, Wednesday and Thursday evening in the Quinta da Boa Vista or the Maracana stadium to vote on the city's laws? Would it be possible to conduct three oral plebiscites a week? Clearly not. Direct democracy, if fallacious in former times, is today impossible.

That leaves representative democracy and its shortcomings – what the candidates promise during the campaign hardly ever reflects their true intentions – the kind appellation for this particular form of lying is 'pragmatism', a very nice word, much nicer than what it designates. Rare is the politician who will confess what he or she intends really to do, since the vast majority of them intend the unconfessable, though they promise plenty of schools, health, transport, work, and general and everlasting happiness. Pure demagogy. It is understood: protected by the secret votes in chambers, the emptiness of public galleries and the bias of the media, the majority of politicians cheat their electors. Pragmatism!

Is there anything to choose between one of these forms and another? No! We can try alternatives. One alternative is the Legislative Theatre, a form of politics which is transitive – it proposes dialogue, interaction, change – like the pedagogy of Paulo Freire and the Theatre of the Oppressed. We are all subjects: pupils and teachers, citizens and spectators.

For it to work, it needs the people's participation. How can this participation be organised, without demagogy? We are trying.

We are in the process of inventing a structure. During the four years of our mandate, instead of applying ourselves to the citizenship 'in general' – as we do in our electoral rallies – we turned our attention to small organic units. Groups of individuals brought together by some essential necessity – teachers, doctors, labourers, students, farmers, domestic servants – and not merely by chance, as occurs at street theatre shows. These groups organised themselves on two levels, 'nuclei' and 'links', bodies which were created within an actual society, in a real city, Rio de Janeiro, and not just on paper.

To understand this experiment it is important to know how and where it was and is being tried. What is the reality of the situation in Rio? In what respects is this reality different or specific?

And, with the citizenship – living, real, actual people – organised in this way, we ourselves are trying to conceive what could one day become THEATRE AS TRANSITIVE DEMOCRACY.

DEAR READER: COMPARING YOUR OWN CITY OR
COUNTRY WITH RIO DE JANEIRO OR BRAZIL, DO YOU
BELIEVE IT WOULD BE POSSIBLE TO CARRY OUT AN
ANALOGOUS EXPERIMENT OUTSIDE THIS CONTEXT?
WHERE, WHY AND HOW? WRITE !!!! SEND SUGGESTIONS!

3 The context

How and where is this experiment being carried out?

Rio is much more than mere Carnival, bronzed women in bikinis (so minute that they are known here as *fio dentale* – dental floss), Bossa Nova and Pelé – it is the eighth largest world economy, ranking alongside the UK, Canada, France and others; but it is a divided society, with a distribution of wealth that is among the world's most unjust, ranking alongside Botswana, Central Africa and Zaire!

Whatever the nature of a popular theatre practice or experiment, there is what is called in military parlance a 'theatre of operations' in which it is enacted. The *Legislative Theatre* is coming into being in Rio de Janeiro. But what kind of city is Rio? What kind of country is Brazil?

SECURITY

ON his accession to the office of Chief of Police of Rio de Janeiro in 1995, the new incumbent, General da Silva, stated that 'only a madman could feel safe in Rio de Janeiro'. This unleashed a chorus of protest: he was the madman, how on earth could he say a thing like that. After all, people said, surely the chief of police, of all people, has an obligation to be optimistic, to calm the population! The situation in Rio – they said – was not as terrible as all that, and one day the Cidade Maravilhosa (Marvellous City) would once again deserve that name. And these severe critics censured the general's frankness.

After his driver had delivered him home, the general sat down in his rocking chair, and reflected on the appropriateness of his pronouncements. The driver bid him goodnight, got into the car and, before he had even parked it in the garage next door . . . he was set upon and robbed.

The general was right. He wasn't mad. He knew that it was

impossible, for him or anyone else, to feel safe in Rio, even in the bosom of one's own home.

KIDNAPPING AND DRUG-DEALING

Commissioner Helio Luz, Head of the Anti-kidnapping Division, also took office in 1995, affirming that: 'From now on, the Anti-kidnapping Division is never going to kidnap anyone again . . .'. He meant what he said. He spoke loud and clear and kidnappings became less frequent.

This hideous practice of kidnapping people – a form of sophis-ticated torture – was re-introduced into Brazil, as the standard method of interrogation, combined with torture, by the military during the dirty war (1964–1979). Kidnapping was subsequently adopted as a tactic by the urban guerrillas (who had been its first victims), who moved on to also kidnapping ambassadors and other personalities to trade them for political prisoners (or for money), and it eventually spread till it became common practice, along with car thefts, bank robberies etc. Today, this method is used by drug-traffickers: when the funds required to 'honour' debts to their suppliers are running low, the dealers need to make money fast. As they cannot resort to the legal banks, at least not when suddenly caught short in this way – which is not to say they are not good customers at other times! – they apply themselves to this lucrative and rapidly achieved activity.

Today, in Rio de Janeiro, everyone gets kidnapped: industrialists, company directors, the children of rich or middle-class people – and even poor people – old people, young men, babies . . . even pedigree dogs: at the end of August 1995, a pure-bred Dobermann was kidnapped and ransomed for a thousand reals (equivalent to a thousand dollars at the time of the incident).

Depending on how much cash is required, anyone can be kidnapped, wherever they may be. In imitation of the government, which claims to 'put out to tender' all its lucrative activities, so the kidnappers also put their work out to tender: one gang picks up the kidnap victim, a different gang does the holding and a third group negotiates the ransom. On earth as in heaven, in the presidential palace as in the streets.

GRANDE PREMIO BRAZIL

There was a curious case recently, shortly before the Grande Premio Brazil (the Brazilian Derby) 'of the century', as the race was billed in August 1995: a man was kidnapped by mistake. The bandits were after the extremely famous three-times champion jockey, Ricardinho, who was going to partner the Brazilian horse, Much Better, which was tipped as the winner and was running against other pompously named horses, such as Emperor of Tijucas, Grand Ducat, etc. It would have been a major outrage, a scandal of national proportions: the prize to be paid to the winner totalled one million reals[1] and the horse had more than five million reals worth of bets on it. If they had carried it off successfully, the kidnappers would have been able to ask the most enormous ransom; they would have been the real winners of the Grande Premio Brazil, without even mounting a horse. They had made the most meticulous plans, followed the jockey for weeks, placed bets, been to the races, hung around the stable and the hotels close to the track, noted where the jockey parked his car . . . all down to the last detail. One little hitch; the jockey decided to sell his car days before the race and the buyer was kidnapped inside his newly purchased vehicle . . . by mistake.

When these delinquents realised that they had kidnapped the right car but with the wrong driver, being compassionate people, they resolved to let the man go, with one condition: 'We've already spent two thousand reals preparing the kidnapping, placing bets on goddam horses, paying for hotels and food, not to mention the time we have wasted. Here's what we are going to do: we are letting you go, on one condition – that you promise to make good the money which has gone down the drain. It's only two thousand reals . . . when we were hoping to make two hundred thousand . . . You can see our point: we can't end up out of pocket.'

It's funny, but horrific. The car ended up costing the poor man another two thousand reals and Much Better came in fourth, confounding the tipsters – and was re-baptised 'Not So Good'.

KIDNAPPING AS AN INDUSTRY

Kidnapping is a complex industry; in the old days, only marriageable young women were kidnapped, with their connivance, in a form of elopement which was called *rapto* (rape), recalling to mind the rape

1. One million dollars.

of the Sabine women. According to the newspapers, today in Rio de Janeiro there are networks of dishonest lawyers who on a regular basis undertake, in return for inflated sums, to guarantee the surrender of the kidnap victims to their families, alive or dead – the going rate is said to be 300 thousand reals a head. A tangled web unites kidnappers, police, drug-dealers and lawyers.[2]

In Rio de Janeiro, all the networks of illegality are interlinked. The illegal lottery barons are the same people who command the kidnapping and the same people who dominate the drugs trade. Recently (in 1995), the drug-dealers decided not to commercialise further the new drug crack, but not on account of humanitarian motives; they had simply realised that crack kills much more quickly than common-or-garden cocaine and that, by selling crack, they were in danger of reducing the size of their consumer market.

All the networks are interlinked, including the police and the criminals. When I was little, we played at cops and robbers: in Rio today, the kids would not know which side to be on, since they would not be able to tell the difference. In 1995, in the Chamber of *Vereadors*, we had to discuss a loan from the prefecture to the state government intended to equip the military police better. We did not know how to vote: whether we should say 'no' and alienate public opinion, which was hungry for more policing, or say 'yes', in the knowledge that many of the police would sell their new weapons to the drug-traffickers.

2. There are of course a great number of honest policemen and lawyers. *AB.*

THE ARMY AS A POLICE FORCE

At the end of 1994, the federal government decided to carry out a blanket operation in Rio de Janeiro to put an end to the violence. The army went into action, staging raids into the hills where the second- and third-rank drug-dealers hid (the higher echelons of the trade live well away from the misery of the *favelas*, many of them even out of Brazil). The sudden repression was savage, incorporating arbitrary imprisonments and beatings.

A commission of *vereadors* went to talk to the general in charge of this 'Operation Rio' to get some explanations and to protest against the disorganised and violent form the intervention was taking. The general, after long conference on strategy, said that 'bandits have no fixed addresses or distinguishing marks on their bodies', and, for this reason, he was obliged to raid *favelas* and pick up suspects. I asked

27

him why, if this was the case, he only invaded *favelas* (i.e., fixed addresses) and only picked up blacks (distinguishing marks). He answered, 'If you want me to put an end to the violence, I cannot promise to keep to the letter of the law . . .'

The operation lasted only a few months and had no visible results, beyond tanks in the streets, machine-gunners everywhere and check-point blitzes causing havoc with the traffic. It lasted till the start of 1995. The violence continues unabated.

WILD LIONS AS DOMESTIC PETS

One of the richest drug-traffickers in Rio – Dozinho – was what could be termed 'eccentric'. Dozinho, a powerfully built man, was well protected in the stronghold where he lived and worked, in Morro de Cerro Cora (the Hill of the White Cliff) in the Cosme Velho (Old City) in the Zona Sul (South Zone) of Rio de Janeiro, surrounded by dozens of thugs armed with machine-guns and bazookas, and a pair of young lions, called Samson and Delilah . . . Quite so: two lion cubs which he personally looked after and trained, in the hope that, when they were bigger, they would offer the most secure form of protection for his domain (*Jornal do Brasil* 25/08/95). And the lions, though young, had learnt to obey their master's voice and knew his basic commands by heart. There are particular breeds of Brazilian mastiff which are known for their extreme ferocity; their use as domestic pets is banned in many European countries, because they are considered wild animals. Dozinho owned several of these, of various different strains – so just imagine, if the dogs can be as dangerous as that, what two real, strong, voraciously carnivorous African lions would be like.

In spite of his veritable arsenal, his human army and his wild animals, Dozinho was killed by a rival gang, from Morro da Mineira (Mineral Hill) in the Zona Norte (North Zone). The drug-dealing gangs fight over the enormous carioca[3] market, zone by zone, hill by hill, inch by inch. These Mineira drug-dealers had destroyed everything they could get their hands on, they had plundered everything they could, and they had occupied the stronghold and taken control of the market. But . . . what was to be done with the two lions? Samson and Delilah had been indoctrinated by the drug-dealer, despite their tender years, and would only obey orders from their master's voice – and he was now dead.

3. Carioca – native to Rio.

There was no way of re-educating them: the animals had been there when the stronghold was overrun, in the middle of all the shooting, and, possibly out of solidarity with their old owner, would not obey their new masters: they remained jumpy, irascible and dangerous. The drug-dealers who had come out on top didn't think twice – they resolved to sell Samson and Delilah to the only possible buyers: the Garcia Circus. Months later, they were discovered at the circus by inspectors from the income tax office, who wanted to know the origin of the poor little beasts (because a receipt was required for tax purposes). The taxes were paid, and today, anyone who wants to can go and see the drug-dealers' lions jumping through flaming hoops and balancing on trapezes.

Lions love the circus!

SOME FIGURES

In Brazil, as in Colombia, the problem of drug-trafficking stands alongside institutionalised corruption, inequitable distribution of wealth (in which the country ranks below Botswana, according to the July 1995 report of the International Bank for Development) and unequal distribution of land, as one of the greatest obstacles to the democratisation of the country.

Drug-trafficking directly employs more than 100,000 people in Rio de Janeiro alone – almost as many as the municipal government itself and twice as many as the giant national oil company, Petrobras (c.f. *Jornal do Brasil* 10/9/95).

WHO LAYS DOWN THE LAW IN THE SLUMS?

As far as law is concerned, the drugs trade functions as if we were living before the Code of Hammurabi, which, in 1750 BC in Babylonia, instituted the first penal code known in the history of humanity, which was carved in stone (and today reposes in the Louvre Museum in Paris). Prior to that, justice was administered at the whim of the king, and in accordance with his power, which was measured by the weight of the club that he carried. So it is with the drugs trade: Pedrinho Maluco, lord of the territory of Campo Grande, owner of machine-guns and AR-15 rifles, resolved to punish a rapist with death followed by quartering, in front of the population of the hill. And that was how it was done. Many commit rape, but only this rapist was quartered. Only God and Pedrinho Maluco know why. We are back in the times before King Hammurabi.

HOW PEOPLE GET USED TO VIOLENCE

Rio de Janeiro is a city where middle- and upper-class mothers ask their sons, when they set off to school or go out for a walk, 'Have you remembered to take some money in your wallet for muggers?' It is prudent to do so; those who have no money when set upon can find themselves even more cruelly treated by their furious assailants.

EXTERNAL DEBT AS A FORM OF MODERN SLAVERY

During the years of the dictatorship, Brazil increased its external debt from 20 billion to 120 billion dollars and it now pays over one billion dollars interest a month to service this debt, which does not stop growing. In the National Budget for 1998 (*Jornal do Brasil*, week of 7–14 December 1997) 37 billion dollars were put aside to pay the interest on the external and internal debts. Precious little remains to serve the needs of the population at federal, state or municipal levels.

The sectors most badly affected are education and health. To give some idea, a municipal teacher or doctor, at the end of his or her career, will earn around 400 to 600 reals a month.[4] Clearly, violence cannot be explained solely by the prevailing economic conditions in a region or country – but by the same token, it is obvious that extreme injustice deepens hatred.

4. Salary in 1996, when a real was equivalent to a dollar.

LAW AND GOD, AND GOD'S LAW

In Dostoevksy's *Crime and Punishment*, Raskolnikov, the Protagonist, reaches the conclusion that God does not exist, and that, if God does not exist, everything is permissible. For this reason he kills an old woman and steals her money, not so much for the money, which is little, as for the enjoyment of the power of killing. Everything is permissible. Why not kill the old lady?

If neither God nor law exists, everything is possible, even random killing, murder at the drop of a hat. In Rio de Janeiro, and in Brazil as a whole, that is how it has been.

THE MASSACRES: PEASANTS, STREET-CHILDREN AND PRISONERS

Wholesale killing is frequent. In the rural areas it passes unnoticed. Only very special cases make the news, like the assassination of Chico Mendes, which became the subject of a North American film, or the massacre of landless peasants in Corumbiara, Roraima in August 1995 – a number of peasants, whose only wish was to work the unproductive land, were violently evicted by judicial order: nine of them now lie six foot underground, their burial plots the only piece of land which fell to them on those estates. Or Curionopolis (Pará, 17 April 1996) where more than 20 peasants were killed, 35 wounded, dozens 'disappeared' and not one police officer was injured.

Sometimes a particularly unusual case is considered newsworthy: a family living on the Brazilian border with Colombia, in the last decade, invited 30 indigenous people for a barbecue, got them drunk and killed them, one by one, with machete blows. In court, the leader of the assassins candidly confessed that he 'did not know that killing Indians was against the law'.

Some recent massacres have achieved world-wide notoriety. In Vigário Geral, a *favela* in the Zona Norte, four military policemen were outside the bounds of their precinct, trying to negotiate with drug-traffickers, when they were ambushed and assassinated; by way of response, a clandestine police organisation, calling itself 'Os Cavalos Corredores' (the Running Horses), went into the *favela* where the dealers lived and shot on sight, at random, 21 people who had nothing to do with drug-dealing or attacks on the police: a factory hand on his way to work, lunch-box under his arm, an old man sitting in front of his house smoking a cigarette, an old woman reading the Bible seated on the sofa of her house, and so on.

Actions like this are not uncommon in Brazil. In Carandiru, the São Paulo prison, to 'gain control' over an internal uprising, the military police, armed to the gills, killed 111 unarmed prisoners, who had given themselves up. The leader of the operation subsequently put

31

himself up for election as one of the MPs for the state of São Paulo, bearing the candidate number 111, and he was elected. It has to be said that a large part of the population appreciates and approves of this type of violence. As evidenced by an 'opinion poll' in Rio de Janeiro, judging the guilt of a military policeman, Lieutentant Flavio, who killed a mugger in the middle of the city, in broad daylight, in front of TV cameras: the result was 50 per cent on his side, 50 per cent against him.

In August 1993, a number of street-children lay sleeping in front of the closed doors of the beautiful Candelaria Church in the centre of Rio de Janeiro: a small group of hooded policemen jumped out of a van and emptied their guns into them at point-blank range – seven children died without waking. A few played dead and saved their own lives.

Why did this crime take place? While many children survive on the streets by selling chewing gum or washing windscreens at traffic lights, it is also a fact that others commit minor thefts, sometimes while armed. The shopkeepers in the area pay the police to rid them of these children. Since the service is easy, the price is modest. Apparently, the going rate for killing a child is between 30 and 50 US dollars. And, as the price is low, they are killed in great numbers. There are people who defend the extermination of minors as if it was a simple treatment of an infestation of rats or ants – malodorous, but necessary.

According to the Brazilian Institute of Social Health (IBISS), in the first quarter of 1995, 378 children died in violent incidents in the territory of the state of Rio de Janeiro, an average of 4.2 children a day. One Candelaria every two days. According to the newspaper *O Globo* (6 September 1995) in the first six months of 1996 in the small dormitory towns around Rio more than 300 people died each month: the wars of Vietnam, Korea, the Lebanon and Bosnia pale by comparison.

In Acari, 11 young men leaving a funk gig were picked up by the police in front of witnesses, and their bodies never appeared. No-one was punished.

To complete the tally of violence, we have to tell of the Mothers of Cinelândia: 26 women who had their young daughters, girls aged between 8 and 12, kidnapped, and, without any doubt, taken to other states, where they would have been less able to defend themselves or flee, and forced to prostitute themselves. Every Monday, like the Mothers of the Plaza de Mayo ('*Las Locas de la Plaza de Mayo*' – 'the

Madwomen of the Plaza de Mayo'[5]), they gather in front the steps of the town hall, with pictures of their daughters, collecting signatures for a petition asking the President of the Republic to take steps to recover the girls. Twice my mandate gave recitals of poetry and music relating to childhood and the mothers made passionate speeches, but even so, after a while, the public lost interest.

On Saturday 9 September 1995, the President of the Republic made a speech condemning such massacres, which continue unpunished. On this same day, 12 young people between 12 and 20 years of age at a party in Morro do Turano were slaughtered. Their killers are being sought . . .

5. The Mothers of the Disappeared, victims of Argentina's dirty war in the 1970s. Every week they parade in a circle in the Plaza da Mayo in Buenos Aires, in white headscarves, bearing the photos of their children; they have done this since 1975, and they're still there.

HISTORICAL PHOTOS: VIETNAM AND AFRICA

Thinking about Rio de Janeiro, some famous photographs come to mind. Do you remember that Vietnamese officer pointing the revolver at the kneeling Vietcong prisoner? Taken a few seconds before the gun was fired, the photo was shown in newspapers and broadcast to the whole throughout the world. Do you remember the Chinese student in Tiananmen Square alone in front of a column of war tanks which had stopped in front of him, impotent? (Days later the same tanks murdered hundreds of students.) Do you remember that tractor in Rwanda shoving dozens of bodies into a communal grave – genocide – during the civil war which killed thousands of Rwandans? Do you remember the 'surgical strikes' of Baghdad, looking like a New Year's Eve party lit up with fireworks, while the bodies piled up on the ground beneath? Do you remember Bosnia? Do you remember . . . do you remember . . .?

None of these photos is so far removed from Rio – it's a question of quantity, not quality. Rio de Janeiro, the place where we are endeavouring to carry out our Legislative Theatre experiment.

A TIME TO STOP, A TIME TO GO ON

In this place and time we are putting the Legislative Theatre to the test. As might be expected, we face serious problems: poverty and physical danger are the two main ones.

6. There are 530 *favelas* (shanty towns, slums) in Rio alone. One of them, Rocinha, is inhabited by more than 200,000 people.

Sometimes we have been forced to interrupt the work because of threats. In Morro da Saudade, a slum in the centre of Rio,[6] we had a women-only theatre group: the participants themselves advised us not to visit them again. In Vigario Geral our van, loaded with scenery and props, was robbed; days later, one of the people who lived there brought us wigs and costumes which had been in the stolen van saying that perhaps we would be able to make use of them, as we did theatre . . . It was a warning.

Other times we persisted, even with difficulties. In Morro do Borel, as soon as you went into the *favela*, there were always two men armed with guns on top of a flat roof: they were the drug-dealers' lookouts. The hill was divided between two rival gangs: the Red Command and the Third Command. We worked with the parishioners of a Catholic church, which, as luck would have it, was in no-man's land. Sister Lucia told us: 'It's very quiet here, except every now and then when you hear the odd burst of machine-gun fire . . . Happens very rarely . . . every other week . . .'.

CICELY BERRY, FROM THE ROYAL SHAKESPEARE COMPANY TO THE VIDIGAL SLUM

When that wonderful teacher, Cicely Berry, Voice Director of the Royal Shakespeare Company, comes to Brazil, she also chooses to work in one of the *favela*s, Vidigal, where there is a very active theatre group – as a rule, they do productions of classical plays in the slum, which is very unusual and very beautiful. Once, during a voice session, machine gun-fire was heard. She went on rehearsing *Hamlet* . . .

SOMETIMES WE GET SCARED, SOMETIMES NOT

Here is an account by Regina, one of the *coringas* (Jokers) of our mandate, of what happened when she went to Borel to help on the visual aspects of the production:

> *Olivar and I went to watch the Morro do Borel play. With those rapid bursts of gunfire, you get frightened, you don't know what'll happen next*

. . . We are hardly out of the van and we hear a salvo of shots. Someone says: 'They are firing a salute to honour our arrival!' As soon as we arrive in front of the church, another rally of shots. The boy who was going with us ran, so in the circumstances I thought that I had better run too, the priest ran, everyone ran, into the church, some even started praying . . . And with real faith!

It was compulsory vaccination day, the church was being used as a medical post and it was full of children, of all shapes and sizes. Every now and then there was a fresh burst of shots, but no-one seemed to take any notice. Till one of the mothers saw her son near the door and shouted to him: 'Come away from there my lad, before you get a bullet in you' as naturally as she might have said 'Come out of the sun, you could burn yourself . . .'

The rehearsal was to have been on the top floor, which had windows and fresh air, but we preferred to rehearse in the ground floor, because it had no windows and was safer. From time to time the shooting started up again, only now it wasn't so far away, each time it broke out it was closer. We went on rehearsing for two or three hours longer. Shots also seemed to be coming from behind, we seemed to be surrounded, with shooting on all sides. From my vantage-point I could see the people outside, by the door which was still open, and I saw a great deal of movement, lots of people running into the church, and I thought that perhaps it was time for mass and that those people were coming for mass, but they told me that there was no mass at that time of day, then I began to think that it would be best to get going soon, as soon as the shots eased off a little and before it got dark . . . We left and there was a crowd outside, around a dead body stretched out on the ground, but we did not want to look at it – and though it was very tense and the people were all talking at the top of their voices, everything seemed very normal, no-one was in the least bit scandalised, except me. When shots were heard, the children ran to take cover, and when the noise stopped, they came back.

When we came down the hill and found ourselves treading on asphalt again – phew, I felt so relieved, it felt like Paradise. We got to the bus and as we were drawing away from the favela *again, I felt a fresh onset of relief. So what must they feel? The people who live there? What about them?*

We are going to continue rehearsing our play, but I hope to God that none of us ends up being mourned in the Chamber. Because at times like that, life hangs by a thread . . .'

35

Her account ends here. I want to make clear, however, that our strategy is never to throw ourselves into 'heroic' actions. If the situation becomes permanently dangerous and risky, we prefer not to persist, not to run pointless risks, and we go and work in other areas, with other groups and other themes. We agree with Lord Byron's poem: 'there is a time for leaving, even when there is no certain place to go ...' The account above refers to one such occasion; when this state of affairs comes about, we abandon the venue or transfer the rehearsals to another place. It has already happened with various groups on various occasions. We definitely don't want to be heroes!

WHY THE LEGISLATIVE THEATRE – WHAT FOR AND WHO FOR?

In Brazil – and so many other countries – the people don't believe in anything any more. We are living through a wave of privatisations, a veritable *tsunami*, one of those gigantic waves that submerge coastal regions of Hawaii three hours after an earthquake in Japan. Which is how it happens here: in Europe the Berlin wall comes down; in England intransigent Thatcherism is victorious; in Mexico they begin to privatise everything which might yield a profit;[7] in Argentina even the Zoological Garden has been privatised, even the monkeys, giraffes, rhinoceroses and flamingos now belong to private companies. Argentina is selling off everything that made a profit and is keeping only loss-making enterprises, following the neo-troglodyte-liberal *tsunami* (in the true sense of the word 'troglodyte', like stone-age man, with no morality); profit is privatised, loss is socialised.

Many politicians who in the past used to defend the poor, today affirm that globalisation is inevitable and modern. They forget that all hegemonic powers have always been globalising and that to globalise is in their nature. From Pax Romana on, or the Incas and the Aztecs, or the British and American empires, or Hitler's Thousand-year Reich, imperialisms have always sought to monopolise the world. There is nothing modern about the modern world; there are still troglodytes![8]

7. This was written in 1996.

8. For more on this, see 'Afterword: The metamorphoses of the Devil', p. 249.

PROSTHESIS OF DESIRE

Today, the only true modernity relates to the technological: computers allow a collapse in the Asian markets to bankrupt Brazilian stocks and shares within a matter of seconds. And what is terrible with modern globalisation is that people are isolated and individualised in front of a TV, for instance, only to have their individuality taken away: the market cannot satisfy the desires of all, so those who manipulate the market seek to extirpate all of our individual desires and make a PROSTHESIS OF DESIRE, they implant the market's desire in us, they would have us believe that we all love the same fast food, the same drinks, the same clothes. In Japan, they have even succeeded in convincing large groups of people to adore one particular pop star, a virtual singer, who receives thousands of love letters every day, and exists only in CDs, cassettes and TV screens: she was fabricated by computers, her voice being a mixture of many different singers' voices, her body a mixture of many other dancers' movements, her mind . . . oh, well, why bother with details?

WHAT IS TO BE DONE?

In the light of all the above, we felt that since our profession – our craft, our art, our duty – was theatre, and not cinema or television, we should create a theatrical form to contribute to the resistance, because in today's Brazil as far as the poor and the unemployed in the cities and the landless in the countryside are concerned, that is what we are talking about, resistance, like that in France under the Nazi occupation. Believe me – it is nothing less than that.

And, step by step, we are trying to invent, to systematise, to structure this new method which we are calling 'LEGISLATIVE THEATRE', but which is still work in progress, a task we are only midway through.

DEAR READER: THOSE OF YOU WHO KNOW RIO DE JANEIRO, DO YOU CONSIDER THIS PICTURE EXCESSIVELY BLEAK? WITH THIS BACKGROUND IN MIND, HOW DO

37

YOU THINK THIS EXPERIMENT CAN STILL BE DONE?
WHAT OTHER ELEMENTS, INFORMATION OR IDEAS
ARE LACKING, TO BETTER INFORM AND STIMULATE
YOU TO TRY SOMETHING SIMILAR?

4 The structure

Our 'Cabinet', that is, our office at the Chamber, is structured as follows:

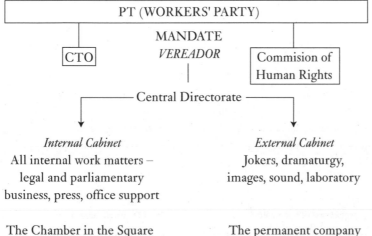

PT (WORKERS' PARTY)

MANDATE
VEREADOR

CTO

Commision of
Human Rights

Central Directorate

Internal Cabinet
All internal work matters –
legal and parliamentary
business, press, office support

External Cabinet
Jokers, dramaturgy,
images, sound, laboratory

The Chamber in the Square
The interactive mailing list

The permanent company
The mandate's shows

NUCLEI AND LINKS
CONSTITUTION: a) by community; b) by theme; c) by both
ACTIVITIES: a) workshops; b) shows for the community itself;
c) inter-community dialogues; d) festivals;[1] e) festive events[2]

Summaries[3]

THE METABOLISING CELL

Projects of law; legal actions; direct interventions

[1] Occurring on specified dates, to coincide with national or local festivals.
[2] More spontaneous or short-notice gatherings, in reaction to events.
[3] Like match reports in sport, combining main points of the show and forum session, and feedback.

OUR PARTNERS

Links and nuclei

Rio is a large city; it has the most extensive urban woodlands in the world, and six million inhabitants, plus another six or seven million who live in neighbouring cities or dormitory towns, close to the city.

Rio is a city of contrasts: extreme wealth around the beach, extreme poverty on the height of the hills – a city squeezed in between the mountains and the sea.

In this city we are organising a network of partners, structured as what we call 'nuclei' and 'links', each with its own particular focus and function.

A link is a group of people from the same community, which communicates periodically with the mandate, setting out its opinions, desires, and needs. This relationship can be enacted by means of a presence in the Chamber, or in the community, or in any of the other places where our mandate's activities take place. It can be a personal encounter, by means of the Chamber in the Square or through our interactive mailing list.

A nucleus is a link which is constituted as a Theatre of the Oppressed group and actively collaborates with the mandate in a more frequent and systematic way.

THE MANDATE AND THE NUCLEI:
THE DIFFICULTIES

It isn't easy. When a group is already in existence – a religious community, for example – it will have its own pre-existing structure, independent of the mandate. Its members will already have solved practical problems like scheduling, location of rehearsals, etc. But of course, the group will also bring its own internal problems.

The principal obstacle to the formation of nuclei is financial. A good example is SEPE, the union for teachers and other education workers. For years we wanted to go beyond the formation of a link with them, we wanted a nucleus. On a few occasions we got as far as making some small plays with few characters. But we always met the same problem: many teachers from the SEPE who were members of the theatre group lived outside Rio and often didn't even have the money for the bus fare. Rehearsals which had been planned were cancelled after hours of waiting around, in which the Jokers and the teachers who were there would pass the time chatting about the situation in the teaching profession, in the hope that the others might turn up.

The destruction of public-sector education and health is part of the politics of the globalisation of barbarity (cf. Thatcher, Reagan, Gingrich, the Brazilian dictatorship).

They know what they are doing

Knowledge and health are power, so economic elites try to conceal knowledge and destroy health. An ignorant and debilitated people is more easily dominated. It was the reactionary US Senator Barry Goldwater who said that poverty is necessary to capitalism, since it facilitates the negotiation of salaries and conditions of work: the workers are afraid of losing their jobs.

Ever since the beginnings of civilisation in Egypt, 3,000 years before Christ, only the powerful have had access to knowledge: the people were taught only how to carve stone and build pyramids. In India, till quite recently – in fact, till the present day – education has been reserved for Brahmins and a few politicians and members of the Kshtriya warrior caste, while being drip-fed to farmers and Vaishya business people and Shudra artisans, and completely denied to the untouchables, the pariahs.

That's still the way things are throughout Brazil. Today, in December 1995, a city teacher earns around 300 dollars a month: s/he would pay more to send a single child to a private school than what s/he receives for teaching a class of 40 pupils in a public school.

Another difficulty is the widely scattered nature of some of the groups we work with. At various times we have started working with streetchildren but since these children do actually live on the street, you can't exactly give them a ring.

INTERVENTION IN THE STREET WORKERS' UNION

Often our partners are people who absolutely reject the idea of theatre. I remember one of the most difficult sessions of my life, when we were invited to work with 26 leaders of the Sindicato dos Urbanitarios (the Street Workers' Union), when their new leaders took over in their elections. They were 25 men and one woman, resolutely a woman amongst so many men. She used to say: 'Sure, I am a woman, but I'll stick my dick on the table with the best of them' – by way of demonstration that she would not cower in the face of any machismo – and that's how she overcame it!

Machismo and theatre

Amongst other things the macho men were embarrassed about doing physical exercises and hostile to the idea of man-to-man bodily contact; in one particular exercise they were standing in a circle with their eyes closed, and when I said I was going to pass behind them and tap one of them on the shoulder to designate 'the leader', their protests were vociferous. 'Don't creep up behind me, mate – stop right there!' they chorused, almost to a man.

The only way to convince them to 'do theatre' was to stimulate their curiosity around images of the campaign and the way they came to power. I asked them to show me the image of the union before they took over – and they all did so, as if they had taken photographs.

They do theatre when they forget that they are doing theatre

Using the bodies of the participants, along with tables, chairs, plant pots and anything else that was to hand, they eventually arrived at a consensual image of bureaucracy and ineffectuality. They argued to the point of shouting, but, since they were genuinely interested in recollecting how the union used to be, they forgot that by making these images they were making theatre, and they threw themselves into it with passion.

The power of images

Then I asked them to make the image of how the union was today. They replied that before they could do that, they would have to show

how they came to take power, and they went on to show, scene by scene, image by image, as if it was a series of photos, every important event that had occurred during the process: the discovery of secret documents (image), the public denunciation (image), the fear of the old leaders (image), the electoral propaganda against the old leadership (image), the convincing of the electors (image), the election (image), the victory (image), the actual flight of the previous leaders (image), the installation of the new ones (image), and the present situation, today, there and then (image).

Images as debate

I then asked them to carry on making images, with the same care and precision, and show how the transformation should be effected from there on in, and they began an exchange of opinions, an extensive and intense discussion, still in images: 'I like this image' – 'Well I don't, I prefer this other one . . .'. And they started to discuss their future strategies through images! They started making theatre when they could forget that they were making theatre!

POLITICS AND THE POLITICAL PARTY

There is also the issue of party politics. I started to feel it as soon as I was elected by the Workers' Party (PT). Before the election, I was seen as a man of the theatre who was seeking to be a politician: afterwards, I was seen as a politician of the PT who was using theatre for party ends, which was not true.

Being a politician of a particular party, whichever it may be, is viewed with a certain suspicion. The population at large, with just cause, rejects the political class in general. There is a joke which always goes down well, about the man who has lost his memory who wants to re-learn arithmetic and, by way of starting point, wants to ascertain the sum of two and two. First he asks an economist and gets the mathematical answer: 'the sum of two and two is situated somewhere between 3.88 and 4.12, with a margin of error of 0.12'. When the lawyer is asked the same question, the response comes – 'If you're talking about funds coming in, two plus two is 22; if you're talking about paying out, two plus two is only 4'. 'How much is two and two?' the man asks an accountant, a specialist in tax matters.

'How much would you like it to be?' answers the competent accountant. And, to the same question, the politician answers: 'How much are two and two? Why, two for me and two for you'.

To sum up: no-one should imagine that our first meeting with new partners is always easy. They do not always welcome us with open arms, and they are usually very suspicious at first, though we almost always become good friends later: theatre brings about this miracle.

CATEGORIES OF NUCLEI

The nuclei fall into three main categories:

- **Community**: defined by geographical community, formed by participants who live or work in the same community and therefore have many problems and preoccupations in common (Morro do Chapeu Mangueira, Morro da Saudade, Morro do Borel, Bras de Pina, Andarai, Rio Comprido, Julio Otoni).[4]

- **Thematic**: defined by community of interest – formed by participants who are brought together by a shared interest, an idea, a powerful shared objective – CENUN[5] (black students), Portadores de Deficiências (disabled people),[6] Meninos e Meninas de Rua[7] (streetchildren), Mulheraça[8] (women), Atoba (a homosexual collective), Mundo da Lama[9] (an ecological group), Tá Limpo do Palco[10] (25 domestic servants).[11]

- **Thematic and community**: participants who combine both of the above characteristics: Sol da Manhã[12] (farm-workers squatting on disused land, without legal documents); Casa das Palmeiras[13] (patients and psychologists belonging to a psychiatric institution); Terceira Idade[14] (old people); Escola Municipal Levy Neves and Escola Municipal Ministro Afranio Costa (pupils and teachers from two schools); the Princesas de Dom Pedro II[15] (patients discharged from mental hospitals); INFA[16] (a group linked to the Catholic Church).

4. Mostly from *favelas* or church groups.
5. O Coletivo Estadual de Negros Universitarios – the Black University Students' State Collective.
6. Literally, 'Handicapped People'.
7. Boys and Girls of the Street.
8. Womankind.
9. World of Mud.
10. A phrase such as a cleaner might use, along the lines of 'I've done the stage . . .'
11. For more information on all the above, see Appendices.
12. The Morning Sun.
13. The House of Palms.
14. Third Age.
15. The Princesses of Dom Pedro II.
16. Integrantes do Movimento Familiar Cristao da Pastoral da Familia da Igreja Catolica.

THE FORMATION OF THE NUCLEUS

The participants

The participants are, for the most part, lower middle class, working class or unemployed. They range from university students (CENUN) to adults on literacy courses. Some groups include, amongst others, teachers, lawyers, biologists, as well as various different professionals with liberal leanings.

What is their understanding of our project? I believe they do all understand what we are doing, though not without some difficulties. We also have our doubts: do we speak a language they can understand? Do they speak a language we can understand? Are we capable of building linguistic bridges with them? What kind of languages might be possible?

Therein resides the enormous importance of images as a medium for clarifying intentions. I would cite the example of the indigenous peoples in Peru – when I worked there in 1973, I suggested we make an image for every significant or sensitive word: family, work, future. . . . And the technique of 'the image of the word' was born.

Words are living entities

Words like 'protagonist', 'oppressed', 'conventional theatre' do not have much meaning for some of these groups. Still less, talk of catharsis. In France, on one occasion, a pupil of a vocational training school told me that he never experienced the slightest oppression; just the odd *emmerdement* (shittiness) . . . and then started talking about these huge oppressions.

Little by little, however, taking care not to rush, we are able to go on to explain what certain words signify and the people begin to understand and take pleasure in increasing their vocabulary. Every word in existence is substantial: no synonym is an exact match of another word, all have their own nuances; even when words say the same thing, they do not mean the same thing.

People like to learn: they are fascinated. Our task is to learn to teach. Without condescension. This can be done easily enough in the calm of rehearsals, but immediately becomes more difficult in the urgency of a Forum Theatre show. Words are living entities and should be treated with the same tenderness as human beings. They

45

are alive, they breathe, they can be happy and they can suffer. We have to teach our partners to love words, to choose the ones they prefer to signify each particular idea or feeling or emotion they have, to utter them meaningfully: words are a language, and so is the voice, and so is the body, and so is the body in space, and so are our eyes, the most vulnerable part of our bodies.

The stage scares them: it is the place everyone is looking at

How do we get people to accept the idea of going on stage? What does the citizen-as-artist feel? Resistances and temptations. There is embarrassment and pleasure, bashfulness and desire, and on top of everything the natural obstacle of people not wanting to speak publicly of their own individual problems. As if to do so was embarrassing, a confession of failure, of impotence.

The Joker must show, by means of examples – preferably solicited from other participants – that no problem is UNIQUE and EXCLUSIVE to one person alone. In one way or another, the problems are pluralised. In the absence of absolute identity, there will be analogy; when there is no analogy, at the very least there will be a resonance, always. The Joker has a duty not to latch onto an individual problem, as if only that individual had that problem – s/he must show how problems are pluralised. But s/he also has a duty not to undervalue the individual, or give the impression that 'it's the same the world over'. It is not: even when alike, the same problem presents itself in different forms in each individual. The participant can feel devalued if something he or she valued as their own personal problem is subsequently revealed as the possession of all. When all is said and done, we all cherish our own difficulties.

A lonely woman was chatted up at the São Cristóvão's subway by a young man who subsequently robbed her of her purse; of course, she was the only one to whom this had happened in a subway in São Cristóvão at that particular time, but how many of the workshops' participants had had something analogically similar happen to them? A young black man had some 'friends' to dinner on the day he got paid, several times, and each time he was robbed: none of us had had this happen in the same way, but how many of us had at some point in our lives allowed some form of abuse to happen to us rather than stay on our own?

The stage scares them: why should they reveal such facts to other people? Perhaps the only answer is: because other people, in other ways, have had similar experiences of aggression.

The workshops

The workshops which initiate our contact between Jokers and community actors can last two hours, two weeks, two months or two years. They can consist of an immediate intervention at the outset or a long preparation to consolidate a nucleus.

Choosing the games

In the workshops the exercises and games of the arsenal of the Theatre of the Oppressed (as described in *Games for Actors and Non-Actors*, Routledge 1992) should be used, the work being adapted to suit the abilities and possibilities of the participants. The arsenal and techniques of the Theatre of the Oppressed are made for the people and not vice versa.

An example of this happened in Bradford when I worked with a group of people with disabilities and their attendants and carers. I was hesitant about using the exercise called 'Pushing the Other Person', in which the actors push against each other, in pairs, in various different positions. On the advice of Tim Wheeler,[17] I proposed they do the exercise, suggesting that each person did what he or she could, or adapted my instructions to his or her own capabilities and desires: this was one of the exercises they liked most – without realising it, they invented their own way of doing it, which varied according to whether the encounter was between two disabled people in their wheelchairs, two so-called 'healthy' people, or a mixture of the two.

The ecological group O Mundo da Lama adapts the rhythm exercises to its own agenda by using, whenever possible, images of animals that live in the mangroves.

17. Director of the company, Mind the Gap, which was hosting this workshop.

Puberty

However, thought needs to be given to which exercises and techniques are going to be offered, which work is appropriate for the particular group: the Arsenal is varied enough, there is plenty to choose from. For instance, I believe that when working with adolescents, exercises in which the participants touch each others' bodies should not be used: with their bodies in the throes of change, they may feel embarrassed about bodily contact.

Blind people can use other senses

But equally one should not hesitate, for instance, to propose an exercise like the Machine of Rhythms to groups in which there are blind people: I've done it, and had the pleasure of seeing blind people go into the machine and enhance it with rhythmic gestures and vocal sounds. Though blind, their other senses often compensate in their perception of outside reality.

The rehearsals

It should be understood that rehearsals are already a cultural-political meeting in themselves. Theatre will be the medium of the encounter, theatre will be enacted, but it is very important to be aware that it is the citizens who will be making the theatre, around their own problems, trying their own solutions. In this context, every exercise, every game, every technique is both art and politics.

Stanislavsky in the slums of Rio

Schedules – the question of the timetabling of the start of an activity, be it a rehearsal or a show, is not only a matter of discipline: it too is a matter of art and politics. The great Stanislavsky transformed the concept of the actor's role, with the elaboration of a system which allowed the actor to abandon the old symbolic style of acting (in which for each emotion there was a corresponding gesture, or physiognomic expression or tone of voice, i.e., a cliché!) and to search for a sinaletic interpretation (in which signified and signifier are united – love is not the hand on the heart, but an emotion which the actor really feels and which, on being expressed, discovers its own form). This same Stanislavsky gave over the whole of the opening chapter of his first book on acting to show how important it is, in this collective artform, that people show due regard for the agreed schedule, which in fact amounts to showing respect for their co-artists.

A poet can wake up at three in the morning and write a beautiful poem in the privacy of his own room; a painter can paint her picture whenever she feels like it, when inspiration comes, and it's up to her whether she paints it all in one go or over a number of years. In the actor's case, this does not apply: inspiration has to come at such and such a time of day or night, and for the whole cast, at the same time. The actor cannot suddenly call up an audience at the crack of dawn to come running to catch his performance, because he only feels inspired at that time of day.

Besides, a scene is not the simple juxtaposition of two actors, but their INTER-RELATION. It is not what each person creates in isolation, but the thing they make together. Love is not the fact of two individuals being crazy about each other, but that which passes transitively *between* the one and the other. The same applies with the theatrical. A boxing match is not two fighters, each fighting in a different ring, *it is one fighting the other in the same ring.*

That is the artistic rationale: that the smallest theatrical unity is two people. And now someone will say: 'What about monologues?'

Once I saw a production of a very beautiful play, which told the story of a woman from the time she got home till the moment of her suicide: the theatricality was engendered by the intense and extreme interrelation between the woman and the phone which didn't ring, the doorbell which didn't sound, the friend or parent or lover who didn't call on her – the interrelation between the woman herself and the powerful presence of absence.

The political rationale is equally strong. In Brazil, we are well used to the notion of 'getting by' – 'We'll muddle through', we say, 'That's the way it goes', 'Never mind . . .' We are used to a total lack of respect; the bus on the street doesn't stop for old people or students, because they are entitled to travel free and thus don't generate income for the bus companies; the private hospitals won't attend an emergency if the victim doesn't have private health insurance or a credit card, and the victim can die at the hospital doors, and they do. Doctors say: 'We cannot save the lives of all patients, we have to choose those better equipped to survive . . .'

Time to work . . . after the work is done . . .

Adherence to the agreed schedule – whether in relation to rehearsal or show – offers the security of a structure in which one can take one's place. It is a sign of respect, a sign of consideration, to which the poor in Brazil are unaccustomed.

But it is also important to understand that failure to stick to the schedule is often justified; other factors come into play, such as lack of transport, or lack of money for transport, or women having to make a double journey (from work back to home and then back out to the rehearsal). Our partners should be encouraged to be punctual, but not punished, nor made culpable, when they fail to do so.

In the days of the guerrilla war, timing was sacred: when a meeting in such and such a city was set, at such and such a place, at the junction of these particular streets, at three minutes past a particular hour, with an injunction that someone would ask the question 'What time is it?' and the right answer would be 'My name is João'; this created a sense of security, of confidence. Sticking to the schedule was a matter of safety: the converse meant lives would be risked. But we are no longer in the guerrilla time, we are in the middle of a long war – seemingly eternal – for the humanisation of the dispossessed. This long road begins with the restoration of the artistic capacity within each person . . . at a particular time, and not half an hour later.

I am convinced that when people are confident that good time will be kept, this contributes to the early development of creative talent in each participant. When I know that the rehearsal will start at seven in the evening, then my preparation starts from now on, at three in the afternoon. Unconsciously, the mechanisms of creativity are engaged.

Concentration

Most professional actors (and most 'professional audience members') do not have any difficulty in concentrating during rehearsals or performances; theatre is their profession, their métier. But with community actors (and neighbourhood audiences) concentration is more difficult. Professionals usually rehearse in a special room, a rehearsal room, and their performance usually takes place in a theatre; communities cannot count on this 'magic' place to rehearse in, and their performances may take place anywhere; usually rehearsals happen in the same places where they meet for other non-artistic activities – political, social or leisure. Professionals shut themselves away to rehearse; communities, as a rule, rehearse with the doors open, anyone who wants to can drop in, selling refreshments, beer or sandwiches. For this reason, communities often ask to rehearse in our base, 'in the theatre', that is, a room with some degree of calm and intimacy.

It is necessary to create conditions in which the cast can concentrate, while at the same time appreciating that a voluntary lack of concentration, people not paying attention, can be an unconscious self-defence, a way of dealing with the fear of acting a role. In the case of community actors, this problem will not be corrected by means of reprimands but by drawing the cast's attention to important aspects of the play, the action or the characters, encouraging discussion and creativity around particular points (studiously diverting attention away from the fact that they are 'making theatre') and emphasising the political importance of making their work aesthetically pleasing. Yes, it is true: many people can start making theatre only when they forget that they are making theatre!

UP TO NOW THIS HAS BEEN A DELICATE PROBLEM: HOW TO BALANCE THE RIGOUR OF A REHEARSAL WITH THE INEVITABLE FLEXIBILITY INHERENT IN NON-PROFESSIONAL WORKING CONDITIONS, ESPECIALLY WORKING WITH PEOPLE WHO HAVE NOT PROPOSED THE PROJECT IN THE FIRST PLACE, BUT MERELY ACCEPTED IT, ALBEIT WITH ENTHUSIASM . . . IN BRAZIL, FOR MANY PEOPLE, THEATRE HAS A VERY LOW STANDING.

The show

The workshop period is in itself already a useful and revealing time; an aesthetic space is created in which the participants can express themselves politically by means of exercises and games from the arsenal of the Theatre of the Oppressed, and by the formation of images, the discussion of themes, etc.

Rehearsal is much more than simply rehearsing but we should not lose sight of the fact that the objective of the rehearsals (which are already a form of political activity in themselves, a way of discussing the problems of the community and the relationships between those individuals and their community) – the end-point of the rehearsals – is the actual show, when the group opens itself to the rest of the community and together, using the language of theatre, they discuss and try to rehearse solutions. And they try to invent the required laws which I, in my role of *vereador*, must present to the Chamber.

Other people have their own oppressions, and we must get to know them, and place ourselves in solidarity with them.

After opening their show to their own community, the group should seek dialogue with other communities, and take part in festivals, where everyone can get to know each other or renew old acquaintanceships, and exchange ideas, information, suggestions, advice, proposals – i.e, do politics. Inter-group dialogues and festivals are important: each oppressed person should try to gain an understanding of the oppression experienced by others and show solidarity with them. More than this, reciprocal knowledge encourages and increases emulation. The ideal would be one day to create NET-WORKS OF SOLIDARITY – one day.

The solitude of rehearsal and the public unveiling of our problems

While the workshop element of the process may evolve in an atmosphere of reasonable intimacy, the performance itself is presented publicly and is therefore open to all the unforeseen events which characterise popular shows. We have to evolve from that intimacy to the public presentation: now, we have to make the show look like a show. We are no longer in dialogue with each other: we are proposing a public discussion, an open discussion, so we must 'make theatre'. On this occasion merely 'to be theatre' does not suffice; we must 'make theatre'!

We have no more excuses: we are going to receive people we have invited: so, we are going to make theatre for them, not only for ourselves! At this point, certain problems frequently recur.

Let's analyse some of these problems and try to suggest some solutions.

5 A compact course on playwriting and theatre arts

The tools of our task, the instruments of our work

DRAMATURGY

FOR seven years I was Professor of Dramaturgy at the São Paulo School of dramatic Art; and over many more I have led seminars on Dramaturgy in many other cities. In all these courses I have always based my teaching on a system of laws, which are not to be understood as repressive as laws to be obeyed at all costs! – but as useful instruments of dramaturgy to be used to resolve problems or detect structural defects.

I was a teacher and my job was to give lessons which were, broadly speaking, clear and useful. These were guidelines rather than prescriptions, suggestions rather than recipes. Later came times of other experiments, in different theatrical forms, along other paths. And now, with the Legislative Theatre, it is once again necessary to set out from a well-structured and reliable scheme; the participants in the experiment are groups of people who, for the most part, have never done theatre. They need some clear directions to guide them as they start out, before they try other ways. This chapter may seem too simple, and in reality it is: but this is the best way to introduce neophytes to playwriting. To assume that in some cases they have never even seen a play!

This system, which applies various theories of theatre, can be summed up thus:

- **Laws and rules**: Brunetière, a nineteenth-century French writer, set himself the task of ascertaining whether writing for the theatre was governed by certain immutable laws or just a number of working rules. He began by analysing Aristotle's famous Law of Three Unities.

In his *Poetics*, Aristotle recommends that all the dramatic action should occur within a single day (the Law of the Unity of Time). And this was the case with Greek tragedy, but not with the Elizabethan theatre. Our guidelines concur with the former – we think that it is advisable to reduce the dramatic action to the shortest space of time – unless of course it is necessary to do exactly the opposite.

Brunetière recalls that, in the Hollinshed version of the Romeo and Juliet story, on which Shakespeare based his play, the story happens over a period of years; the lovers' passion is not so ardent or instantaneous, it takes time to grow. By compressing the time-scale, Shakespeare intensifies the dynamic of the plot, the emotions, the conflicts. Therefore, concentrating the action into the shortest space of time is generally a good rule to follow, as long as the piece does not call for the exact opposite, as is the case with Ibsen's *Peer Gynt*, or Strindberg's *The Voyage of Peter the Lucky*. In our work, we frequently encounter the tendency of groups to relate sagas stretching over time and space. People love to tell their life-stories, detail by detail. So the first rule should help us concentrate the action in time, instead of breaking it down into fragments and telling the story chronologically, the way it actually happened in reality. We have to explain to the community groups that the important thing is the reality of the image, and not the exact image of reality. The important thing is to show what things are really like, as Brecht used to say, rather than merely showing what real things are like.

The second Law, the second unity Aristotle speaks of, is the unity of dramatic (or tragic) action, which should be a single action, the main action, with all other actions referring back to it, as happens in Sophocles *Oedipus Rex*, for instance: everything that happens in it relates directly to the quest which Oedipus undertakes to find the murderer of Laius, his father – i.e., himself. This is what happens, as a general rule, in Greek tragedy, or in the plays of Racine, such as his *Phèdre*. But exactly the opposite can be done, as can be seen in Brecht's *Fears and Miseries of the Third Reich*, in which the multiplicity of dramatic actions, of storylines, produces a cumulative, kaleidoscopic effect; or Shakespeare's *King Lear*, in which the parallel dramatic actions of the two fathers,

Lear and Gloucester, and their respective daughters and sons, are essential: each course of action throws the other into relief, reinforcing the characters by comparison of one with another. Thus, the Law of Unity of Action is more a suggested possibility than a rule; but it is a useful suggestion for community artists, who tend to want to include everything in their plays, just as it happened in real life: their lives.

And, as every member of the group always wants to include some element of his or her own story, even though it may have little to do with the main theme or body of the play, there is always a danger of producing a patchwork – which is something to be avoided.

The last of the three so-called laws, which was not formulated by Aristotle, though it is attributed to him in deductions made by his obedient disciples, refers to a possible Law of Unity of Place: the play should take place entirely within the same setting . . . always a good idea when possible, unless of course it should be necessary to do the opposite, as in Shakespeare, Brecht and so many others. When working with community artists it is a good idea, not least because of the practical difficulties of changing sets: they don't have stagehands.

Aristotle systematised his theory starting out from a practice current in his time and from the tragedies he knew, which tended to be concentrated within a single place, with a single action unfolding within a single day. Concentration (of time, action and place) is without doubt a good general rule, but not a coercive, prescriptive law.

For us, in the context of this experiment in Legislative Theatre, we have to concentrate on the essential, on the subject we really want to discuss with these communities, however great the tendency of groups to include events which actually happened, but have no relation to the more essential matter which needs to be talked about. The three unities are useful, not as laws, but as general rules, guidelines, suggestions.

- **Plot or character?** Later, Brunetière discourses on the dramaturgical disputes of his epoch. What should originate and guide the creation of the play – *fable* (the story, the plot) or characters? Do characters construct their history or does the story mould its characters? Supporters of the former position would seem to include writers like Corneille and Ibsen, and of the latter, Racine and Chekhov. And all are excellent dramatists, whatever their point of departure.

- **Chinese crisis**: As far as our work is concerned, though we seek to create characters which are recognisable to the communities, we always have to strengthen the story, the plot, the structure, of the play, so that certain politically meaningful facts will be thrown into clear relief: what is the nature of the problem we are seeking to resolve, and what openings does the piece allow for 'Chinese crisis'[1] – moments where there is danger and opportunity. However rich the characters, we must keep in mind that in the Forum we will be discussing a situation which could happen, or may already be happening, or will happen in the future, to any member of that community, whether they are a character in the play or not.

- **Genres – pure or not?** Another discussion: should genres be pure (as is the case in tragedies such as *Phèdre* and *Oedipus*) or can one follow a tragic scene like the murder of King Duncan (by the Macbeths) with a comic scene in which the drunk porter babbles nonsense (what some North American professors of playwriting term 'comic relief'?). In fact, the asinine utterances of the porter serve to intensify the macabre revelation of the deaths, which follows soon after. Phèdre's Nurse is a serious woman – Lear's Fool sings daft songs. It doesn't matter: the important thing is for the characters to be true, not in the way they look, but in their essence.

    For us, in the Legislative Theatre, we always run the risk of trivialising: the risk of cracking jokes or poking fun just for the sake of it. Certainly, we shouldn't make shows which are all doom and gloom, but equally we should not be satisfied with mere criticism by caricature of the world we are trying to transform. Comedy's function in our work should be to throw light on the oppressive situation, and not disguise or excuse it by superficial censure.

Is there, then, any one element which is so essential to theatre, so necessary, so absolutely obligatory, that without it theatre would not exist? The image – light – is the essence of photography: without it, there would be no photography. Photography requires no more than the image: the rest is framing. The image in movement is the

1. Apparently, in some Chinese languages and in Korean there is no single ideogram for the word 'crisis' – there are two, one which would translate as 'danger', the other as 'opportunitues'.

essence of the cinema: the static camera in conjunction with immobile objects will produce photographs, rather than cinema, however many rolls of film are used up. Nothing more than the image in movement is essential to cinema: even actors are not necessary, a leaf and the wind will suffice. Sound is the essence of music; sound allows us even to listen to silence. Music has no other prerequisites, though Mozart may be better heard in the Opera de la Bastille[2] and the samba song best appreciated in Morro da Mangueira.[3]

What then is the essence of theatre, if such exists?

2. Paris's second opera house.
3. A *favela* in Rio de Janeiro.

The law of conflict

The philosopher Hegel replies: – 'The essence of theatre is the conflict of free wills!' That is to say: a character is a will in flux, a desire in search of its satisfaction, but it does not obtain its object immediately: it is the exercise of a will which collides and conflicts with other, equally free, but contradictory wills. Nothing more than this is essential to the theatre: not sets, nor costumes, nor music nor buildings – without all of these, theatre can still be made, even without a theatre, but not without conflict. All these other elements can strengthen and intensify, they can embellish the theatre, which simply would not exist without the conflict of free wills and, adds Brunetière, 'wills which are free, and conscious of the means they will employ to attain their goals'.

And even this definition is too ample and inclusive. Within it can be included a dialogue by Plato or a boxing match: in both cases the characters exercise free wills to defeat their opponents, whether by means of reason or by force.

The objectivity and subjectivity of goals

John Howard Lawson, a US writer, specifies the necessity: 'That these goals be at the same time objective and subjective'. It is this requirement that is lacking both in the boxing match (purely objective, since it is a matter of flooring the opponent as quickly as possible, knocking him out) and in the dialogue by Plato (which treats as a matter of pure subjectivity the question of the nature of heroism or virtue).

There is however one of the Dialogues – which coincidentally is frequently performed as a piece of theatre – which revolves around a discussion of whether, from the aesthetic point of view, Socrates should or should not have accepted his condemnation to death or whether, on the contrary, he should have availed himself of the opportunity offered to him of fleeing and taking refuge abroad. Here, the moral concepts which are discussed have an objective dimension: will Socrates live or die? And the dialogue becomes theatrical! It is theatre! Equally, there are plays about boxing matches in which the important thing is not the punches traded, objective and bloody as they may be, but the subjective significance of this physical violence: the Protagonist wants to prove to himself or someone else his bravery, he wants to prove that he is the champion again, etc. This is theatre!

Equally in either case, the goals become both objective and subjective – and thus we can arrive at a complete formulation: 'The essence of theatre is the conflict of free wills, conscious of the means they employ to attain their goals, which must be simultaneously subjective and objective'.

Thus, the theatrical will should not be reducible to vague statements of desire – to want happiness or to seek the good of all mankind and universal peace and harmony – but must be concrete: to desire the good of this particular person, in this form and at this time. Peace by this means or that means. Concretely.

Equally the goals must be important, they must be necessary, and the more important they are, the greater the intensity and inclusivity of the piece.

In our experience of Legislative Theatre it is important that the will exercised by the Protagonist – the character who will be replaced in the forum by the spect-actor – is a desire which the intervening spect-actors feel and will be ready to exert themselves to achieve, since they must enter into sym-pathetic relationship with him or her (they must share the same emotions, desires and ideas). The will belongs to the Protagonist, but must be shared by the community; it must be simultaneously an individual desire and a social will.

Free will

Hegel writes extensively on the subject of free will in his book on *Aesthetics*. Animals, according to him, are totally dominated by the environment around them, by constraints of a physical nature, biological necessities, by genetic programming. And, being an animal, man is too. And, though his actions are conscious, they are limited by fear. Only the Prince (in whom all powers are combined) can act without fear of the consequences. Hamlet would not murder Polonius, Laertes and the King if he feared the police.

Thus, for the will to be really free, according to Hegel, its impulses must be able to materialise, to come true. The ideal tragic character is the Prince, says Hegel.

However, the freedom of a character should not be confused with a lack of physical constraint. Prometheus is bound and yet is a free god: he continues his condemnation of Zeus, even as his liver is consumed day by day by the vultures and, even then, he affirms his devotion to man, his repudiation of gods. And Hegel observes that in a picture by Murillo a child gets a whipping for having stolen a fruit and, even as he is being beaten, he eats the fruit.

Hegel is insistent that the wills of the characters (not their whims) should be exercised around what is essential, rational and universal, and not around the accidental or the particular. But, as a drama is woven through with particularities, particularity must be inscribed on the universal.

There are various forms in which the will can be manifested:

1. THE SIMPLE WILL: This is the character will which takes a form of great intensity, always seeking the same goal, in a single and unvarying manner: Iago, from first to last, desires Othello's perdition; Richard III, from start to finish, seeks power; Tartuffe thinks only about money and Orgon's wife.

2. THE DIALECTICAL WILL: In this case, the character carries within him or herself, with variable intensity, a will and its opposite. Here the paradigmatic character is Hamlet and his 'to be or not to be'; equally Brutus, who desires happiness and the death of his protector, Caesar; or Mark Antony himself (who wants to be soldier and lover).

3. THE PLURAL WILL: Here we are dealing not with a single character but with various characters who share the same will, in the same or similar forms. The people against Mark Antony, soon after the death of Caesar. Though they may not be absolutely identical, the transformations the plebeians go through – they are shown as an ignorant rabble – are slow and gradual; like the people against Coriolanus, they have varying degrees of intelligence, but all desire rebellion; or the people against Dr Stockman in Ibsen's *Enemy of the People.*

4. THE FUNDAMENTAL WILL: This is what Stanislavsky termed 'the super-objective', and referred to as the 'secondary wills' within the same person, which must be subordinated to the primary will, the more persistent and permanent will. Hamlet's fundamental will is to avenge the death of his father. His secondary wills are: in relation to Rosencrantz and Guildenstern, to make himself pass for mad; in relation to Polonius, to madden him, to confuse him; in relation to his mother, to convince her to give up his uncle; in relation to Ophelia, a dialectical will, since he loves her and sends her to a convent.

5. THE LUNAR WILL: By Etienne Souriau's definition, this is when one character's will is directly related to another's, as Horatio's is to Hamlet's; Siro's to Calimaco's (in Machiavelli's *Mandragora*); Oenone to Phèdre's (in Racine). Clearly, for the actor, there should never be Lunar Wills, since as far as each of us is concerned, each of us IS ALWAYS the PROTAGONIST of our own lives.

6. THE NEGATIVE WILL: Sometimes the character's will manifests itself in a negative form: he does not want to do a particular thing – i.e., he wants to do exactly the opposite of what other people want him to do. In Erskine Caldwell's *Tobacco Road* there is a wonderful character, Jeeter Lester, who desperately wants to stay in his shack, in opposition to a positive invasion of his lands by land-grabbing speculators who want to build on it. In the last scene we see the tractors advancing, and Jeeter Lester, dozing on a rocking-chair on his veranda, barely opens his eyes as the tractors begin to demolish his house.

7. THE WILL AND THE COUNTER-WILL: To a greater or lesser extent this duality is present in almost every character and it is a quality which should be sought by anyone who writes, directs or acts a character. The counter-will is the desire which emerges in the character in counterpoint to his will. At the same time as he declares his love, the character fears rejection; though he leads a strike, he fears the sack. Or the will itself constructs its own counter-will; Romeo can be madly in love with his Juliet, but can feel repelled by her when she contradicts him in everything; the same can happen with a striker, who, however sure he may be about his case, can experience doubt about the legitimacy of his action.

It is essential for the actor to work not only on the most evident counter-will of his character, but also to try to analyse the whole rainbow of his desires. The better acquainted he is with it, the more he will be able to enrich his performance.

The counter-will ensures that the character is in a permanent state of unstable equilibrium and this is theatrical; every second his expressivity shows him to be slightly different from how he was the moment before, and this attracts and maintains the audience's attention. The actor without a counter-will is always the same; minutes pass, scenes end, and he is immutable. And uninteresting. The dialectical actor, by contrast, is always moving, drawing us in.

8. THE SUB-DIVIDED WILL: Some characters, in Chekhov's work for instance, are so rich that they seem to possess diverse fundamental wills in an intricate network. Wonderful writer though he may be, his plays are very difficult to use in Forum. In this book, we are dealing exclusively with this form of theatre as politics. I love Chekhov, but not as material for Forum; I don't want a spect-actor to replace his characters and find better solutions. Chekhov is wonderful as he is.

9. THE WILL AS EXPRESSION OF NECESSITY: All characters' wills should be, above all, related to necessity, rather than mere caprice. More than this, they must be justified in terms of ethics (as in the confrontation between Creon and Antigone; she, defending the right of the family to bury their dead, her brothers; he, defending the right of the state to apply sanctions against those who have died fighting against their own city).

The will must always be justified, but it will not always be just . . . The wills of the antagonists (the oppressors) should be justified, without necessarily being just – justified by the economic, social and political characteristics with which they oppress. To justify does not mean to accept.

Clearly, in our current experiment all the characters' wills are identified as the demands of the communities we work with – unions, schools, etc. Because, in the case of the Legislative Theatre, we are going beyond mere discussion and rehearsal of the themes we are treating; for us it is a matter of REALLY trying to change the law.

As the essential element of theatre is the will, it follows that the dramatic structure must then be a conflictual structure of several wills, which express different social forces. All the characters must form part of this structure, which must be centralised in a central conflict, which in turn must be the CONCRETION of the CENTRAL IDEA of the play. This is not as complicated as it seems.

The central idea or theme

It is important that the group decides what the central idea is, what the subject of the play and the subsequent forum is to be. The tendency of many communities is to include in the play 'everything that the participants can remember' about an event. The result of this is that often we do not know what we are talking about. A Forum is a question posed to the audience, seeking answers. The question has to be clear. If the spect-actors are to be able to intervene and offer alternatives, and if the Forum is to enrich our understanding, the central idea must be perceptible to all. It can happen that an audience will decide to 'forum' other parts of the play than those relating to the central question being asked.

THE LAW OF CONFLICT is the first law of dramaturgy. Coincidentally, it is the first 'law' of dialectics.

The obstacle

An intense free will, unless it meets an equally powerful obstacle, is soon satisfied – this does not produce theatre. Thus it is vital that the Protagonist – the oppressed person whose place is to be taken by the intervening spect-actor – encounter one or more oppressors, who are his or her obstacle. This search for suitable oppressors must not be random; the group which is creating the play must have genuine knowledge of the problem and must present an organic vision of the situation in which all the elements are true. Theatricality must not sacrifice truth.

It often happens that the actual obstacle is either too immovable or is invisible, imponderable. For instance: Oedipus's actual obstacle is

Zeus, the all-powerful god. However, a conflict of this nature, between the finite human and the infinite divine, would be an unequal match. In this case, the dramatist resorts to a 'displacement' of the conflict: Oedipus fights first against Tiresias, then against Creon: the theatricality is born out of these conflicts and not out of the conflict of Oedipus versus Zeus. Out of the secondary conflicts, displaced conflicts and not out of the principal thematic conflict.

The same thing happens when the obstacle is Society, the Education System, the Power of the State. The dramatist must pit the Protagonist against the representatives of these abstract powers. Sure, society is the oppressor, but who are its agents? One cannot present a character called 'Society' or 'Education' or 'State Repression': we need to personify, to concretise in a person, a character, the means by which society, the education system, or the repressive power of the state, oppresses the Protagonist.

The classic theatre is full of examples in which the Protagonist confronts unknown obstacles: this is the case with Messer Nicia, the Protagonist of Machiavelli's *Mandragora*, in that all the characters conspire against him, while he thinks he is in conspiracy with everyone against an unknown person – whose identity is, in fact, known to everyone except him. The antagonist, the obstacle, does not necessarily have to be a known and actual person, but he must exist as a concrete character and not an abstraction.

The nucleus of the conflict

The nucleus of the conflict must always be the concretion of the abstraction which is the Central Idea or Theme of the play. If we are going to write a play on racial prejudice the nucleus of the conflict must treat precisely that: a victim of prejudice struggling against the prejudiced discriminator.

The nucleus of the conflict must be a kind of synthesis between the Protagonist's thesis and the antithesis represented by the Antagonists, his oppressors. Both must form an organic part of the same system: the family, business, the ownership and non-ownership of land, the community and the forces acting to repress it, etc. The two elements should be a unity of opposites, as with Antigone and Creon – the rights of the family, which Antigone is defending, are set against the rights of the State, as represented by Creon.

63

The nucleus of the conflict must be a system in equilibrium, which becomes unbalanced: it cannot be made up of extreme weakness at one pole and omnipotence at the other. An unstable equilibrium which is dislocated. This system must allow a great variety of displacements (Hamlet v. Claudius, Hamlet v. Rosencrantz and Guildenstern, Hamlet v. Polonius, v. Laertes, v. the actors, Claudius and Gertrude, Laertes and Polonius, etc. etc. etc.). However all these displacements must always be referential to the central conflict.

The theory of crisis

William Archer articulated a 'theory of crises'. According to him, we always observe the waves of the sea with great fascination, because the waves seem to be successively larger, and as each wave grows and dissolves a new wave takes its place, and grows and disappears, till the last wave dies on the sand – and after the 'last' there will always be another . . . This should be the model for the dramatic development of a play: not merely a single enormous wave which never falls back, but a succession of them, each one: 1) assembling the framework of the conflict; 2) unleashing the climax, the explosion; 3) producing the outcome; and so on, in succession, with greater intensity each time.

The structure of a scene or play should be designed in such a way that the action does not start too close to the crisis; this is what we call the 'counter-preparation'. At the start of *Romeo and Juliet*, Romeo is not yet in love with Juliet and proclaims that he will love Rosalind for ever. His change of love makes for theatricality.

In the same way, if Shakespeare started Richard III's extraordinary courtship scene with Lady Anne by showing her to be in love with him, there would be no 'qualitative variation' in his scene with her: they would immediately fall into each others' arms. But in Shakespeare's play, the reverse is the case – Lady Anne starts by spitting on him, i.e., a million miles from tender kisses.

In the case of Legislative Theatre shows, the principal crisis – the moment at which the spect-actor will be called on to intervene – must be clear and must have the characteristics of 'Chinese crisis'. Why do we call it that? Because in Mandarin Chinese, (and also in many other Chinese languages, and even in Korean), the word 'crisis' is represented not by a single ideogram, but by two: the first signifies 'danger' and the second 'opportunities'. Thus, the origin and function of our 'Chinese crisis'; it is the moment at which the protagonic character enters a situation of danger and at which, depending on what choice he makes, there will open out in front of him different opportunities.

And back to Hegel once more, who says that 'the greater the intensity of the wills exercised, the more urgent the necessity of victory; and the smaller the chance of this victory, the better the play'.

The motivation of the will and its characterisation

The motivation is the will itself and its necessity – the motor for wanting its object, its aim, and the reason the will must be exercised – and the latter should never be a matter of mere caprice, *it must be a necessity.*

The motivation is what the character wants and does; the characterisation is the way she does what she does. Characterisation must never be revealed by means of spoken information alone: the audience will not pay the slightest attention when told that a particular character is this sort of person or that sort of person, but will watch with interest everything that she does, which *shows* this information. 'Doing is the best way of saying', wrote the Cuban poet, José Martí.

In one of our group's plays, the father character said at a certain point that the mother was a hypochondriac: that was how the information was conveyed in the first version of the play. No-one took any notice. They changed it. In the second version, we saw the mother taking pill after pill and no-one needed to talk about it, unless they did so as part of an action, rather than merely to inform the audience. The hypochondriac is shown in action.

PLAYING A PART

The first problem which confronts us when rehearsing a play with community groups is the absence of a shared frame of reference. Most of the members of our groups have never been to the theatre, and if they have, it was to see a boulevard comedy. When we utter the word 'theatre', what they actually understand is TV soap opera.

The Brazilian TV soap operas habituate viewers to a type of acting which we might term *epidermic realism*; the actors imitate the cariocan way of speaking and a loping cariocan gait which involves dancing from foot to foot without leaving the spot, mixed with what they have seen of certain actors formed by the 'Actor's Studio' – but, of the latter, they ape only the tricks.

Obviously there are always honourable exceptions, but, as a rule, the television actor is a mere imitator, he is playing 'let's pretend'. This is aggravated by the fact that the majority of TV soaps take place in a social class different from that usually inhabited by the actors who perform them, and we see these actors wandering through scenarios which they would never have encountered in real life, meddling in plots which are never anything like their own experience, exhibiting passions they have never felt.

When we talk about 'theatre', what we mean is the theatre which our community actors have within themselves, but, in the first instance, what they take the word to mean is the false theatre that they see on television. When we manage to show them that *theatre is they themselves* and not the TV soaps, the results are always wonderful.

But it takes time ... Initially there is embarrassment, the mumbled voice directed to the floor, dropping at the actor's feet, the inhibited gesture tying up the body. The actor must learn the difference between just talking to another actor and talking to that actor for the audience's benefit. In normal dialogue there is a direct line between those engaged in the dialogue; the same dialogue in the theatre is a triangle, the third point of which is the audience.

Similarly in relation to the body, we have to convince the actors that an actor doesn't cross his arms unless the character would cross his arms (arms are so expressive, arms are language – arms are made to float in the air and not to be strapped across the chest: let our arms breathe!)

However, the art of playing a character can be very difficult or very easy. For Alfred Lunt, an actor from the early part of the century, who was married to a famous and excellent actress (so they say – I don't know, I never saw her), Lynn Fontaine – for Lunt, performing a role was a very easy task. His (possibly apocryphal) advice to actors was to 'speak loud enough for everyone to hear and don't bump into the furniture'.

It is not quite as simple as that, but when the community actor stops thinking about trying to imitate the actors on the eight o'clock soap and concentrates his energy on showing what the people he himself knows are like, what the real situation he himself lives in is like, acting becomes much easier and more pleasurable; it is a pleasure to relive on stage vivid scenes from real life, and by reliving them, to understand them.

The spect-actor and his relationship to the show

The theatrical ceremony is well defined: away from the prying gaze of others, a number of people prepare themselves, and organise an event – a reproduction of scenes from real life, with varying degrees of authenticity, that is, as these scenes happened or as they were experienced, remembered, imagined. They then invite other people to immobilise themselves in front of a raised stage or an arena (the 'aesthetic space') and there, they reproduce the event rehearsed.

The theatrical ceremony has as its first premise the division of the space into one area where the actors move around and another where the spectators are immobilised. Though juxtaposed, they do not penetrate each other, nor is one superimposed on the other, and even when the latter space (the spectators') is fragmented and the former (the actors') dispersed around the room, these smaller segments maintain the same relationship to the surrounding space as that of the large stage to the large auditorium. Very occasionally, shows make actors and spectators revolve in the same area, embrace one another or perform common tasks in a common space, as happened in some of the theatrical events directed by Richard Schechner or Julian Beck, amongst others, during the 1960s.

The Theatre of the Oppressed breaks with this ceremony and has, as its first premise, the intention to democratise the stage space – not to destroy it! – rendering the relationship between actor and spectator transitive, creating dialogue, activating the spectator and allowing him or her to be transformed into 'spect-actor'.

This transformation can come about in two main ways: either by the citizens themselves (the 'Oppressed' activated as artists) creating the show – the images to be presented – or simply by their intervention during the part of the show denominated 'Forum', when actors and spectators, on equal terms and with equal powers, improvise solutions or alternatives to the problems put forward by the show. In either or both these two forms, the citizen transforms himself into 'artist'.

What is the effect of this transformation?

In the first place: where was the artist the spectator has transformed himself into before? Within himself, clearly. The spectator 'act-ualised' that capacity which, within himself, was only 'potential'; it is as simple as a person learning to ride a bicycle, to swim, to dance the waltz or to beat a drum: the dancer and the athlete were inside him, they were potentialities contained within that person's body.

Thus, the theatre creates a space in which potentialities can be 'act-ualised' or developed: the potential becomes actual. The person can re-dimension himself, investigate himself, find himself, recognise himself.

This special space is propitious to discoveries. And the person who discovers or is discovered, is transformed. What effect does this transformation produce? Let us analyse some exemplary cases.

Lillian Gish in the Chapeu Mangueira

4. In *The Rainbow of Desire*, using the analogy of the pressure cooker, Boal writes of the 'person' as being the container of all angels and devils – the angels are the characters within the person which we release; the 'personality', that which we show to the world; the devils are other possible characters, which theatre can enable us to experiment with and, if we choose, add to our personality. A.J.

In the Chapeu Mangueira group, they did a piece about refuse, dealing with both the city's negligence and the residents' own responsibility for the matter: one Saturday afternoon, they were about to start the show, entitled *Garbage!*, for the local community, when they realised that one of the principal actresses was lacking. They searched all over for her till finally they found her at her home. What was she doing? Taking a bath and perfuming herself with soap. They were amazed.

But these people were wrong to be shocked by this: the actress, instinctively, had accurately perceived that she was an actress *playing* a character, whose habits, whose customs, were very different from her own. She was capable of playing the dirty neighbour, capable of creating a character[4] – and when we play a character we all draw the material from within ourselves, from our 'person' – however, that character had nothing to do with her personality and, when performing in the show, she wanted to be absolutely clear about the fact that she was playing the 'neighbour' and not herself dissolved and degraded in the neighbour's dirtiness.

It might have seemed simple-minded but in fact she had intuitively understood something essential to the art of performance: clean, she would be a genuine actress playing a dirty character; dirty, she would be *a dirty actress playing herself*, which she wanted to fight against.

The actress of the silent screen, Lillian Gish, apart from being known for her talent, was also renowned for the fact that when she played roles of poor bedraggled women, she made a point of dressing in pure silk underwear. And so it was with our beloved Lillian Gish of Chapeu Mangueira.

The Oppressed Recognises the Mechanisms of the Oppression

This happened one Sunday afternoon at the base of Atoba, a homosexual organisation. A play was being rehearsed which had been written by the actors themselves, about an actual occurrence: one of them had done a written test to obtain a particular job. He passes and is called for a personal interview: on seeing him, the interviewer seems to find it strange that the man is wearing an earring, and passes comment on his rings and his clothes. The young man replies that it's just a question of taste. Finally, because of his 'peculiarities', the young man is not taken on, in spite having achieved the best mark in the written exam.

The open rehearsal began: there were a hundred or so gays and lesbians there, people who habitually met there, and a further 10 or so assessors from my office, invited to attend and debate. At the end of the play, when he hears the manager say that he will not be given the job, in spite of his excellent exam, the Protagonist silently weeps, without protesting. The scene was performed with great authenticity and emotion, and the audience enthusiastically applauded his sincere tears in the face of the injustice.

Except that the actor wasn't acting; he was being. And we only realised this when one of the Jokers went on stage to comfort the actor. The scene as rehearsed was not supposed to have ended like this – on the contrary, it was supposed to have ended explosively with the oppressed homosexual responding with a violent outburst. In the heat of performance, the actor became genuinely overcome with emotion, forgot the lines he'd learnt and wept in silence.

How might we explain what happened between actor and character?

HYPOTHESIS (or better, HYPO-THESIS, hypo = less than)

The young man was used to discrimination and knew how to defend himself. In daily life he knew his enemies and knew the weapons to confront them with. He was used to 'living' this scene in real life and now, as actor, he had to 'experience' it on stage, he had to 're-live' it, on stage in front of us. In the street, the scene occurred always 'for the first time', so the actor 'lived' it; on stage he had to repeat what had been rehearsed, predetermined, and for this reason he 'experienced' it. He re-lived. In real life we live, in theatre we re-live and observe ourselves better.

When he was actually performing it and saw the mechanisms of oppression – the contempt, the disgust, the loathing – deployed fictitiously against him, by a homosexual like him – a victim of the same oppression! – the actor 'lived' this discovery and could not use, in front of his fellow, the defences which he habitually used against his real oppressors, such as for instance cynicism, flippancy, caricature. This discovery was lived 'for the first time', which brought forth the actor's uncontrolled emotion, hence the shock.

The Girl Speaks to her Oppressors by means of Interposed Person

The Rio universities' black student group, SENUM, was presenting its play, *The Peg*, for an audience made up predominantly of younger black students from schools and colleges. The piece deals with a black girl and her oppressions when she is looking for a job and is discriminated against on account of her colour, and also in her own house, in childhood, when the family forces her to wear a peg on her nose to try to make her nose thinner, like a white girl's nose. In one of the shows, a young girl who had come to the theatre in a party from her school came on stage because in the actors she saw her own companions, other members of the school party: the actors were treating the character the way her schoolmates treated her: name-calling, using words like black bastard, nigger, Zulu, half-caste, fuzzy, monkey. She became fearful and angry, seeing her real companions watching the scene at her side, and she came on stage and said to the characters everything that she would like to have said to her real schoolmates, who were watching in shamed silence. From that moment on, the children never made fun of her again: they had seen that it was no laughing matter; it hurt.

The Woman Discovers that She Has Always Been an Actress

In one of the groups linked to the Catholic Church, a fat woman was chosen to play the character of an irate, pugnacious, aggressive fat woman. She was radiantly happy. Later she was given another role: a peevish and aggressive father. She was even happier and said: 'Now I have discovered that my whole life I have been actress and I never noticed. Except from now on I also want to play parts more different from my self, because my husband challenged me: "Don't you see? They are giving you parts which suit your face; you only play crazy women, and even when they needed a short dumpy man, they chose you. Go and play a nice, happy character . . . At least try being like that at home: play a nice wife! You're a good actor, you can do it. Try!"'

THE IMAGE OF THE STAGE

The aesthetic space is the area where the scene and the accompanying Forum are played out. The aesthetic space is the creation of the audience: it requires nothing more than their attentive gaze in a

71

single direction for this space to become 'aesthetic', powerful, 'hot', five-dimensional (three physical dimensions, plus the subjective dimensions of imagination and memory). In this space, all actions gain new properties – dichotomisation, plasticity and tele-microscopy: the actor in this space is dualised (he is himself and he is the character); the objects no longer carry only their usual daily signification, but become the stuff of memory and imagination; and every tiny gesture is magnified, and the distant becomes closer.

The aesthetic space is a creation of the spectators. Why? Human beings relate to the world, constantly, in a binary way, perceiving the world and responding to the stimuli they receive: according to the variation of light intensity, the aperture of the eye increases or diminishes, the body contracts or expands in response to cold or heat. In the same way, to a question we ask, we imagine an answer – even silence is action. We are in permanent dialogue with the out-side world, receiving stimuli and producing actions. At the moment when the human being becomes the spectator, he suspends his need to act, his urge for action. This energy does not cease to exist – so where does it go? It goes into the place where the object of his attention is located, be it a person or a thing: and in the area around this object, the aesthetic space is created. The more people looking in the same direction, the more intense is the space. This phenomenon can occur on a stage, in an arena, or anywhere around a 'real-life' incident.

The Chamber as circus

Recently, the passing of the annual budget in the Chamber culminated in a brawl; *vereadors* broke windows, threw chairs in the air, they even pulled guns and hurled a microphone in the face of the person chairing the session, who bled.[5] During the tumult, mini-conflicts broke out throughout the assembly: stimulated by the violence, people who had scores to settle started parallel confronta-tions around the room. The attention of the spectators present was centred on the speaker's table, where the major fracas was happening: some wanted the session to go on, others wanted to interrupt it. Whenever a fresh row exploded, part of the audience directed its gaze towards it for a few moments and, that in itself created a new mini-aesthetic space. The newly created dichotomised actors (man and *vereador*, one involved in the brawl, the other showing how brave

5. I told the aggressor that he had misunderstood Marshall McLuhan, who wrote that 'the medium is the message'. *AB.*

he was) were energised by the audience, which inevitably led to 'over-acting'; phrases like 'Don't push me!' 'Get your hands off me' clearly denoting a subtext along the lines of: 'Please, get me out of here . . .'

Till eventually one particular *vereador*, a squat fat little man, one of those whose normal procedure was to enter mute and leave in silence, one of those silent voices which abound in the assembly – this man who had till that moment been comfortably ensconced in his seat – suddenly became aware of the photographers and TV reporters with camera in hand, and, unable to resist the lure of free propaganda, jumped on top of his bench, giving vent to stertorous guttural shouts which would have put Johnny Weissmuller, the famous Tarzan, to shame. His gestures seemed to indicate that he was about to jump, even without the aid of a creeper, all the way from his bench onto the speaker's table, 30 metres away. Everyone turned in his direction, but when they saw who it was, a completely insignificant and uninteresting person, they soon stopped looking. The miserable *vereador*, who had enjoyed a brief initial moment as the centre of attention, gesticulated even more extravagantly and amplified his voice, but, pretty soon, seeing that he had been abandoned, he became discouraged, climbed down from his bench, and having learnt his lesson, sat back in his usual place, crestfallen, murmuring: 'It's only because I'm short . . .' And then he shut up, as always.

This is the tremendous power of the aesthetic space – the spectator's creation, put to use by the actor. And because it is so powerful, there is all the more need to democratise it.

The image of the scene

One of the most important aspects of the Forum Theatre show is the image of the scene – and I use the word 'image' advisedly, rather than 'scenography', or even worse, as the French say, 'décor'. Image is a totality, it includes both the things and the people involved in the event, even passing things and people. In the image of the scene one must be able to discern where the aesthetic space is, how it is configured, where it starts and finishes. In theatres, this area is marked out by the black or neutral colouration of the rest of the space, the auditorium, the walls, the aisles. In the street, in the open air, one has to take into consideration passing buses, outbursts of barking from startled dogs, the inevitable drunkard who feels compelled to pass comment on every scene or speech, and continually applauds, usually at the wrong points, etc.

So the first precaution which must be taken is to clearly delineate where the aesthetic space is – it exists without such delineation, but is reinforced by it. The aesthetic space can coincide with the stage but it is not the stage: it is the concentration of the eyes of the spectators on one area.

The aesthetic space has special properties: apart from its dichotomising, plastic and tele-microscopic aspects (which I explain in my book *The Rainbow of Desire*), it is magic. Especially in poor communities, it exercises a power of enchantment. And, when precisely defined, it comes to signify an inaccessible area which will later, in the Forum, be invaded: an invasion which symbolises transgression. And we know that transgression is necessary if oppression is to be ended: if the oppressed accepts rules, habits, customs, traditions, that everything is just the way it is because it has always been that way, then he will never free himself from his oppression. (One of the arguments used against agrarian reform relies on the idea of 'acquired rights' to land, as if all acquired rights or titles were legitimate: the slave owners had paid for their slaves 'legally', therefore they had 'acquired rights': if we were to recognise this as a legitimate argument, we would still have slavery today.)

In their name or in their place

For this reason, when the first 'spect-actor' comes on stage, he transgresses, like a member of a church congregation who takes the place of the priest and celebrates the mass himself. And, since the spect-ator is one individual rising out of the audience, he does not make this transgression *in place* of the other spectators, but *in their name*. The actor acts in place of the spectators; the spect-actor acts in their name, because each member of the audience can decide whether she feels represented by this intervention or not, and, if she doesn't, she can go on stage and give her own version of things.

It is important that the aesthetic space be well defined, especially because we almost always work in visually polluted places: football pitches or basketball courts, flights of steps at public buildings, etc. On seeing the aesthetic space, everyone should be able to see its physical limits, so that the transgression will be more distinct. It is not enough simply to hang a cyclorama or a coloured drape at the back, and sling a canvas on the floor. These elements need to have been given an 'aestheticising' treatment; they should not, cannot, look like objects we would encounter in daily life – even though they are made out of such things, they must be treated aesthetically so that they are differentiated from them. A sheet of cloth should be treated in such a way that it doesn't look like a sheet of cloth bought in the local store. This treatment can relate to number, or shape, or colour, as we will see.

Joker scenography

We have to develop a 'joker scenography'; we are working with poor communities, our shows should neither seem nor feel expensive. All the set materials must be made out of recycled or re-used objects. Things which have been thrown out. Or cheap things. But with creativity. We should especially try to use materials which are easily found in the community itself. And transform (aestheticise) them.

Rosa Luiz Marquez's group, Los Teatreros Ambulantes de Puerto Rico, made a show populated by a mass of people in wedding dresses and bridesmaids' costumes, and bishops' robes and soldiers' uniforms, all beautifully dressed in newspaper clothes. All, absolutely all, made out of those rolls of paper left over by the big newspapers, who sell them at second-hand prices.

During the 'Land and Democracy' event we did a scenography laboratory which used plastic bottles to make large wine goblets with delicate stems, outsize syringes and other surgical tools, machine-guns, etc.

In the Chapeu Mangueira *favela* group, all the wigs were made out of metal strips from beer cans and the whole scenography of the play, which was dealing with the subject of refuse, was made out of exactly that. Clean rubbish, obviously, hygienic rubbish, but rubbish all the same.

We did a show during the elections, with Benedita da Silva, our candidate for senator and Conceição Tavares, who was standing as MP (they were both elected!), in which the two of them engaged in dialogue on stage, and also sang to each other in dialogue form. At the end of the show, a school of samba came on: all the participants' costumes were made out of newspaper sprayed with silver.

The German group, Spect-Act-Ulum, did a play which required four telephones. These were all made out of papier mâché (from old newspapers) and each phone reflected the power of its user, from the smallest, which nestled in the palm of a hand, to the largest, which was larger than its user and wrapped itself around him.

Often it is enough to stick some coloured paint on objects for them to be 'joker scenography' – that is, scenography which simultaneously reveals the origin of the object and its present usage.

In the old Arena theatre, Flavio Imperio and Marcos Weinstock, in memorable shows like Lope de Vega's *The King is the Best Justice*, and the multiply authored *Paulista*[6] *Fair of Opinion*, used to make sets and costumes totally based on throw-away things and yet the impression that came over was of glorious nobles and princes and princesses in the former piece and gaudy and ostentatious television programmes in the latter. Everything was used, even old bits of donkey harnesses thrown out by the São Paulo council, stairs and window-frames raided from demolition sites, remnants from the animal hide trade, everything.

In a play done by CTO Paris, a mother carried a cross made out of kitchen utensils, the son's bed was a coffin, and the father did his accounts on a pile of adding-machines.

The function of 'joker scenography' is also to allow the audience to see and not merely look. If they look at an actual telephone on stage, they won't see a telephone; but if they can see an object (larger or smaller, or different colour or texture from a 'genuine' phone) representing the absent phone, then they will see the absent phone. Things which are as they are are not seen; we only see absences. The 'joker scenography' should deliver the spect-actor to a reality which is not present, except symbolically. We are light years away from the scenography of Antoine,[7] the French master of hyper-realism who, when producing a play set in a slaughterhouse, went and bought fresh carcasses every day.

6. 'Paulista', relating to São Paulo, as 'carioca' is to Rio.

7. André Antoine (1858–1943), French actor and director renowned as a pioneer of naturalistic sets.

THE STAGING

The staging (the *mise-en-scène*) is an important part of the image. Often groups have a tendency to have their characters come on stage, say 'Good morning' or 'Good Evening' to the other characters and then sit down at a table to start conversing; however interesting the dialogue, the image of three or four people seated round a table – we should be aware that this image is also language! – certainly is not saying anything particularly intelligent or interesting, and runs the risk of making the show monotonous and devaluing the dialogue by not emphasising it, or underlining or pointing it.

How do we get round this problem? It can happen that the actual 'ritual' of the action shown on stage is already visually rich and very theatrical. In such an instance, it is enough to reproduce it, trying to reinforce it. Work scenes tend to be in this category, for instance. Weddings and baptisms, solemn ceremonials, social gatherings, fables, etc.

But the opposite can happen; the ritual can be static and un-expressive. When this is the case, we can resort to all the rehearsal techniques around working with images, such as, notably, the 'Rashomon' technique: each actor makes a sculpture using himself, the other actors, and any objects to hand. A subjective sculpture which shows things not the way they are, but the way he feels them. Each actor will make his own subjective, unique, individual sculpture, and the scene will be replayed as many times as there are actors. This will provide the director with a repertoire of images to choose from.

Another way of arriving at a rich and stimulating 'image of the word' was also used by the actors from Spect-Act-Ulum. The theme of the show was bureaucracy and the whole show was created from images made by the group members themselves on that theme and that word: what is bureaucracy. The final image was a synthesis of all these images, filled with the dehumanised and defunct gestures of the bureaucrat.

Categories of image

There are various categories of image. I will cover some of them below.

- **The sensory image**: In public shows, I like to do a demonstration showing myself first just as myself, my body, and asking the audience what they see. A man. I show them a chair and repeat the question: a chair, they answer. That is the sensory image, the first category of image. Something which people see and agree to call by the same name.

- **The mnemonic image**: This is an image in which the observer completes what he is actually seeing with elements which existed in other circumstances but are not now present: I sit on the chair and do the actions of a person typing, and even without the machine being there, the observers 'see' the typewriter which exists in their memory; or I play an imagined or remembered piano, or speak into a microphone, or drink from a glass or a bottle, etc. And the spectators see objects which don't exist, but once existed, and still exist today in their memory.

  The actions must be precise for the observers to revive their memories. Once, at a workshop out in the country, I was doing a demonstration of the mnemonic image and I extended the parade of images to include a steering wheel, and, to the best of my abilities, did a motorist driving a car; but, since I have never learnt to drive, my motorist actions must have been on the imprecise side, because when I asked: 'What do you see?' they all answered: 'A man milking a cow!'

- **The 'imagined' image**: This is another category of image. Except when the actions are inadequate, imperfect, or badly executed, the observers are all able to complete with the aid of memory, the sensory, objective image, which is actually in front of them. But sometimes an image may be presented in such a way that completing it from memory alone is either impossible or insufficient: in such an instance, the observer resorts to his imagination. For instance, a man standing on a chair with his arms apart as if he was about to strangle someone, can provoke completely different 'visions' in those observing: a horror film monster, Dracula, King Kong, a madman, a person who has just painted the floor and can't get off the chair without smudging the paint, etc.

  In this case, we are dealing with a 'projected image', that is, each observer projects onto the existing image memories, desires or fears he carries with him, consciously or unconsciously. Any 'interpretation' of such an image is not in the image but in the observer: the image is in the eye, not in the object. In fact, any image whatsoever is polysemic, carries many meanings, which is precisely what leads to the richness of Image Theatre: if the spectators already know what an image is supposed to signify, they cease to project other possible meanings onto it.

- **The symbolic image**: A flag, nation; green, hope; red, danger; finger and thumb joined in a circle means 'OK' in the USA, but is pornographic in Brazil. National images: the gestures that accompany or signify *ma que* in Italy or *bof* in French. These are images of this type, where such and such an action means such and such a thing; they have no value as prospective language, they denote only the signification which is attributed to them.

In search of the subjunctive image

Now I would like to make a few observations on the uses of coercive images that we suffer in day to day life.

It is said that we live in a world dominated by images, and it is true that images do dominate us, mainly those emanating from television, with which a transitive dialogue is well nigh impossible: there is only monologue. As far as newspapers are concerned, a minimal freedom is left to the reader, who can choose his reading rhythm, which page, which news, in what order, and can, to a certain extent, imaginatively rearrange the whole newspaper to suit his preference. With the TV, no such space is allowed us. Obedience is the only option left us, all we can do is respectfully salute the screen, like a soldier to his superior officer.

The truth is that the television does not allow itself to be seen. Looking is a biological act: open eyes look. Seeing is an act of conscience.

Images can be conjugated like verbs

The person who watches television, 'sees the television', but does not 'see television'. Television does not allow itself to be seen, it obliges us to watch it, and that is very dangerous. Because the images which television shows can be conjugated in at least three modes and four tenses. Let us look at some examples.

First: in the present indicative. This happens when, for instance, the TV shows us live, by direct transmission, events happening at that moment on the football pitch or in the street, in the governor's palace or in the slum.

In spite of the appearance of objectivity, even in the present indicative the image is manipulated, firstly by the camera operator

79

who selects what he thinks should be seen; secondly by the TV director, who chooses from the various images generated by different cameras which will be shown to the viewers, and when. Thus, even in the present indicative, the image shown is only, as it were, that of one side of a chess game: it is impossible to understand the game, to have one's own opinion, if one cannot see the whole of the board.

Second: the perfect indicative, as happens, for example, in the national news, which give us a resumé of the news and relates what has happened, in its own way; here the selection of images is still more restrictive and directed, and is more a reflection of the desires of the TV channel's proprietor, who shows us what it is important for him to show, magicking away what he doesn't like.

One example will suffice; the famous debate between Lula[8] and Collor[9] in 1989. All that was eventually broadcast was a big lie, fabricated from fragments of truths. It was like broadcasting a boxing match and showing one contender's direct hits and the other's bruised face. The images shown are genuine, but the montage of these images is deceitful. In the indicative mode and the perfect tense, the manipulation of the images is total and absolute – with images of reality, the TV director creates a new reality, more convincing than its model.

Above all, images on the TV are conjugated in the imperative mode: 'Eat this, drink that, everything else will make you sick, buy the lot, right now, our telephone operators are waiting for your call, if the lines are busy call back another time, don't waste a minute, don't be a fool, why have you still not bought this stain-remover which is exactly the same as the one you can buy much more cheaply in the shops, but by telemarketing you will, at the very least, feel only as stupid as everyone else.'

In the cinema, as on the television, the sound-effects can stimulate us to feel certain emotions. The TV goes further and, in imperative mode, even tells us what we should find funny, and when, and even how much, we should laugh. The majority of comedy programmes direct the viewer's responses. I freely admit to having often thought I must be stupid when I haven't detected the slightest hint of humour at moments when the roar of canned laughter has clearly indicated that this was supposed to be a funny bit.

Rhythm on TV is equally imperative: a single image cannot last longer than a few seconds on the screen; this even goes as far as making the speaker change angles, change cameras, so that the viewer doesn't have time to get used to a particular image and

8. Luis Inacio Lula da Silva, universally known as Lula, the leader of the Workers' Party (PT) and challenger for the presidency against Fernando Collor.
9. Fernando Collor, Brazilian President, who was elected in 1990 and subsequently impeached in 1994 on corruption charges.

actually see it, rather than merely watching it, in a hypnotic trance. This is one of TV's most powerful weapons: the use of time. A picture by Van Gogh shows, as logic would lead us to expect, that particular painter's vision of the world; between the viewer and the picture, there is a partnership: the former is granted the possibility of seeing the picture when and how she likes, at her own rhythm, choosing which angle to look at it from, which part of the painting to observe more closely.

Rarely – perhaps only on a few educational programmes – does the televisual rhythm become less frenetic and allow the viewer to interact, and even digest the information instead of merely swallowing it whole.

The TV hardly ever presents Subjunctive or Conditional images, that is, images which allow us to think, to imagine, to invent, images which instil doubt or allow fancy. And when the TV gives the impression of democratising, it does so in an even more authoritarian manner: I, the TV, decide that you can only decide between option A and option B. You decide . . .[10]

It's not true: it's already been decided. Why reduce the viewers' creative capacity to a simple heads-or-tails dreamt up by the producer? Who do you like more, mummy or daddy? How many children will no longer think of saying: – 'I like the next-door neighbour better, 'cos she's got fat legs . . .'?

And the TV viewer, however imaginative he or she may be, is converted into a mere recipient of orders, behaviours, fashions and idioms, thoughts, customs.

Television – as it currently exists – is the opposite of art, since the artist is a person who helps us to see what we tend only to look at, and to listen to what we tend only to hear. And I think I should go further: the true painter goes beyond the mere mixture of colours and shapes, and manages to see darkness: manages not only to see things in darkness, but actually to see darkness, as Rembrandt does; the true composer transcends the mere ordering of sounds and manages to hear, and make us hear, silence, as Beethoven does. Just as the true psychoanalyst is able to hear the word which is not spoken.

Television, by contrast, blinds and deafens us. Television is the antithesis of psychoanalysis.

10. 'You Decide' is the title of just such a programme on Brazilian TV, which presents only options A and B for the viewers to choose from.

Map showing the locations of the mandate's interventions in the city

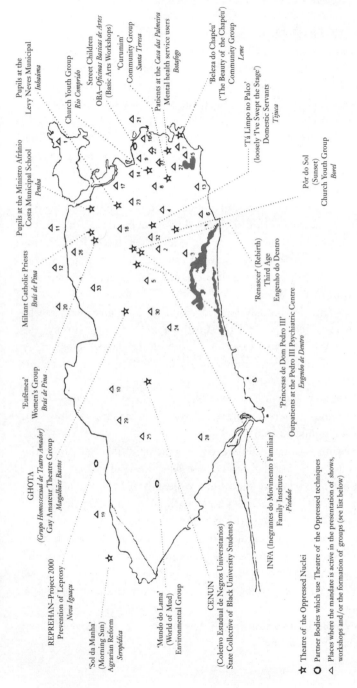

Pupils at the
Levy Neves Municipal
Inhaúma

Church Youth Group
Rio Comprido

Street Children
OBA–*Oficinas Basicas de Artes*
(Basic Arts Workshops)

'Curumim'
Community Group
Santa Teresa

Patients at the *Casa das Palmeira*
Mental health service users
Botafogo

'Beleza do Chapéu'
('The Beauty of the Chapéu')
Community Group
Leme

Pupils at the Ministro Afrânio
Costa Municipal School
Penha

'Tá Limpo no Palco'
(loosely 'I've Swept the Stage')
Domestic Servants
Tijuca

Militant Catholic Priests
Brás de Pina

Pôr do Sol
(Sunset)
Church Youth Group
Borel

'Eufêmea'
Women's Group
Brás de Pina

'Renascer' (Rebirth)
Third Age
Engenho do Dentro

GHOTA
(*Grupo Homossexual de Teatro Amador*)
Gay Amateur Theatre Group
Magalhães Bastos

'Princesas de Dom Pedro III'
Outpatients at the Pedro III Psychiatric Centre
Engenho de Dentro

REPREHAN–Project 2000
Prevention of Leprosy
Nova Iguaçu

'Sol da Manhã'
(Morning Sun)
Agrarian Reform
Seropédica

'Mundo do Lama'
(World of Mud)
Environmental Group

INFA (Inegrantes do Movimento Familiar)
Family Institute
Piedade

CENUN
(Coletivo Estadual de Negros Universitarios)
State Collective of Black University Students

☆ Theatre of the Oppressed Nuclei

○ Partner Bodies which use Theatre of the Oppressed techniques

◁ Places where the mandate is active in the presentation of shows,
workshops and/or the formation of groups (see list below)

1 Secondary school students – *Ilha do Governador* (Governor's Island)
2 Health sector professionals – *Jacarepaguá*
3 Workers – *Rio das Pedras*
4 PT (Workers' Party) militants – *Praça Saens Pena*
5 Community *Sulacap*
6 Adolescents – *Rocinha*
7 Children – *Chapéu Mangueira – Leme*
8 Adolescents – *Candelária – Mangueira*
9 Street children – *Maracanã*
10 Artists – *Vila Kennedy*
11 Neighbourhood group – *Caxias*
12 Cultural animators – *São João de Meriti*
13 Members of the local community – *Vidigal*
14 Teachers linked to the Union – Various locations round the City
15 Women's groups – *Morro da Saudade – Botafogo*
16 Street children – *Centro*

17 Members of the local community – *Caju*
18 Animal rights group – *Jacarezinho*
19 Students at the Rural University
20 Afro-Catholic movement – *São João de Meriti*
21 PT (Workers' Party) militants – *Niteroi*
22 OJL (Organization of Youth for Liberty) militants – *Catete*
23 Members of the local community – *Complexo da Maré*
24 Therapists – *Jacarepaguá*
25 Cultural animators – *Campo Grande*
26 Adolescents – *Vigário Geral*
27 PT militants – *Largo do Machado*
28 Disabled people – various locations around the city
29 Health sector professionals – *Realengo*
30 Members of the local community – *Colônia Juliano Moreira*
31 Children – *Morro da Saudade*
32 Church Youth Group – *Andaraí*
33 Adolescents – *Pavuna*

SOUND AND VOICE

This is a delicate problem: if the environments in which we show our plays are always visually polluted, the same can be said, with even greater justification of noise pollution. It is no accident that Shakespeare always began his shows by making more noise on stage than there was in the audience: fights between servants or popular revolts (*Romeo and Juliet* and *Coriolanus*), witches (*Macbeth*), ghosts (*Hamlet*) or monstrous characters (*Richard III*), are placed right at the beginning of the first act, because in those days they could not count on the effect of concentrating lighting on the stage and turning the house lights down, or on pliant and well-behaved audiences in the court of the King Louis XIV.

The same applies to us, as we frequently have to compete with the hooting of car and lorry horns. And in the same way as the aesthetic space must detach itself from the rest of the space, so too, the sound space must separate itself from the general din. How? This is where music is of the greatest importance.

A show must have rhythm, which should not be confused with speed. Rhythm is not speed, though our community groups do tend to gallop through the script when they feel that the scene 'has no rhythm'. Rhythm is the organisation of infinite time, just as image is the organisation of infinite space.

Life, as we live it, is incessant. Its essential activities are ceaseless. Some are rhythmical, like the beating of the heart, or melodic, like the blood coursing through our veins, some follow the circadian rhythms, like hunger, menstruation or other periodic activities, while others are more aleatory, like sex.

The world is rhythmical: day follows night, summer follows spring, the tide ebbs and flows . . . And human life moves in harmony with the universal rhythms. A solar eclipse disorientates animals, especially birds, which can even die from such a disturbance, unable to adapt their rhythms to the curtailment of day. The same happens with jet lag.

Some human activities are not rhythmical, but are still incessant, such as perception and action. We are always perceiving and always acting as a result of our perceptions, our desires, our wills. Even asleep we feel cold or heat and turn over or change sides.

When for whatever reason – for instance watching a show – the human being suspends his incessant activity, all this energy is transferred to the area of his attention: the aesthetic space comes into being, as we have already seen. With sound and voice we have to break the rhythms of the street, and create the rhythm of the scene.

This aesthetic space is IMAGE and SOUND.

6 The show and the community

IN one community, a participant asked us to make posters advertising the show, and she wanted to distribute them not only up on the hill where she lived, but also on Copacabana beach, just below. She did not want the actors to interrupt other community activities by presenting their shows without prior warning. She wanted publicity.

It might have seemed like vanity: it wasn't. She wanted to give the event its proper significance, by advertising the date and time it was to be presented, by naming the actors, by giving the play a title. She wanted to make the show stand out from other run-of-the-mill activities . . . She wanted it to be respected by her neighbours and she wanted to take on this responsibility.

The opening of the show for a community is an important moment, a big step. If the rehearsals are already a form of political activity in themselves (the citizens talk to one another and try to pinpoint their oppressions, to understand them by means of aesthetics), the shows are the moment of social communion, in which the other members of the community are invited to participate in the debates, still using the same theatrical language.

The inter-community DIALOGUES are also important, when the participants of one community show their work to another community, whose members intervene in the Forums of their plays. Sometimes, by being outside the situation, they can see better, as happened for instance when a member of CENUM visiting Chapeu Mangueira came up with a solution no-one had thought of: if it was impossible to persuade a philanthropic society (the equivalent of a charity) to act as intermediary for the granting of state funds to their project, because of the unpaid work that this would involve. The spect-actors from Chapeu Mangueira replaced the Protagonist but no solution was found. A young man from CENUM intervened, abandoned the dialogue with the manager of the charity, and made a proposition: nothing was stopping this and other communities from creating their own philanthropic society with this specific purpose. So he proposed they create their own charity. Which was precisely what was done, with the help of the advisers from our cabinet, who wrote the statutes and took all the necessary legal steps. Apart from bringing in a fresh view from the outside, these dialogues help to create a 'network of solidarity'.

Apart from these dialogues, it is important for us to mount FESTIVALS at least once a quarter, the primary goal of which is to allow contact between each community and the majority, or all, of the others. And, by extension, with the population at large: as a rule, these festivals take place in busy squares or public gardens on days when there are crowds.

FIRE AND THE THEATRICALISATION OF THE STREET

Often, especially for commemorations or demonstrations, it is necessary to theatricalise the streets and the squares. To this end, some spectacular methods must be used.

In Ipatinga, on the anniversary of the police attack on the Metal Workers' Union headquarters, in which several workers were killed, the members of the union's theatre group, in collaboration with a group of German actors who were doing a workshop with us, showed a scene in which this assault was symbolised by balls of fire (made out of newspapers) and barricades made out of burning tyres.

On another occasion, in Rio, in a procession we did through the streets to the steps of the legislative assembly, we performed a ritual washing of the steps (symbolically the cleansing of corruption) in mimicry of the annual ceremony at the Church of Senhor de Bonfim, in Bahia, and we used fire to cremate the urns of corruption (in this case, ballot boxes). In Bonfim *baianas* (generally very fat black women) wash the stairs of the church, singing religious songs, symbolising the cleasing of the souls.

In front of the Souza Aguiar Hospital, we did a parade of *sem-terras* (landless people) bearing a corpse (a rag doll) singing 'Funeral do Lavrador' (The Ploughman's Funeral), by Chico Buarque with words by João Cabral de Melo Neto, then we set fire to the doll.

During the ceremonies to commemorate the award of the Pedro Ernesto Medal to the bishop Don Mauro Morelli (a man who devoted his life to the protection of streetchildren) we used candles in a procession, like a Catholic procession, and each person carried a symbol of a profession: book, spade, stethoscope, etc. At the foot of the altar, these were exchanged for a stalk of wheat. Then the procession entered the Chamber to award the medal. And we did the same in a syncretic mass sung for the dead of the massacre of the Yanomanis.

ASCESIS: FROM THE PHENOMENON TO THE LAW WHICH GOVERNS IT

The most important aspect of all theatrical research resides in the means by which it can be extrapolated to other realities. An experiment carried out in a single place, once only, however marvellous it is in itself, may be finite in its effect. When doing research, the important thing is to share this research and its results. In the case of the Legislative Theatre, all the shows must travel from the originating community to other communities, so that everyone may share their knowledge.

From practice, we must arrive at a theory, in order to understand what we are doing, so we can do it better and so that we may be able to apply the experiment to other places: which is of course the purpose of this book.

We are trying to carry out this research by two means.

BY MEANS OF THEATRE

- **Inter-nuclei dialogues**: One group visits another, and the two groups show their plays to each other. This is a good thing because they get to know each other and they begin to form a 'network of solidarity'. When the group of black students went to dialogue with the Chapeu Mangueira group on the hill, it was illuminating to see that though there were many black people in Chapeu, their problems were far removed from those faced by the black students at the university.

  One day, the Terceira Idade (Third Age) group showed its play on love affairs in old age specifically for the children of the Curumim group. The children were fascinated to see 'respectable' women of advanced years talking about lovers and safe sex and condoms, etc.

'My mum should have seen this play', commented one of the children. Imagine the good it must have done for this bunch of youngsters, in the dawning of their sexuality, to see old people speaking of love. A form of absolution for their own thoughts and fantasies.

- **Parables**: When a community group is proposing a play, it is natural that its members should think of those stories which most closely concern that community. Natural and desirable. However, it is equally desirable that it should seek to call the attention of the participants to the problems of other communities, which is what we try to do by means of the inter-nuclei dialogues, or by means of the suggestion of PARABLES: a word or a phrase is decided on, for instance, 'agrarian reform', a subject which is most pertinent to one of our groups, O Sol da Manha (The Morning Sun), which is made up of landless peasants; we suggest to other groups that, even without their being aware of it, they also suffer the consequences of the monopolistic ownership of the land (according to the newspapers, in the territory of Acre, a man named João Coto is the owner, the sole proprietor, of a stretch of land larger than the whole of Portugal). And we ask these groups to make a show on this subject, on their understanding of the subject, preferably a parable play, preferably without text: everything must be shown by means of fable, action, images, movements, sounds, etc. One day all the groups are invited to present to one another the shows that they have prepared on the same subject; this meeting will enhance the debate around the chosen subject-matter.

- **Denunciations**: Once a show exists, it can be shown on political demonstrations or other non-theatrical occasions, as happened with O Sol da Manha, in Brasilia, during a gathering of peasants demonstrating about land distribution: our group also did shows when there were demonstrations about the Mothers of Cinelandia, or the Ianomamis who had been massacred, or on marches against the privatisations, or protests about the Tivoli Park incident, where a 9-year-old girl was raped; or protests about the park itself, where the roundabouts and rides were far from safe, being inadequately consructed and maintained and often broke, causing fatal accidents.

89

- **Festivals**: Twice a year we organise festivals in which the groups show their work and discover the pleasures of shared experience. In 1995 a festival brought together 14 groups, starting at ten in the morning and running till six in the evening, when the traffic started up again through the middle of the gardens – the gardens are closed on Sundays and open only for public leisure use. Festivals are points of meeting designed to give a sense of the extent of the Legislative Theatre movement.

  We also did a number of smaller festivals around the town, during the Seventh International Festival of The Theatre of the Oppressed in 1993, when a number of groups from abroad mixed with national groups, showing work at the Vila Kennedy, at Bangu, on Ilha do Governador, in Morro do Macaco (where blond Swedes were received by the local black population), and people could exchange experiences with people from different countries and cultures.

- **Fiesta-festivals**: These are festivals which include cultural manifestations other than just theatre, encouraging all cultural creators, offering them a space to show their art, music, pottery and other crafts.

BY MEANS OF THE CABINET

The methods employed here are mainly the Chamber on the Square and the interactive mailing list.

The Chamber in the Square

At this point of our research we have already established certain essential elements as necessities for the structuring of 'Chamber in the Square' consultations.

The first requirement is a certainty about the question. We must know clearly what we are going to ask. Only a question of crystalline clarity will lead to precise and relevant answers. For this reason, before any session of the Chamber in the Square we have to have a preliminary session amongst ourselves, in the Cabinet. We have to have an internal discussion to clarify our own doubts.

Second requirement: the presence of a legislative assessor who is completely *au fait* with the legal aspects of the matter to be debated – this is indispensable. He or she will not necessarily be the co-ordinator of the session, but must be present to clarify the legal niceties relating to the theme, and to translate the possible suggestions into legal terminology.

Third requirement: the distribution of written material. Participants who are in possession of written material on the law being discussed will more easily understand the direction of the debate, and will at the same time grasp the seriousness of the project and its systematic nature – they will see that this is not just a random debate, that it forms part of a larger scheme. This written material must be identified with a 'Chamber in the Square' logo, to enable it to be recognised as part of the democratic politics of our mandate; as part of an attendant structure, and not merely an isolated act.

The written material should be distributed well before the start of the session, to allow the participants time to speak freely on the subject, without inducing them to take a stance prematurely. After an open discussion, the text of the law to be voted on or the stance to be taken by the *vereador* on laws presented by other *vereadors*, is discussed in greater depth and detail.

Fourth requirement: the return visit. It is vital that, some time after the Chamber in the Square session has taken place, the *coringas* (Jokers) go back to the nucleus – or the group consulted, when we are dealing with an organised community which was already in existence – to deliver feedback on the steps taken, in relation to the suggestions received. Thus, for instance, a law on which the *vereador* will have to express his opinion is discussed by various nuclei; at the end of all these debates, the wording of this opinion must be taken back to all those nuclei so that they are aware that their opinions have been taken into account, and can know the *vereador*'s reasons for accepting them or not. When the report-back concerns concrete suggestions accepted by the *vereador*, then an account must be given of what actions have been taken as a result.

Fifth requirement: documentation. A fundamental feature of the project is the writing of SUMMARIES of the work carried out. These summaries do not need to be written out in full, containing the phrases uttered by the participants, but only the enunciation of themes, and a resumé of the suggestions. The summaries should contain every piece of information which could be of use to the cabinet in drafting legal projects or preparing concrete actions.

These summaries, together with those done during the shows, are intended to feed into the mandate's internal political activities.

THE CHAMBER IN THE SQUARE can in fact happen anywhere, at any time – it is just a name we give to one type of consultation. In its most formal manifestation, the interested parties are given prior notice of the event and its subject-matter. In the Levy Neves School, for example, teachers, pupils and parents were warned long in advance what we were going to discuss (as would happen in the Chamber itself), i.e., the legislative project proposed by the mayor, who wanted to arm the Municipal Guard.[1] At the agreed time and place, around a hundred people came to debate the project, including some municipal guards who, to our surprise, turned out to be against the proposal. The reason was very simple: armed – with weapons which would always be inferior to those wielded by the criminals – their lives would be seriously at risk; unarmed, they would be more likely to be spared. The vast majority of the parents thought the same way: they would be safer without weapons since if the guards were armed this would inevitably lead to shooting matches. The vast majority turned out to be against the plan and that was how I voted in the Chamber.

The Chamber in the Square sessions are also a means of trying to resolve local problems, as happened in the communities of Julio Otoni and Chapeu Mangueira, who discussed how to resolve a problem relating to refuse collection; whether or not they wanted the council to recruit dustmen for their area from within the local community itself. It turned out the answer was no, because, in spite of the apparent convenience of this arrangement, the young men selected felt ashamed of wearing the orange-coloured dustmen's uniforms in their own communities . . . Or when lesbians and gays were discussing how to set about demanding a standard rate for the hire of hotel rooms: as things are, a heterosexual couple usually pays the normal price, a gay couple pays 50 per cent more and a lesbian couple 100 per cent more. The reason given by the managers is that the price rises according to the level of fear the couples inspire among so-called normal people.

Another series of very important Chamber in the Square sessions was about the practice of cutting of fallopian tubes in the municipal hospitals. The subject was controversial because it dealt with a matter which is clearly in the area of women's rights and, at the same time, involves danger: in the middle of a difficult birth, for instance, women are more inclined to take the decision to be

1. Something between security guards and police, employed by the city.

sterilised, without being aware that this process is definitive – and they can regret it later. My opinion as President of the Commission for the Defence of Human Rights took into account all the details and suggestions which arose in the Chamber in the Square sessions, such as, for example, the need for the woman to declare that she understands the consequences of this surgery; and that this declaration should be made in front of witnesses and some months prior to the onset of labour, which is when the operation is most often carried out. In the law which is still in the process of being voted on, we have added an obligation for the hospitals to offer women, free of charge, other birth control options.

The participants must not only vote but must also explain their positions, and this must be reported in the summary. And we have observed that the more theatricalised and the better prepared the session of the Chamber, the more pains the participants take to set out their thoughts and suggestions with care and precision. The theatricality of the scene stimulates creativity, reflection and comprehension.

The interactive mailing list

A simple strategy, but no less effective for that: whenever possible, we send out thousands of letters to our mailing list, soliciting opinions on laws to be voted on. The curious thing is that this process provokes intense interest and has the effect of making the citizens feel more personally involved and less excluded from our politics: they are an integral part of it. Often our interlocutors themselves organise Chamber in the Square sessions before replying to us by letter.

The summaries

These are an indispensable part of the process. Summaries should be more than mere accounts of what took place, they should also attempt to *understand* what happened, to theorise. The obligation to produce the summary obliges the joker to think.

SYNTHESIS: THE METABOLISING CELL

Metabolism is the process by which the organism separates the 'wheat from the chaff', the stuff which will serve the human body from the stuff which will be expelled in faecal matter.

93

In our Cabinet, this metabolising cell has one permanent constituency (which includes the general administration and the legislative assessors) and one occasional and changing constituency, i.e. all those interested in the particular subject. The first stage is the *GARIMPO* (prospecting for diamonds) – which involves the careful reading of all the summaries; this is followed by the process we call METABOLISATION, which includes catabolism (the elimination of the superfluous) and anabolism (the utilisation of everything which could be necessary to the human body).

A careful reading of summaries (a *Garimpo*) will reveal, for example, that a particular Joker mentions bus delays on a number of occasions: this calls for an appeal to the council to establish whether the bus companies in the area are actually keeping to their agreed timetables or not. And in the latter case, it calls for protest.

A Forum Theatre show always seeks to understand the law behind the phenomenon. But with Legislative Theatre we go beyond this, trying not only to discover the law but to promulgate it in the Chamber. Or to discover it and modify it. When we talk of law we are talking about written law or law to be set down in writing. To be written into legislation. This is the main conquest of our experiment.

The three paths

The development of a bill or a legislative decree

At the time of writing, two suggestions emerging from our shows have been transformed into 'amendments to the law'*:

- **Amendment of the Law of Budgetary Directives**: making it an article of law that raised platforms must be built under telephone kiosks; a suggestion made by blind members of our group, Portadores de Deficiencias Fisicas (People with Physical Disabilities), who are constantly banging their heads on the kiosks because of the lack of indication at ground level of these raised obstacles.

* For other laws and amendments passed subsequently, see Chapter 7.

- **Amendment of Law of Budgetary Directives**: making it an article of law that entrances accessible to disabled people be constructed in metro stations; this was also raised by the above group.

The first great and total victory was: *The Law of Geriatric Care – Law no. 1023/95*, which obliges municipal hospitals to offer specialist geriatric treatment: doctors and nurses. Old age is not an illness in itself, though many illnesses appear most frequently after 70 years of age: osteoporosis, Alzheimer's, Parkinson's, etc. Besides which, corporeal frailty dictates that the treatment of an old person should not be the same as that of a child or a 35-year-old adult. However, in hospitals in Rio, there used to be no specialists in geriatric care. Our law was developed starting from the show by our Terceira Idade (Third Age) group, which is made up of people over 60, some even over 80. In their play, the old person was attended to by an inexperienced doctor, a dermatologist to boot. Obviously the young man had no idea what to do with the old person and prescribed inappropriate medication. This story wasn't made up, it was based on an actual event.

The Metabolising Cell gathered information about the municipal hospitals and we made the law which was approved in primary and secondary readings. The mayor, however, vetoed our law, alleging 'concord between departments' (i.e. an overlap between legislative and executive powers) and 'defect of initiative' (a procedural mistake). It was his job, not mine, to propose a law like this. I proposed that he should make an identical law and put his own name to it and not mine. The only thing that concerned me was that the law be passed, not its paternity! The veto came back to the plenary session, our old people went to lobby on the day of voting and we won by 25 votes (22 votes were necessary, that is, more than half of the *vereadors* of the Chamber).

This was the first law which exemplified – and concretised – with its promulgation, on 22 November 1995, the Legislative Theatre project.

The Law relating to Hanging Rubbish Bins

At the end of the year we went on to approve a law which obliges landlords to make a small platform on the ground below suspended

2. People use
hanging bins to
prevent dogs and
cats scavenging in
them for food

rubbish bins,[2] to allow blind people to steer a path around them rather than banging their heads against them, which happens all the time. Once again the law was vetoed by the mayor and, once again, we overturned the veto and we promulgated the law!

The development of a Judicial Decree

For example, the mayor illegally authorised all the private banks to receive the salaries of council employees: by law, only the state bank, Banerj, is able to do this. (Employees can transfer their money to another bank if they wish, but payment must be controlled by the official bank.) The Bench started proceedings against the mayor and brought his liberality with the public purse to a halt.

On another occasion, the mayor made declarations in the press threatening to order the municipal guard to beat street peddlers if they resisted being moved on. This constituted a crime according to the Penal Code, article 286: 'incitement to violence'. As President of the Commission for the Protection of Human Rights, I did what I was obliged to do: I presented a crime report on the mayor's pronouncements to the Ministerio Publico.[3] Will the Ministry carry out its obligation in this? We'll soon see, in the next edition of this book.

3. A body which
examines the
actions of the
Executive.

Direct action

- **Racism**: A young man of around 30 years of age went into a shop, bought some CDs and tapes, went to the counter and paid the price of around 100 reals with a cheque. The cashier accepted the payment. When he was already in the street, the man was stopped by the shop's security guards, taken back inside, searched, beaten up: the staff believed that the cheque was stolen. After having beaten him up, they telephoned his home and his mother confirmed that her son was employed and that he earned a good wage: they telephoned the bank and the cheque was supported by funds. The security guards apologised to the young black man. Ah, yes, I forgot to say that he was black.

  It was an outrage; various members of the Cabinet were mobilised, we went with a loud-speaker car and demonstrators to protest in front of the record shop. The shop closed very early that day. The young man entered into a legal process and almost a year later, at the end of September 1995, the shop was obliged to pay 200,000 reals for physical and moral damages.

- **Child prostitution**: We did two intervention shows on behalf of the Mothers of Cinelandia with a play entitled *A Piece of Me*, with music, plastic arts and poetry, about the realities of child prostitution and the abduction of children for that purpose.

As President of the Commission for the Protection of Human Rights I must also offer localised assistance: visits to the Department of Town Planning, for instance, to deal with the case of the Fazenda Modelo (Model Estate), a miserable place to which they transfer beggars, who live there in conditions worse than those endured by factory-farmed pigs, or to try and secure basic sanitation in the Mandela de Pedra slum. I visited the Talavera Bruce women's prison which resulted in a meeting with the judiciary and thence a surprising act of dedication[4] by the judges, who worked throughout the weekend, without interruption, to analyse all the cases that we had denounced and then freed 21 prisoners who had already completed their sentences and were still being held in prison.

4. The word used is actually *mutirao*, which refers to a tradition by which all a person's neighbours work throughout the day for them, without payment.

The Municipal Chamber – where the struggle takes place

In the present mandate, we have to confront an authoritarian right-wing prefecture: the mayor himself admits that he works for the electors who voted for him in the first round. *Ipso facto*, the mayor prefers to rebuild a square in the Ipanema for the thousandth time to make it more pleasing to the eye, even if this is at the cost of paying teachers employed by the municipality the minuscule starting salary of less than 200 reals a month.

In the present Chamber, it is known and openly stated during sessions that some *vereadors* receive salaries from certain lobbies, and get higher payments in return for voting for laws exempting particular activities from taxes, etc. This is actually said during the sessions of the Chamber and is reported in the Official Diary itself. None of these denunciations is ever followed up.

This is the environment we are working in.

97

Strait-jackets

When I enter the Municipal Chamber building I feel like someone putting on a strait-jacket. The moment one goes in, one's identity is lost: the staff do not greet us by name, but by title: 'Good morning, *vereador*'. That is, when they greet us at all, because a good part of them detest the PT and look the other way. Some I have never even made eye contact with.

Inside the Chamber, I feel that I lose my personality and transform myself into a mere *vereador*, just one among so many. I am obliged to perform tasks which are supposed to be the duties of the *vereador*. For instance, if a tractor is needed to flatten the ground of the Mandela da Pedra slum, the natural thing would be for the president of the Tenants' Association to speak directly to the department of City Hall whose obligation it is to see to such things, and ask for a bulldozer. But no: if he telephones them, neither the director, the deputy director, nor anyone in a position of power or authority will take any notice of him. So the *vereador* has to waste time telephoning, exchanging a few pleasantries and, then, as a personal favour, especially for the *vereador*, couched in meaningless formalities and polite small talk, the directorate of the cleansing section agrees to carry out its duty.

Telephoning the chief of police, going to talk to the director of such and such a department, going here, going there, talking with such and such a man, responding to Mr So-and-so – the mental pollution resulting from this infinity of daily requests is more tiring than the São Silvestre[5] race.

5. An annual marathon which takes place on 31 December.

In the plenary, it's even worse. The relation of a single episode will suffice to give some idea of the frightful absurdity of the *vereador*'s duty, the way a *vereador* is supposed to conduct himself. The plenary was going to have to vote on an amendment which the *vereadors* had made to the Teachers' Salaries Plan. In the morning, on the radio, the mayor had given notice that he would certainly veto our project. So, everything was already cut and dried: we would vote on the project that evening (all the *vereadors* had agreed to vote yes) the project would return for a second reading which once again would approve it (albeit with some votes against) and finally, in the third round, we would have to reject the mayor's veto. The final stage we knew would be problematic, because this review of the veto is done by secret ballot. But that evening, the voting was peaceful.

Though everything had already been resolved, since the galleries were full of teachers, those *vereadors* who did not often have an audience at their disposal, took the opportunity to launch into a useless, repetitive, irritating discussion. Everything could have been resolved in five minutes, but, at seven o'clock, closing time, there was still a long list of eager orators queuing up to say the same things and to swear fidelity to the teachers' cause. A prorogation of the session for one more hour was sought and a further idiotic, insincere discussion took place.

Having myself already made my speech at the appropriate time, before four o'clock, I tried to think what we would be able to do on the day we would vote on the veto. I had an idea which made me happy. I thought that we should convince all the *vereadors* that since they would undoubtedly vote to reject the veto, they should openly declare their vote, which is permitted by house rules, and would be equivalent to an open vote. Why? Because the great majority of the *vereadors* who would actually vote with the mayor, would say the opposite on the platform – they would lie, as is their wont. If challenged to declare their votes, there would be three hypotheses: in the best of these hypotheses, they would lie, the result of which would be that the sum of the *vereadors* declaring would be greater than the official count of the poll; in the second hypothesis, they would tell the truth and expose themselves in front of the full galleries, revealing their true colours; in the third hypothesis, they would refuse to make a declaration, asserting their right to the secret ballot – but, in the process, their allegiance to the mayor would be made manifest.

In the first case, a legal and procedural impasse would be created: the number of those declaring would not tally with the official count. How would this impasse be resolved? Only by means of an open vote. In the latter two cases, the ideology of the treachery would be brought out into the open, for all to see.

I was happily contemplating this solution, which struck me as excellent, when I realised that it was already seven o'clock – at which time I had a very urgent prior appointment a long way away. And another *vereador* asked for a further prorogation of another hour so that more *vereadors* could execute their oratorical pirouettes. I waited till half past seven. More pirouettes. And then I left without even voting . . . having to signal a thousand explanations to the crestfallen faces of the teachers who watched me leave, though they knew perfectly well that my vote was not necessary, that the outcome of the vote was guaranteed. What seemed to be necessary was a physical presence, the raising of one's hand, saying yes and being applauded!

I understand the process, I know why it is like this, but to me it feels like a strait-jacket! Do this, do that, get up, get down, come here, go there . . . That is the unbearable part of the day-to-day grind of councillorship.

You pay dearly!

During my mandate, I have experienced all sorts of political violence, on account of my work at the Chamber. I am writing on 29 December 1995 and still the legislative session is not over because the mayor refuses to increase the teachers' salaries and the *vereadors* of the left refuse to vote in the Budget, while he won't vote in the Plan of Salaries and Duties of Education. To this very day I have been the target of further violence (excluding the day-to-day slings and arrows):

- **The defamatory campaign**: launched against me by a newspaper which, every day for three weeks, published daily articles attacking me on its front page, accusing me of having signed an illegal contract with the prefecture for the mounting of seven popular festivals of Theatre of the Oppressed. For another three weeks it published similar pieces on its third or fifth pages. The newspaper's allegations were lies: I did sign a document, not a contract, but a covenant of accord, the difference being that there was no payment of wages or any financial gain whatsoever, just the covering of expenses: lighting, sound, transport, etc., which was perfectly legal. The plenary session of the Chamber judged the case, twice, and on both occasions I was completely absolved. The Audit Tribunal of the municipality also judged it and I was absolved unanimously. But the newspaper never retracted. And many of its readers still don't know the truth: I was innocent!

- **Legal proceedings**: brought by a lawyer of a rival party, based on the same covenant. Such processes take years. In this process, I have still not even been heard. I may have to wait till after the year 2000.

- **Legal proceedings**: brought by the same lawyer, requiring me to vacate a building I have never yet set foot in. Before I was elected, the State government had offered me a building as a base for my Theatre of the Oppressed Centre, in the same way as it offered other buildings to other popular theatre companies, which went on to occupy them. The one which fell to me never became vacant and I was never able to enter it. Even though the covenant was signed before I came to power and, more significantly, even though I have never set foot in the building, a legal process was in train against me, to which I had to respond in due course, and present a defence, proofs and counter-proofs. Two years later I was acquitted. The judge agreed that I could never leave a building I had never entered. But, to arrive at this obvious legal conclusion, I had to hire lawyers (and they are very expensive in Brazil).

Besides these, I still have four lawsuits against me relating to income tax – since I have never done anything wrong in this area, I am sure that I'll be acquitted – but lawyers have to be hired – I love them, they are the best available lawyers, but they are expensive.

The cost is high, but it is worth the pain. Today we have 19 popular theatre groups. Each with 10–15 participants. They are happy. They are creating a new way of making theatre: Legislative Theatre.

It hurts deep inside, but it's worth the trouble!

P.S. – This book was written up to here before my mandate was over in December 1996. Now, I want to tell you about two experiments that I did after that time, one in Santo André, a city near São Paulo, and the other in Munich, in Germany.

7 Laws promulgated during the mandate

And one which wasn't

1 Law 2384/95

All municipal hospitals must have doctors specializing in geriatric diseases and problems; *this was the first law we approved – before this, no municipal hospital had specialists in old age.*

2 Law 2384b/95

All municipal hospitals must have at least a certain number of beds equipped for geriatric attendance; *before this, old people would be taken to hospital by ambulance, with no possibility of being able to stay overnight.*

3 Law 1174/95

All municipal hospitals must provide facilities for elderly patients to be accompanied by relatives or friends; *we know that if a relative or friend keeps the old person company this helps rehabilitation – some* vereadors *only approved this law because of the potential economic savings.*

4 Amendments to the Constitution of the City: 33, 35, 36, 37, 38 and 42/95

All treatments for mental illness which produce irreversible consequences are prohibited; *these include 'imprisonment' in high-security cells, electric shock treatments, any kind of physical or psychological aggression, etc. (in reality these were six separate laws addressing the same issue, with slight variations).*

5 Law 35/95

All public telephone kiosks must have a raised concrete platform below them so that blind people can detect them with their canes; *the 'orelhões' (big ears) – telephone kiosks mounted on inclined pillars*

– have been the cause of serious injury to many blind people; the platforms will be shaped like the shadow cast by the kiosk.

6 Law 848/96

All suspended rubbish bins (designed to keep their contents out of reach of cats and dogs) must also have raised platforms, for the reasons detailed above; *elevated rubbish bins are used particularly in wealthy quarters of the city.*

7 Law 2449/96

The name of 'Free Timor' is given to a Rio state school; *at the time almost no one in Rio had heard about the Indonesian genocide in East Timor.*

8 Law 2528/96

7 December is declared Day of Solidarity with the people of East Timor; *this is only a symbolic act, but helps remind people of the issue.*

9 Law 1308/95

The City is obliged to supply plastic bin bags to street traders to clean their pitch after a market; *this is intended to put an end to the nuisance of rotting debris, the subject of constant complaint by residents. The poor traders claimed that such a provision would solve the problem.*

10 Law 2493/96

The Casa das Palmeiras (the House of Palms – a mental health facility) is declared to be of 'public utility'; *this implies legal privileges such as certain tax exemptions and things of that nature.*

11 Law 1119/95

All motels must charge the same price for all couples, regardless of their sexual orientation; *these are hotels specializing in short stays of up to four hours for love liaisons, so that clients don't have to pay the rate for a whole day's stay. Some motels used to charge 50 per cent higher for gay couples and 100 per cent more for lesbian couples: a prejudice (against homosexuals) inside another (against women!).*

12 Law 1485/96

All state schools must have crèche facilities for the children of their teachers, workers and students (parents may choose to use the school they work in or the closest one to their home); *this should be common sense and yet even today, after the law has been passed, it is*

103

still not enacted by all schools, in spite of the fact that it is so easy to implement – all state schools have plenty of space and personnel.

13 THE MOST IMPORTANT LAW: Amendment to the Constitution of the City 43/95 to allow the promulgation of Law 1245/95 – 'the law that protects the witnesses of crimes'
This creates an obligation for the City to protect witnesses in accordance with Law 1245/95, which supplies the means for that protection; *among other items, the City must provide accommodation away from the danger area, a new job, a new provisional and fictitious identity during the danger period; it must make agreements with other cities to transfer the witness/es under threat; it must conceal the witness's real address, etc. This law, the first of its kind in Brazil, was subsequently used by Chambers of other cities and is being considered for the national law dealing with the issue of witness protection.*

Besides those laws that were presented by the mandate itself, I also put my name to many more collective bills of law (along with other *vereadors* of the same and other parties) and around thirty more bills which were never voted on, before the mandate came to an end, or were not approved.

I should make it clear that, in Brazil at least, laws do not apply in themselves; even if they are promulgated, they are not necessarily enforced – the persons or institutions concerned always need to have pressure applied in order for them to obey the relevant laws. The law is only a tool to be used by the oppressed, to help apply this pressure.

Also, laws in our city and country are volatile, and are frequently reversed. Some laws live long; some die at a tender age.

MY ONLY LAW

Some friends of mine suggested that I should try and compose a law all on my own, from my own head, rather than just passing laws which came from the people's desires. If I didn't do it, they said, people might think that my democratic method of legislating was due to my own incapacity to think up good laws, rather than my genuine desire to help the people enact the laws they wanted.

So I went home, and remembered that, in Sweden, the green lights at pedestrian crossings are accompanied by a particular noise when they are illuminated, and the red lights are accompanied by a different noise. By these means, blind people know when it is safe to cross the road. I wanted to oblige the City of Rio to do the same to protect our own blind citizens! I was very pleased that this memory had come to me and I wrote out the text of the law myself, refusing the offer of help from my assistants (who included my lawyers and a legislative specialist!), in order to show that I myself was a very capable lawmaker. When I had finished, I went in person to deliver it to the Justice Commission.

Later when the blind people in one of our theatre groups heard about 'my' law, they came running to my office.

'Boal – do you want to get us killed?' they said, furious with me.

'Why? It's a marvellous law; in Sweden it has saved many lives. Blind people like yourselves hear these noises and cross the roads in perfect safety! It works wonderfully!'

I was flabbergasted with their unexpected reaction!

'In Sweden, they are Swedish!' they told me.

'So what?' I asked in amazement.

They answered furiously:

'Swedish drivers stop at red lights! Here, they don't!'

I tore down the three flights of steps from my office and arrived breathless at the Justice Commission, just in time to withdraw my only law.

I am a lawmaker who has never made a law!!!

Appendices

---

i The history of the theatre of the oppressed nuclei

Groups with whom we worked but which did not reach the stage of becoming nuclei

1. Pref. Mendes de Moraes Street School Ilha do Governador (Governor's Island) – Northern district – work carried out with secondary students who wanted to theatricalise the problems which students encounter on a day-to-day basis.

2. Cardoso Fontes Hospital (Jacarepaguà – Western district) – professional people working in the hospital who organised a nucleus to discuss, in a ludic and didactic manner, the serious problems of education.

3. Rio das Pedras (Western district) – journalists, carpenters, housewives and community workers wanting to debate the question of basic sanitation in the region.

4. PT from Rua da Praça Saens Peña (Northern district) – this group's objective was to bring the PT's proposals to the street in an alternative form, for which reason they decided to do a Theatre of the Oppressed workshop.

5. Sulacap (Western district) – community artists who mounted two Theatre of the Oppressed festivals in the neighbourhood and started a workshop in their area.

6. Rocinha (Southern district) – with the help of the Rocinha Community Centre we organised a Theatre of the Oppressed nucleus made up of youth from the community, which started a piece on teenage pregnancy.

7. Children from Chapéu Mangueira (Leme – Southern district) – children from the community did a Theatre of the Oppressed workshop, in addition to developing the work with puppets.

8. Candelária (Mangueira – Northern district) – young people from the community put on a play about 'Operation Rio' (the army occupation of the *favelas*).

9. São Martinho (Central district) – street children who attended the 'World of the Street' project which took place in Maracanã, formed a nucleus.

Old nuclei (which no longer exist)

1. Article 288 (Vila Kennedy – Western district) – nucleus formed by artists living in Vila Kennedy, in the west of the city, treating the question of police violence in the area.

2. Caxias (another municipality) – members of the Movimento de Bairros (Neighbourhood Movement) formed the nucleus which discussed the problems surrounding the rubbish dump known as the 'Caxias dump'.

3. São João de Meriti (another municipality) – made up of workers and cultural animators of a CIEP (Popular Education Centre) in the area, the nucleus theatricalised the difficulties confronting the inhabitants after the rains.

4. Vidigal (Southern district) – inhabitants of the *favela* constituted a nucleus which used the Theatre of the Oppressed to work on the problems faced by the slum-dwelling population in matters to do with housing.

5. SEPE – For three years the TO nucleus of the Sindicato Estadual dos Profissioais de Ensino (the State Teachers' Union) used Theatre of the Oppressed techniques to discuss education.

6. Morro da Saudade (Botafogo – Southern district) – a group of slum-dwellers formed the Women in Action nucleus which took a play all over the city which treated the problems faced by women in

the community. The growing violence within the community made the continuation of the work unviable.

7. Meninos e Meninas de Rua (Boys and Girls of the Street) – Central district – with the aid of the National Movement of Boys and Girls of the Street, we formed a nucleus of adolescents (who came from the streets and from community care establishments) which theatricalised the life of one of its members. After the Candelária massacre we did not manage to continue the work.

8. Caju (Central district) – members of the community treated the problems caused for the community by the rains and the failure to mobilise the inhabitants.

9. Animal Protection – members of various groups which fought for the protection of animals, using Theatre of the Oppressed techniques as one of their tools. They put on a play about domestic animals in residential areas.

10. Universidade Rural (Rural University) – Itaguaí – another municipality – students at the University created a piece about the oppression of women. Difficulties around promotion, and long periods of strike action, made work difficult.

11. Afro-Católicos (Afro-Catholics) – Baixada Fluminense – a greater Rio – members of the movement which is trying to introduce Afro culture into Catholicism formed a Theatre of the Oppressed nucleus to make their ideas better known.

12. PT Niterói (another municipality) – militants belonging to the Niteroi Workers Party did a piece on health (specifically cholera).

13. Organização da Juventude pela Liberdade (Youth for Freedom Organisation) – Central district – militants organised a Theatre of the Oppressed nucleus which discussed the question of compulsory military service, and the lack of democracy in schools, which hinder the creation of unions.

14. Maré (Northern district) – inhabitants of one of the *favelas* in the Maré complex who were interested in creating cultural projects for the community, formed a nucleus which worked on the question of land ownership within the favela. The increase in violence in the area brought our work to an end.

15. Therapists – a group of therapists from various health institutions in the city formed a nucleus which did a play about the situation *vis-à-vis* public transport in the city.

16. Campo Grande (Western district) – cultural animators from the Campo Grande formed a nucleus which worked on two plays: one on AIDS and another on the family.

17. Vigário Geral (Northern district) – after the massacre of Vigário Geral, our mandate made contacts in the area through the Commission for the Protection of Human Rights. We organised a nucleus made up of adolescents who put on a play about the difficulties confronted by young people in a poor community.

18. João Cândido Nucleus – PT – Largo do Machado – Central district) PT militants decided to do Theatre of the Oppressed to discuss the power of media influence on the population. The group's intention was to use theatre techniques in the Lula's campaign for the Presidency.

19. Disabled people – a group made up of disabled people (blind people and people with cerebral palsy) organised a theatre nucleus with the aim of diversifying the means used by the movement in its struggle. The play spoke of the discrimination suffered by disabled people in work and education. This group was responsible for two amendments to the Municipal Budget and one Legislative Bill.

20. Health (Realengo – Western district) – white-collar workers from the Albert Schweitzer state hospital organised a nucleus with the aim of discussing with professional people working in their field the main health problems.

21. Colônia Juliana Moreira (a prison farm in Jacarepaguá – Western district) – parents of inmates of the colony formed a nucleus to discuss the question of the privatisation of the colony.

22. Children from Morro da Saudade (Botafogo – Southern district) – the children and grandchildren of the Women in Action group

decided to set up an infants' theatre nucleus and did a play about the question of basic sanitation in the area.

23. Andaraí (northern district) – members of the youth group from the Churches of São José and Nossa Senhora das Dores (Our Lady of Sorrows) theatricalised the difficulties encountered by young Catholics when they are open about their Christianity in social situations.

Theatre of the oppressed nuclei currently in operation[1]

1. In 1996.

1. Grupo Galera da Penha (Penha northern district) – pupils of the Escola Municipal Ministro Afrânio Costa – are working on the question of free travel for students on buses within the municipality, reclaiming their rights.

2. Grupo Renascer (Born Again Group) – Engenho de Dentro – Northern district) – members of the Third Age Club which takes place inside the Pedro II Psychiatric Centre discuss in their play the problems faced by old people. This work gave rise to the law of 'compulsory provision of geriatric services' we created and we put into the Bill that it should authorise an escort in cases where old people went into municipal hospital.

3. Grupo Pôr do Sol (The Sunset Group) (Borel – Usina – Northern district) – the Pastoral group for young people in the community of Borel, linked to the Catholic Church, put on a play about the discrimination suffered by inhabitants of deprived communities in daily life in the city.

4. Grupo Galera da Levy (Inhaúma – Northern district) – students from the Escola Municipal Levy Neves theatricalised the day-to-day problems in the state education system. The group was responsible for the organisation of the 'Chamber in the Square' session on 'Should the Municipal Guard be armed or not?' and took two suggestions for Bills to the Cabinet: 'crêches in municipal schools' and 'provision of buses for extra-curricular school activities'.

5. INFA (Engenho de Dentro – Northern district) – members of the Movimento Familiar Cristão da Pastoral da Familia da Igreja Católica, a Christian family movement attached to the Catholic Church, did a play on family planning and prepared another on 'Brotherhood and Politics'.

6. Grupo Beleza do Chapéu (the Beauty Group of Chapéu) – Chapéu Mangueira – Leme – southern district) – a community group which has already done a play about community health centres and now has another piece about household refuse and its implications for the community. This second piece has generated two petitions for information to COMLURB.

7. Pavuna (Pavuna – Northern district) – adolescents, linked to the residents' association, whose play discusses the lack of political will to bring the Metro into their neighbourhood.

8. Grupo As Princesas de D. Pedro II (the Princesses of Dom Pedro II Group) – (Engenho de Dentro – Northern district) – a group formed by women who were clients of the Pedro II psychiatric centre and today are accompanied by mental health professionals of the institution. They have a play which talks about the oppression of women with psychoses.

9. Grupo da Casa das Palmeiras (Botafogo – Southern district) – a group made up of clients of the Casa das Palmeiras Institution run by Dr Nise da Silveira did a play on the oppression experienced by users of the psychiatric system. Members of the group are militants of the movement against mental asylums.

10. Mundo da Lama (World of Mud) – Mundo da Lama is a non-governmental organisation which is dedicated to environmental education and to the preservation of the mangrove swamps. In search of a new language to use in the discussion of environmental themes, they mounted a play about the preservation of the mangrove swamps.

11. GHOTA (Grupo Homosexual de Tectro Amador) – GHOTA is a homosexual amateur theatre group, linked to ATOBÁ, which theatricalises scenes about prejudice and discrimination. With this work as the starting point, we presented a Bill which proposed the penalisation of commercial establishments which discriminate against homosexuals.

12. Grupo Tá Limpo no Palco (the 'I've Done the Stage' group) – Tijuca – Northern district) – housemaids, pupils on the supplementary course of the Santa Teresa de Jesus college, made up a group which looked at the problems faced by domestic servants.

13. CENUN (Colectivo Estadual de Negros Universitarios) – the Black Students State Collective organised a Theatre of the Oppressed nucleus, to take the discussion of racism to the far corners of the city.

14. Grupo Curumim da Júlio Otoni (Santa Teresa – Central district) – adolescents from the community theatricalised the family conflicts they experience around the subject of funk gigs. Now they have a piece about drugs in adolescence and the discrimination suffered by the inhabitants of the *favelas* relating to the presence of drug-trafficking activities in these communities.

15. Grupo de Brás de Pina (Brás de Pina – Northern district) – Catholics who are members of various movements within the church make up a nucleus which is dedicated to making a piece of theatre every year around the theme of the Brotherhood Campaign. The group uses Theatre of the Oppressed techniques to intensify discussions within the parishes of the city: its subject is 'life in society'. Apart from the traditional techniques of the Theatre of the Oppressed the group, which works intensely and is one of the most creative groups linked to our mandate, uses a variant of Forum Theatre: the play is shown and the audience is then divided into small groups which must discuss it and then improvise a scene which presents a solution to the problem. This group, as well as the work which it undertakes directly with the communities, is already giving rise to the creation of other groups also linked to the Catholic Church.

16 Grupo do Rio Comprido (Rio Comprido – Northern district) – members of the youth group of the Church of Our Lady of Sorrows theatricalise the family conflicts experienced by adolescents.

17. Grupo MULHERAÇA (Vila da Penha – Northern district) – members of the women's movement use the Theatre of the

Oppressed to discuss the problems confronted by women in the present day (the double day's work, the division of domestic duties, etc.)

18 The peasants' cultural group Sol da Manha (the Morning Sun) – (Seropédica – another municipality) – militants belonging to the Movimento dos Trabalhadores Sem-Terra (the Landless Workers' Movement) make up a nucleus which theatricalises agrarian questions, to promote the cause of agrarian reform. The nucleus is responsible for the Bill which obliges the municipality to distribute free refuse bags to market traders.

19. MORHAN (Nova Iguaçu – outside the municipality) – Members of the Movimento de Reintegração dos Hansenianos (Movement for the Re-integration of Lepers) use the language of theatre to popularise discussion of Leprosy.

At the time of writing,[2] many other contacts are being made with a variety of communities. Hope is the first thing to be born! **2.** 1996.

ii The dreamt future: Legislative Theatre without the legislator

This is the text of a letter I wrote to Richard Schechner to be published in the *The Drama Review*, March 1998.[3] **3.** Since this was written in English, I have not altered anything, apart from correcting spelling.

RIO DE JANEIRO, OCTOBER 1ST, 1997

Dear Richard,

You asked me to update our experience on Legislative Theatre for TDR, and I am happy to say that we are, slowly but steadily, advancing towards another stage.

At first, it was very hard to take it, very painful. No one loves to lose! We were absolutely conscious that we had done a beautiful and important work, during the four years of our mandate, at the Chamber of Vereadors, both in the legislative and in the theatrical fields.

We had formed 19 permanent theatre groups of "organized oppressed" all over the city; we had promulgated 13 laws that came directly from those groups, from their dialogue with their own communities and with the population in the streets; we had made, in 13 cases, desire become law!; we had intensely fought against all sorts of injustices, economical, social, political, sexual, etc. We had made good theatre! We were happy and proud with ourselves and with our work, and . . . and we failed.

In 1992, when I was elected vereador, no one believed it could happen. Including myself. All we wanted was to help the Workers' Party and their campaign. We had a project — to do theatre as politics and not merely political theatre — but no one understood very well what that might be or mean. Surprise: even so, I was elected!

In 1996, everyone was sure I would win again. Many people even asked me for whom they should vote, since it was certain that I would easily be re-elected. Inside the Party, I was considered to be one out of 3 or 4 vereadors that would obviously be re-elected. In the public opinion, now everyone knew what we meant by theatre as politics: they had seen it in action! Surprise: even so, I was out!

At first, we were very sad, discouraged, disappointed, melancholic. Ungrateful population!!! Unattentive voters!!! Alienated citizens!!! We had offered our work, our sacrifice, our talent, and we were rejected! Better stop. They don't deserve us . . .

But we are not used to giving up. We decided to go on, to go further!

The new stage was — and is — difficult to structure. Like every new experience.

Beginning March, after finishing at the Chamber, all the "jokers" — (the cultural and theatrical animators of the Center of the Theatre of the Oppressed, the CTO-Rio) — had lost their jobs. The Chamber had paid their salaries for four years. They worked for free for 19 stable communities, and other aleatory ones, all of them very poor. Many groups were formed with people that lived in slums. The mandate (me and my assistants at the Chamber) was even obliged, in most cases, to put its own money to finance theatre activities: make settings, transportation, and even food.

The mandate lost, suddenly everyone had to get their subsistence elsewhere, and could no longer work for free for so many groups. Sadly, we saw most of them being dismantled, one by one: only a few are still at work – the peasants' group, some others related to the church, some in poor communities . . . Slowing down.

The Center of Theatre of the Oppressed was then legally constituted, with only five members (Bárbara Santos, Claudete Felix, Helen Sarapeck, Geo Britto, Olivar Bendelak) and became a Non-Governmental Organization, to try to get funding in Brazil and abroad. Some institutions have already promised to help. We will see.

Contacts were made with governments of other cities, with the Union of the doctors, the State University, and some others. We entered the new phase: Legislative Theatre Without Legislator!

With the doctors' union, we made a play about women at hospitals, in all aspects related to sex: sexual relations, contraception, abortion, pregnancy, giving birth, etc. How women are treated in Rio de Janeiro's hospitals, and what should be done to better their situation.

With the students, we made a play about cruelty against freshmen at the universities. In Juiz de Fora, we made a play about garbage in the streets, hygiene. In other cities, we made workshops.

These plays and shows did not lead to create any new laws. In this aspect, the most interesting experience we are doing is in the city of Santo André, which is a very important city close to São Paulo, with more than 900,000 inhabitants, a great number of workers in the steel industries, and traditionally a very combative population – it was in that region that the Workers' Party was founded some 18 years ago. Also, that was the birthplace of the CUT (Workers Central Federation).

Here, the experience, extremely fruitful and rich, has followed these steps:

1. In May, two "Jokers" of the CTO-Rio conducted a 10-day workshop about the essential techniques of the Theatre of the Oppressed – 50 people participated, most of them working for the government in the areas of education, public health and culture. This group produced a Forum Theatre play about complaints of the citizens, and we presented that play in the streets, with intense popular participation: more than 20 "spect-actors" entered the scene. I was the "joker" of the first presentation.

2. These 50 participants divided themselves in small teams, and reproduced the first workshop for about 15 different communities – these communities, in most but not in all cases, produced their own plays about their own problems and discussed them in their own communities.

3. The city government started a project called "Participatory Budget", which was the trademark exclusively of the Workers' Party, and is now being used also by other political parties in power. Basically, the government proposes a division of the Budget according to the regions of the city and according to the different activities that involve the whole city, like health, education, transportation, etc. Each region and each section of society that will handle a certain amount of money, organises itself in assemblies, and decides how that money shall be spent: which are their priorities.

4. Here, the two processes merged: all public sessions, in which the population was invited to give their opinions and vote, always started with the presentation of a Forum Theatre play depicting problems and inviting everyone to find out solutions. After the play and the Forum, the normal assembly discussions followed, stimulated by the theatre presentation. In this aspect, it was different from the experience in Rio, when the texts of the law were produced by the Forum itself.

5. At the end of this process, the government collected all suggestions and all indications, and produced the Budget of the City – by law, the Budget has to be delivered to the Chamber by the last day of September.

So it was: last 30th of September, at 6 pm, according to the law, the CTO-Rio organised, together with Santo André's population, a "school of samba", or parade, or procession, in which all sections of society that had contributed to the Budget were represented in "Wings" (like in a school of samba). The Budget, in theatre prop book form, was carried on an altar (like in a procession), and the whole was animated by a "battery" of drums and percussion (like in a parade).

This group crossed the town announcing the first Budget made with popular participation, and inviting the population to go to the City Hall, where the mayor was awaiting, where he received the Book of the Budget, crossed the square, and entered the Chamber of Vereadors to deliver it to the President of the House.

It is true that this process was not entirely theatrical, or mainly theatrical; it is

true that some important elements of the Legislative Theatre were not used –
like the interactive mailing list – but it is also true that we have already began
this new stage of the experience of democratising politics through theatre:
Legislative Theatre Without the Legislator.

We can do more, and better, next year!

Next time, where? When?

Of course, in Brazil where we are intensely believing in this method, and
intensely working for it to happen. But this should not be a Brazilian
experience. It should spread out in other countries. We want democracy: theatre
can help in this process – why not?

When I started the Theatre of the Oppressed movement, many people used to
say: "– Yes, it is very nice for Latin America, but in other countries it will not
work . . ."

Today the TO is practiced all over Europe, North America, Africa . . . Last
May, more than 45 countries were present (with shows, videotapes, or other
manifestations) in the 8th International Theatre of the Oppressed Festival,
organized in Toronto by Mixed Company. At least twelve books have been
written by other people about their own experience with TO, in politics,
psychotherapy, education, social work . . . TO is not Brazilian, not Latin
American – it is a process that can be used – and further developed! – in all
societies where a minimum of freedom exists. Of course, it is not recommended
to Afghanistan . . .

Before the end of this year of 1997, I'll try two other experiences outside
Brazil. The first one in Munich, during a workshop organized by the Paulo
Freire Association, end of October. The second one, beginning December, with
my own Centre of Theatre of the Opressed in Paris.

In this one, sponsored by the French Government, 15 children in difficulties
will follow a three-months' workshop, and will be joined by another group of 20
adults and, together, they will try to propose projects of law, using Forum
Theatre and other theatrical means.

Perhaps, dear Richard, if you want, I will write some more about these French
and German events, in one of your future editions of TDR.

And . . . perhaps . . . about something similar that we can try in the United States . . . I would love it!!!

All my real best wishes.

Augusto

P.S. – By the way: recently, I was acquitted of the fourth lawsuit against me, provoked by conservative right-wing people, during my stay at the Chamber; there are still five more under trial. So, the legal (and also moral, spiritual, psychological, metaphysical, etc.) consequences of my mandate will still last for more two or three years . . . It is not easy to make Legislative Theatre in these areas . . .

iii Symbolism in Munich

As detailed in his letter to Richard Schechner, Boal's failure to be re-elected has not dented the enthusiasm for the Legislative Theatre experiment both within and outside Brazil. The following are his accounts of the related experiments he has since undertaken in Europe and Brazil, demonstrating the hunger for and the potential of Legislative Theatre in other contexts. *AJ.*

THE Paulo Freire Association, so named in honour of the great Brazilian educator, invited me to show some examples of Legislative Theatre in the city of Munich. I explained that our experience in Rio had taken us four whole years, to approve 13 new laws, and that the most we could do in only four days would be a pale version of this, a symbolic event, a hint of what that theatre form might be in the future, in the city of Munich, or elsewhere.

We started our work and, over four days, we prepared five small scenes about oppressive situations revealed by the 35 participants of the workshop to be directly or indirectly concerned with them. As just one example, one of the scenes prepared by the group dealt with a very common problem in Germany – and, as far as I know, in many other European countries: some men choose a wife through matrimonial agencies, by looking at photos, CVs and other information. These women are recruited in countries like Romania, Thailand and even my own country, Brazil.

Once the bridegroom has chosen his 'wife', she is imported by the agency with promises of marriage and a wonderful life, European-style, the life of a princess. Of course, these young women are very poor and full of hope and also very naive.

Arriving in the country, part of the agency's promise is fulfilled: they marry. Once married, the 'husbands' – in most cases, not always! – behave as though they had bought a slave, and treat their 'wives' as such, in the kitchen and in bed. More often than not, these women don't speak a word of German, and have difficulties learning the language. They have no friends and are sometimes forbidden to go out without their men. The 'husbands' keep strict control over them. Masters and slaves.

If the 'wife' decides to leave her 'husband', this is not easy but it is possible – the only problematic thing is that she automatically loses her German nationality, and is sent back to her country by the police. She is punished: not him!

During the Forum we did within the group, the participants expressed their opinion: if a crime has been committed – through a marriage of convenience, with the woman's purpose being to acquire German nationality and the man's to acquire a slave – both persons are responsible for that crime, and not just the woman.

The following proposition for a project of law emerged: the woman should be punished with the loss of nationality, yes, but not with deportation from Germany: most of these women not only had economic problems back home, but also political ones – in some cases, their lives would be in danger if they were deported. And the 'husband', considering that he is also responsible for having faked a marriage, should be punished with a short term in prison, to discourage him from going on to marry other foreign women in need, as some of them are in the habit of doing.

Other short scenes were made about issues such as social security, homosexual marriages, the use of public spaces for private activities, etc.

On the fifth day, Fritz Letsch (from the Paulo Freire Association) obtained permission to do the Forum Theatre show inside the City Hall (Rathaus), and invited many polititians, including the Mayor of Munich, who could not come – it was his birthday that day! – but he sent his Deputy Mayor, who attended the session at the side of the Secretary of the Green Party for Bavaria: those two were the only 'authorities' present. Of course, we had invited everybody else but, understandably, they had more urgent things to do.

The publicity material advertised the wrong start time for the session and some people came to the Rathaus at eleven in the morning, when we were rehearsing for the presentation at 1.30 pm. Among them was an old lady with completely white hair, who had to use a walking stick to move around. This lady had been at the public lecture that I had delivered on the first day of the workshop, during which I had explained how the Legislative Theatre worked.

I remember that, during the dialogue after my lecture, another woman said that this process might have worked well in Brazil, because in Brazil we are Brazilians (meaning by that statement that we dance and sing, which is not necessarily true for some of us . . .) and that we are extroverted people. But – according to her – it could not work at all in a country like Germany, where the people are more introverted, less expansive. Maybe she was unaware of the Oktoberfest!

I replied that when I introduced the Theatre of the Oppressed in Europe, frequently I heard the same prognosis . . . and yet . . . today, TO is practised in almost all European countries, and very actively to boot. Of course, in each country, people have to adapt the method to their own culture, their own language, their own desires and needs. TO is not a Bible, nor a recipe book: it is a method to be used by people, and the people are more important than the method.

The same can happen with Legislative Theatre: in each country, it has to find its own form of application to the prevailing realities in that country. But the woman, that night, held to her opinion. And the old lady with white hair and a beautiful cane at her side, said nothing.

When we started the show at the Rathaus, I explained that what we were going to do had only a symbolic value: we had not gone through the whole Legislative Theatre procedure, we had not done many shows for many different kind of audiences, we had not done the 'Chamber in the Square' about the problems presented in the scenes, we had not used the inter-active mailing list to consult people who might be useful in preparing a law, and whose knowledge could enlighten us. On the contrary, we had composed the projected laws ourselves, which positively is not the right thing to do. So, if anything, the presentation at the Rathaus would have only a symbolic value.

After my introduction, we did the scenes, the audience chose three of them, including the slave-wife scene, and we did the Forum session on those three. Many people intervened, even the Deputy

Mayor's secretary! In the slave scene, most of the interventions were similar to ours.

To close the event, we delivered our proposed laws – someone had painted them in beautiful letters on beautiful paper, to enhance the effect – to the Secretary of the Bavarian Greens. She was very nice to us, and said that she understood the symbolic character of the event but, even so, she would really take these projects of law for the consideration of the Green legislators.

We were very happy. On her way out, the old lady with the cane and white hair approached me: she was one of the first to come in, and one of the last to leave. She greeted me and said:

> It is very entertaining what you have done. I agree with you and I know that this is just a symbolic action. But it was very important for me: you have shown that this is possible. Law is always the desire of somebody, but never our own! And it had never crossed my mind to imagine that people, common people, people like us, could get together, make theatre about our own problems, discuss them on the stage, and then sit down and propose a new law . . . I agree with you: Legislative Theatre can help us make our desire become law!

I was very happy.

The Civil Society, in Paris

October–November, 1997, with my own Centre du Théâtre de l'Opprimé, in Paris, we did a two-month long workshop with 20 children in difficulty: drunken and violent parents, sexual abuse, drugs, etc. At the beginning of December, I took over the work and with seven of those children and 20 other participants, we made a few scenes of Forum Theatre about racism, and, on the last day, we presented them to the MRAP (Mouvement pour le Rassemblement et l'Amitié Entre les Peuples) audience of a hundred activists. They had been discussing the major problem of racism in France throughout the day and, in the evening, they came to our show. At the end, we delivered them some texts of laws that we would like to see promulgated: of course they have no power to do that, but power enough to influence some legislators.

CTO-Rio de Janeiro

In Rio de Janeiro, our plans include work with the FORUM FOR A DEMOCRATIC CITY BUDGET, an umbrella organisation which includes many other organisations and is trying to enact, from the point of view of the community, the same as is being done in some other cities which are more democratic than ours: the participatory budget.

This work will be led by myself, and also Bárbara, Claudette, Helen, Geo and Olivar, the present members of CTO-Rio, to whom I dedicate this book.

The
'No-one Here is an Ass!'
Book

Prologue
'No-one here is an ass!'

I was outraged! I was sure something very serious was happening. Against all sense, the majority of *vereadors*[1] had just voted in a law exempting private companies from the payment of taxes they owed. It was not right. It was not fair! Everyone had to pay, poor people had to pay: why not rich health insurance companies? Why not tourist hotels? Why should the rich be exempted?

As a rule, I am polite and try to treat everyone with courtesy. That evening was the exception: I was furious. I asked to speak and, once on the speakers' rostrum, I bellowed: 'Those of your Excellencies who voted for this outrage are all either crooks or asses!!!'

I went back to my seat, ashamed of my outburst. I asked my more experienced colleagues what I should do to put things right. Make an apology? Stand my ground? Walk out?

Soon afterwards, various *vereadors* went to the microphone to protest. One of them very calmly said: 'His Excellency, the honourable *Vereador* Augusto Boal, exaggerates. He says that those who voted in favour of the exemption are all either crooks or asses. His Excellency knows perfectly well that no-one here is an ass!'

It was a slip. The *vereador* in question is universally thought of as honest and upright. So could it have been fine irony? Whatever it was, it was a good suggestion for the title of this book.

A book which gives vent to views and feelings, mostly originally delivered in the form of so-called '*pronunciamentos*'[2] in the Chamber. I have chosen those which transcended the particular event or deed which occasioned them. They are all about Rio de Janeiro, its people and its leaders. I have tried to trim them of all the formal trappings of the Chamber, all the 'ladies and gentlemen', and 'honourable such and such' etc.

In speaking of the Chamber, my hope is to speak of Rio de Janeiro. Of Rio and of Brazil. Of Brazil and of that unfathomable wonder, the human condition.

Augusto Boal
Rio de Janeiro, May 1996

1. *Vereador –* legislator at city council level.

2. *Pronunciamento* means proclamation or manifesto; another usage of the word means insurrection or rebellion.

1 Paulo Freire, my last father

In early 1996, as had happened for the previous two years, the University of Nebraska, at Omaha, USA, presented a Pedagogy of the Oppressed conference, including a Theatre of the Oppressed Section. Nearly 1,000 teachers and scholars came from all over the US and from many other countries. I had been there both the previous years, but this time Paulo Freire came for the first time. This was the first and last time that the two of us really worked together, during a round-table session which closed the event.

Furthermore, the University decided to bestow on both of us the title of 'Doctor Honoris Causa in Humane Letters'. During the preparation, we were backstage, waiting to be called for the ceremony, dressed up in the black regalia designated for this solemn occasion, and my hat[1] would insist on sliding forwards – when the organisers had asked me the size of my head, in order to make a hat which would fit me, in the E-mail I sent by way of reply I had supplied the right amount of centimetres, but instead of 'circumference' I had written 'diameter', a measurement which would have made my head bigger than my waist, so they did not have a new hat made for me, and the only one they could find was a little larger than my head, and was held in place with several uncomfortable hair-pins . . . Holding my hat, I asked Paulo if he remembered when we had first met. Neither of us did. We had been friends for so long, it seemed like forever . . .

But our friendship must have dated from 1960 when, for the first time, I and my Teatro de Arena de São Paulo went to Recife, in the state of Pernambuco, where he was trying out his method. There we met. Paulo was 10 years older than me.

1. A mortar-board, presumably – this introductory note was written in English for this book. I have only tidied it up. *AJ.*

On this occasion, I asked him if he would accept the Medal of the City of Rio de Janeiro, which I was empowered to award him, as I was member of Rio's Legislative Chamber. He accepted. Later that same year, we did a ceremony at the Chamber to award him the medal. Instead of just speeches, we also had a musical session, in which *repentistas* (guitar-playing singers who improvise their songs) from the north-east, where he was born, sang for him and for us, telling of remarkable episodes from his life and work.

It was very moving and beautiful. As president of the session, I had to make a speech. We had agreed that the whole ceremony should be short – Paulo was not in the best of health. This text was my speech on that night.

IN Babylonia, many centuries before Jesus Christ, a man observed an apple which had fallen from an apple tree rolling down a slope into a ravine, and he saw something which till then all had only watched unseeing: the apple rolled along, touching the ground with its circumference. Only one part of its surface touched the ground. The man realised something which no-one had noticed before: in order to roll, the apple did not need to be spherical, if it was circular that would be enough. And he invented the wheel.

The wheels we see rolling along all around the world, down lanes, round race-tracks, through markets, in our homes, in the street, were invented by a genius, a man who saw something that hitherto everyone had only watched.

Another apple, centuries later, fell onto Newton's head. Any one of us would have let out a yelp, made an imprecation, uttered a swearword, cursed the vegetable kingdom. Newton, by contrast, saw the obvious: 'matter attracts matter in direct ratio to mass and inverse ratio to the square of the distances'. This is logical and crystal clear. Because, if it was not so, the apple would never have fallen on Newton's head; Newton and the earth would have fallen onto the apple. Today this is easy to understand. But it took a genius to see what everyone had until then only watched unseeing.

Archimedes, taking a bath, noticed that his leg had a tendency to float. A strange thing! And, in a flash, 'Eureka!' – he discovered the obvious: 'a solid body immersed in a liquid receives an upward thrust

127

equal to the weight of liquid displaced'. Nothing could be more elementary. Only, till that moment, no one had translated into theory the practice of floating legs. All the users of all the baths, swimming pools, lakes, were used to seeing their legs floating, thought it entirely natural, but only Archimedes deduced the law which governed these phenomena.

That is the nature of geniuses, they discover or invent the obvious, which no-one has seen. The same happened with Paulo Freire: he discovered that *o vovô absolutamente nao viu o ovo*[2] (Grandpa most certainly did not see the egg), *nem a vovó viu a ave* (nor did Grandma see the chicken), whilst, by contrast, it was absolutely certain that the stone-mason saw the stone, the cook saw the *feijão*,[3] the farm-labourer the spade, the soya, the wheat. And the worker and the peasant did not see the wage, holidays nor the right to schooling and health for their children. The worker did not see the time to rest. The hungry, the time to eat. The poor, the time of deliverance from poverty.

The act of learning to read is learning to think, and thinking is a form of action. Thus, notwithstanding the respect due to the grandpas and grandmas of the old textbooks, nor the care due to chickens and eggs, the peasant needs to know how to write the name of the scythe with which he works the land, the builder the name of the bricks with which he constructs the house, the cook the names of the ingredients with which he flavours the *feijão* and the *farinha*.[4]

And thus, representing in letters and words the pain that the poor felt in the flesh – but without forgetting to represent their dreams and hopes! – Paulo Freire invented a method, his method, our method, the method which teaches the illiterate that they are perfectly literate in the languages of life, of work, of suffering, of struggle, and that all they need to learn is how to translate into marks on paper that which they already know, from their daily lives. In Socratic fashion, Paulo Freire helps the citizenry to discover by themselves that which they carry within them.

And in this process, teacher and pupil learn: 'I taught a peasant how to write the word "plough"; and he taught me how to use it', as a rural teacher put it. It is only possible to teach something to someone who teaches us something back. Teaching is a transitive process, says our master, a dialogue, just as all human relations should be dialogues: men and women, blacks and whites, one class and another, between countries. But we know that these dialogues, if not carefully nurtured or energetically demanded, can very

2. Negative versions of phrases of the kind traditionally used in literacy teaching, pre-Freire.
3. Beans, an integral part of Brazilian national cuisine, particularly for the poor.

4. Coarse-ground flour.

rapidly turn into monologues, in which only one of the 'interlocutors' has the right to speak: one sex, one class, one race, one group of countries. And the other parties are reduced to silence, to obedience; they are the oppressed. And this is the Paulo-Freirian concept of the oppressed: dialogue which turns into monologue.

King Alfonso VI of Spain once said: 'If God had asked my opinion before creating the world, I would have recommended something much simpler.' Paulo Freire, in a way, 'de-complicated' teaching. Though, according to the official histories, God made no such request of him (but inside I am convinced that he did ask him!) Freire created something simpler, more human than the complicated authoritarian forms of teaching which placed obstacles in the way of the learner.

With Paulo Freire, we learned to learn.

In his method, over and above learning to read and write, one learns more: one learns to know and to respect otherness and the other, difference and the different. My fellow creature resembles me, but he is not me; he is similar to me, I resemble him. By engaging in dialogue we learn, the two of us gain, teacher and pupil, since we are all pupils, and all teachers. I exist because they exist. To write on a white sheet of paper one needs a black pen; to write on a blackboard the chalk must be a different colour. For me to be, they must be.

For me to exist Paulo Freire must exist.

January 1998. If I had to repeat these thoughts, I'd say the same words. In sadness, I would add only this: Paulo Freire has died. But he will always exist, like my other fathers, all now deceased. Like José Augusto, who taught me to live and work, and to live working; like John Gassner, who taught me dramaturgy; like Nelson Rodrigues, who gave me a hand into theatre.

With Paulo Freire's death, I lost my last father. Now I have only brothers and sisters.

2 Clementina's turn

During the period of my mandate, the mayor of Rio was somebody who loved to be talked about in the press. He would enter a butcher's shop and ask for an ice-cream, just to have this foolishness reported by the press. He would invite the Beatles to re-form and come and live in Rio – the unfortunate death of John Lennon being only a detail in this brilliant plan. He invited a famous Italian opera director to stage a Brazilian samba show on the sands of Copacabana. He would do anything for press coverage.

Among these eccentricities – let's put it kindly! – he loved to dub important streets with the names of recently deceased famous persons – knowing that there would be protests and legal challenges to restore the traditional names. He had no consideration for the feelings of their families, on seeing the names of their loved ones being put up and taken down on the corners of all those streets.

So it was with Antonio Carlos Jobim, our great composer, whose name, for a few days, graced the most famous avenue bordering the beach of Ipanema, where he lived, then another central avenue in the same quarter, and even today has still had no serious homage paid to him. For weeks, the press spoke of nothing but the mayor and his manias.

MONTHS ago, a journalist suggested that the Chamber of *Vereadors* introduce a bill changing the name of Visconde de Parajá street, named after the forgotten figure of an owner of mills and slaves during the Paraguayan War – to the glorious name of the valiant and heroic Zumbi, to mark his tricentenary. Zumbi was the last king of Palmares, the Black Republic, founded in the north-east of Brazil, larger than the Iberian Peninsula, that existed for almost a century and was destroyed by the Portuguese army when it became so strong it would no longer accept Portuguese market forces. Zumbi died with all his people, slaughtered to the last man, woman and child.

Charmed by the idea, I imagined what the beautiful Alameda Zumbi dos Palmares would look like – yes, the alameda, since, in my dreams, the ex-viscount street would become a grove lined with leafy poplars – or in their absence, splendid coconut palms from the north-east! – as set down in the bill which I started to scribble down.

I desisted from presenting it, however, on consideration of the immense complications entailed in these changes of nomenclature: the number of rubber stamps which have to be thrown in the bin, the amount of headed notepaper which has to be reprinted, not to mention visiting cards and credit cards, and all the letters which go astray.

Then, lo and behold, all of a sudden, without the slightest hesitation, the mayor decides to pay another homage to one of the great names in our music, Tom Jobim, and, after the defeat he had suffered when he had tried to do the same to the Vieira Souto Avenue,[1] in the dead of night, the viscount becomes a genius. The master of slaves becomes one of the inventors of Bossa Nova. This act of homage is more than justified, and yet, might the choice of a public park not have been better? Jobim loved trees. Is it not obvious that the family of the viscount will make a fuss again, just as the family of Vieira Souto did? Or will it prove to have been just another example of our mayor's fondness for the dictum 'speak ill, but speak of me'.

If that's what it's about, the mayor is not going to stop there, and it is certain that he will carry on naming and de-naming the beloved Tom in all the streets crossing Vinícius de Moraes[2] Street, named to honour one of our most popular poets, till the mayor has the brilliant idea of baptising the two little cable-cars of the Pão de Açucar,[3] Vínicius and Tom, and, since cable-cars have no family to take umbrage, it might well come to be.

This unexpected renewed outbreak of naming rekindled my own nomenclatural fancy. And, for this reason, I have set out to write this open letter to the mayor, and the inhabitants of Copacabana and Ipanema, proposing – since it is not in my power to promulgate these changes – radical modifications in our naming of streets, with many nominations, as well as transfers of homages already doing service in Tijuca, Ramos or Brás de Pina.

I might start by once again changing the name of the Vieira Souto, which will henceforth be known as Avenue Maestro Heitor Villa-Lobos, for two main reasons: in terms of hierarchy, an avenue is

1. Vieira Souto Avenue, named after an illustrious family, was the first street to be renamed Tom Jobim Avenue, until the surviving Vieira Soutos objected.

2. Vínicius de Moraes, a popular poet.
3. The famous 'sugar loaf', a Rio landmark.

superior to a street and, without any doubt, Villa was the father of them all; Vinícius and Tom would have parallel and not perpendicular roads, like their lives – and so, for that reason, I would de-name Joana Angélica (who I didn't know – that is, if she even existed) and name it Tom, whom I admire for what he was; we loved him! In this way, the two poets would be next door to each other, the poet of strings and the poet of letters.

And, carrying on from Villa, in place of Delfim Moreira, I would introduce the poet of Vila Isabel, Noel Rosa, who was one of the early fathers of the samba, who died so early, so young, so poor; Avenue Noel Rosa sounds as nice as his music. Coming out of this Samba avenue, instead of Linhares, Guilhem, Guilhermina, Afrânio, Lira and Góes, I would put the musical names of Lamartine Babo, Nelson Cavaquinho, Pixinguinha, Cartola, Sinhô, Mário Reis to go on naming some of our best ever samba poets. In the case of Ataulfo, it will be enough to change the surname, from Paiva to Alves[4] – a huge economy for the coffers of the prefecture which will then be able to pay doctors and teachers better.

4. I have no idea who Ataulfo Paiva was; Ataulfo Alves was a wonderful singer and composer.

Starting with the Via Villa, we could pay homage to Lima Barreto, Mário Peixoto and Glauber Rocha in recognition of the fact that cinema has been a considerable force in the development of our popular music.

In Copacabana, no more Siqueiras, Figueiredos, Rodolfos, Hilários – no more saints and queens, no more of Elizabeths, English or Belgian: let us open the way for Nara Leão, Ellis Regina, Dolores Duran, Clara Nunes, Silvinha Telles and Maysa.[5] All starting from the Avenue Carmen Miranda, the Brazilian bombshell, ex-Atlantica.

5. All popular musicians.

The Rodrigo de Freitas Lagoon? Who was Freitas? No name would sit better on these stormy waters than that of Clementina de Jesus, that beautiful black singer, who became known only at the age of 70, after a long life as a domestic servant. The Lagoa Clementina! In this way, no one would need to ask any more 'Clementina, where are you?', as the lyric of her best-known samba goes, since everyone would know with absolute certainty that Clementina was everywhere: in Ipanema, Leblon, Jardim Botanico, Fonte da Saudade and in our hearts. Clementina is in heaven, with her heavenly voice. Awaiting her turn for a proper homage here on earth.

3 *Saudades*[1] for the chicken thieves of yesteryear

1. The word *saudades* is untranslatable, a very Brazilian and Portuguese concept combining longing, yearning, hope and nostalgia.

Brazilian governments have always been known for their corruption. But we have also always had serious and honest politicians. The climax of blatant, positively extrovert corruption was certainly the period of 1990–1992, which culminated in the impeachment of the President of the Republic, accused by his own brother of being the brains behind a complex criminal gang which stole billions of dollars from the country. This speech was delivered during the outbreak of one of these cyclic periods of explicit corruption.

I AM a nostalgic person; I like thinking about old things, the distant past. During the Second World War, Brazil had a national project: the Allied victory. And the people worked together and I remember the huge mountains of tin cans piled up on patches of waste ground – the famous iron pyramids – which, the papers used to say, without further explanation, were necessary for our war effort.

As children, we erected pyramids of empty sardine tins, Argentine peach cans, punctured pans and bent cutlery, convinced that, in this way, we would win the war. We were soldiers. 'What are all these cans for?' I would ask myself. But answer came there none, and the satisfaction of struggling to pile up cans was greater than that afforded by previous contests, in which the youngsters of my street, Lobo Júnior, in Penha, would pride themselves on their prowess in hunting – or should it be fishing – for frogs larger than those caught by the youngsters in the nearby streets, in their storm drains and ditches.

I remember when Brazil won world championships in team sports, basketball and football, from 1955 to 1964, the time when the Bossa Nova came into being, along with new cinemas and theatres, Brasília and the New Architecture, and even those famous so-called *inferninhos* (little hells), nightclubs. Ah, Maria Ester Bueno,[2] Eder Jofre.[3] How I cheered, how happy I was cheering. I had something to be proud of.

But the most intense memory I cherish from my childhood and adolescence is of the chicken thieves – men who, literally, stole chickens. When they were caught in flagrante delicto, in the middle of the night, they were nearly lynched, they were humiliated and expelled from the neighbourhood in shame.

With the benefit of hindsight and the maturity of age (oh, yeah!) – I see now that those brave men were subjected to the most outrageous injustice. In reality, the chicken thief was always a respectable family man, whom we called 'head of the family', whom the vicissitudes of the market economy had left without work or with meagre funds to support his family.

To beg for alms would have been a degrading admission of failure. With a chicken, you can make broth. The respectable man opted to run the risk: the theft of chickens was very risky; it was an art, a science, almost a military operation, a solitary act of guerrilla warfare.

In our neighbourhoods, people cultivated kitchen gardens and kept animals for the table – birds, goats, pigs, rabbits.

The dangers facing the nocturnal thieves were many and various. They had to jump over walls or fences, struggle through the darkness into the chicken coops without making a sound, crossing back yards and avoiding mouse-traps and – holding their breath – administering the *coup de grâce* which only the most skilful could carry off perfectly; they had to grab the chicken round the neck with such speed that the element of surprise would counteract the bird's instincts for self-defence – all this without making any noise which might awaken the unhappy victim's companions, since the fearful clucking in the chicken coop, the barking of the dogs, the baying of the goats and the grunting of the pigs would certainly alert the owners and their families, who would then rush out in their underclothes, pyjamas or pants, and the life of the heroic thief would be in serious jeopardy.

They were thieves, sure, but their enterprise required a certain degree of heroism and they were not short of cunning, in their choice of timing, of a vulnerable chicken coop, and of the right chicken.

These days people don't steal like they used to. Nowadays chickens are bought already dead and plucked, frozen in supermarkets, trussed up, anonymous, without the element of chance or risk.

This art has disappeared, like so many others are disappearing day by day, like the knife-sharpeners with their tools for cutting and hole-punching, who still chant their calls in the street; the wandering fish-sellers, with their wicker baskets and street-cries; the blackened coal-men who used to feed the iron furnaces, and the budgerigars which would tell your fortune, with envelopes clutched in their beaks.

But a few unpatriotic people continue the tradition; they continue to steal chickens – this time, the ones which lay golden eggs: the golden eggs which belong to the country, the people, the Treasury. And, even when they are found out, the cowards hide.

They have made hundreds of millions of dollars, but they have lost their honour. And, without honour, a man is not a man!

4 Elizete

The woman and the mirror

1. *Carioca* – relating to Rio, as *Paulista* relates to São Paulo.

ACCORDING to a *carioca*[1] newspaper, during the encounter, skirmish, debate – I do not know what name it should be given – between the head of the Department for Social Welfare and the ex-inhabitants of the Favela da Maré, who, 20 months earlier, had been transported from where they lived and dumped on a patch of waterlogged ground in Pedra de Guaratiba, accompanied by some of us, members of the Commission for the Defence of Human Rights of the Chamber of *Vereadors* – according to the paper, at a particular point during the dialogue, my voice was choked with emotion and I cried out.

Maybe, rather than crying out, I actually wept. I have always revolted against the dictum that 'men don't weep': it's a lie; we do. Our machismo obliges us to hide our weeping, so we cry out. Men weep, women weep, everyone who has any sensitivity weeps. It would have been shameful to have remained steely-faced through all that we heard there. And I am sure that not one of us, who were there carrying out our duty, was not affected by what we heard.

And what was it that made me weep, that Friday evening, when the horrors that we heard were already known by many? No new truth was revealed, only the same tragic litany, repeated for the millionth time by those exhausted women and men, who mumbled the same doleful text, which we could hear even before it was spoken, so used we were to those same words, same complaints, same sorrows.

No surprise. So, why the upset? Our hearts are turned to stone. We no longer suffer when confronted with the pain of our brother, we are no longer shocked in the face of injustice: having seen so much of it, we can no longer see it at all.

When we see a whole family, people who used to sleep in the squares of Copacabana and Ipanema, and now sleep outside its fences – real, solid fences built to keep them out! – when we see those families lying at the gates of the same squares, feeling the same cold, the same hunger, the palms outstretched for a coin or two . . . – when we see them and their despair, we can no longer see them. The dew comes down, says the romantic song . . . – and we think of the song, not of tuberculosis.

When we hear accounts of prisoners in São Paulo, locked away and left to rot, stories of prisoners who ask to be tied to the bars of their cells so that they can sleep standing up, since there is no space on the floor – we have heard these stories so many times, the same words so many times, that we can no longer hear them at all.

So many times now we have heard stories of child prostitution, children of 12 or less, pre-pubescent prostitutes – so many times now we have heard this crime against humanity, so many times that we can no longer hear.

Mad words, deaf ears. We are deaf, blind. This way we protect ourselves and manage to go on with our lives, we can go to the cinema or out to a party. Thank God, we are alive, blind and deaf, which suits us. But we have a voice: by God, let us not be mute! For us, tomorrow will be another day: for them, it will be the same. Always the same.

So, what horrors did they relate to us? What dark terrors did they reveal? None. The everyday, the daily grind. The horror goes in one ear, the fear goes out the other.

They told of commonplace things. They used to live in Bonsucesso, Favela da Maré. The construction of the Linha Vermelha[2] (the Red Line) was a matter of urgency, urgency redoubled when it was known that 100 heads of state or of government, kings, queens, princesses, sheikhs, tyrants and would-be tyrants, dictators of all shades and continents, were to visit our beautiful city. It was necessary to render it *maravilhosa*[3] again – at least for four or five days. The Red Line was traced, erasing the houses of poor people, without anyone asking who lived in them. In the plans drawn up on paper no-one lived there, no-one loved, no-one felt the trials and tribulations of life. From the urban planner's point of view, it seemed to be the best route, as appropriate as it would have been considered inappropriate to run a viaduct through the windows of the Sheraton or the Caesar Park.

So, 280 families were condemned to exile, to the abandonment of the place where they lived, some of them since birth. It was for the good of Rio. They were taken to Pedra de Guaratiba, an hour and a half or more away. People whose places of work used to be ten minutes walk from their houses now have to take a two-hour bus

2. The Linha Vermelha is a high-speed road running across the city. It was built to make life easier for the world leaders who came to the Earth Summit in Rio in 1992.
3. As in *Cidade Maravilhosa*, the Marvellous City of the tourist brochures.

journey, in the bus which they were promised would run every hour, but which leaves at dawn and returns late at night. Only one bus a day, into which must squeeze a mixture of men going to work and children going to school, along with others looking for work and a few just going in to town to idle away the time.

They told stories of the humdrum: men losing jobs and, having no wage, abandoning their wives and children to the mercy of God. Banal stories: about families breaking up, the unhealthy nature of the place, ridden as it is with snakes – not majestic snakes as in the plumed cobra of literature; real snakes, the sort which kill, prosaically, without dignity; the liana, the water-snake, the grass-snake. And – still in the realm of the banal – children are dying, an average of four or five a month; they have been there for 20 months already, add it up, that's almost 100 dead children. They used be called *anjinhos* (little angels) – nowadays they are called 'another one'.

The prefecture promised packages of so-called basic necessities to compensate them for this transplantation, and the loss of work. And these packages arrive – not once a month as promised, but every three months; not sealed up as they should be, but with the seals broken. Who tampers with the packages? No-one knows. All anyone knows is that the packages are handed over to the Fazenda Modelo (the Model Estate) – the model of a concentration camp, Soweto, Rwanda, Eritrea – the place inhabited by poor people cleansed from the streets of the city and people made homeless by the floods expected every year between January and March, who have been dumped there since the destruction of their dwellings. The poor against the poor!

Is it the functionaries of the Fazenda Modelo who tamper with the seals of the packages? Are the wretches of the Fazenda fighting against the wretches of Guaratiba?

It was at this point that, for the first time, I was overcome with emotion. There was a girl called Elizete, like the singer. As thin as anything. This young woman said that two little birds, even two good-natured birds, two peaceful, quiet, sweet birds, good singers – two birds of peace, Picasso's doves, white against the blue sky – when confined to the same cage, and put to the test by hunger, can change into ferocious fighting cocks, struggling to the death for the same scrap of bird-seed.

I don't know if this is true or not. There are animals that are stoics and accept death rather than giving fight. But Elizete's literary image is beautiful and powerful: two peaceful birds bleeding in the cage, without water or food. And the birds of the Fazenda and those of the

Pedra de Guaratiba, neighbours, old friends, come to blows with each other: they fight, they steal, they stab one another for a piece of bread. This is not literature; this is cold steel.

This is a social structure which is disintegrating. The implosion of a human group. Of Brazilians. Like us.

Elizete told her story. She enrolled on a course of study, got work, made her way forward, got a better salary, took pride in her achievements, fell in love. By the standards of her ambitions, she was a woman who had achieved a degree of fulfilment, her goals were modest: she wanted a house, a husband and children. In Bonsucesso.

But she was deported to Guaratiba, like the Nazis transported the Jews from one country to another. They uprooted human beings taking no account of the fact that, like trees, we have roots. In Bonsucesso, 280 families were uprooted from their soil – their roots exposed to the elements – uprooted from their land, from their houses, their streets, their neighbourhood, their memories, their desires, their loves, and thrown far away, into a snake-infested swamp. For the good of Rio de Janeiro – we are good hosts; a hundred heads of state, *noblesse oblige.* Long live the Linha Vermelha and long live the foreign leaders who honour us with their presence.

Elizete lost her job, her love and her hope. For one year and eight months she hung onto her dream: house, husband, children. And a person who dreams has hope: Elizete hoped. They had promised that this transplantation would last only six months, a short time; after the months of suffering were over, peace and prosperity would beckon: new houses in the urban district. That was the promise.

After six months they went to protest at the town hall and the response was another fine promise: they should wait another six months. And they waited another six months and another six, and still they were waiting. And they waited for the food packages, growing skinny. They waited for the doctors who didn't come, and the teachers who didn't come. They waited for anyone who might come and no-one came.

Elizete lost hope. The prefecture changed, the government changed. She and her neighbours – maybe 50 or 100 of them – decided to try one last time, to state their case; they went to the city hall to seek out the mayor, who was elsewhere – it's a big city.

The prefecture protected itself. It was perfectly normal that these men and women, tired of a year and eight months' worth of promises, tired of waiting and travelling, it was normal that they should be on edge, excitable; normal that they should fly off the handle; normal

139

that the police should protect property and lives; but it was not normal to beat the belly of a woman who was six months pregnant. They didn't tell me this; I saw it with my own eyes. It was not normal to give such a hiding to such a small group of unarmed people.

A group of the swamp-dwellers' representatives went to talk with the head of the Department for Social Welfare who came to hear these despairing people. Elizete was spokesperson – she no longer had the job she used to, nor the dream she used to dream, she no longer had hopes of husband and children, but still wanted at least her house, like any animal which has a right to a territory, a place to shelter: the dog seeks a kennel. Elizete told her life-story, which was the life-story of 280 families, 1,800 *Cariocas*.

And there we were, with hard faces, unbending, listening to these piteous tales, the same stories repeated over and over. Déjà vu! Till, in an attempt to describe her present state, Elizete said:

'These days, I am afraid of mirrors. Mirrors terrify me.'

She said that she was afraid to look in the mirror, to look at herself in the mirror, to see herself. She was afraid of her own image.

Not like those of us who are afraid of the dark or of heights, or of looking back or looking behind the door, or behind a church. Not like those of us who are afraid of night, or silence, or the future, or afraid of the words we might say or words we don't want to hear. Not like those of us who are afraid of other people or of ourselves, afraid of speed or immobility, afraid of God or the Infinite, afraid of the sea or the rain, afraid of being alone or being in a crowd. Fear of life – living is very dangerous – fear of life or fear of death. She was afraid of the mirror.

She was afraid of the mirror when so many men and women love the mirror above all else. The mythical Narcissus was in love with himself, he loved to see himself in the mirror of the waters. And as all love is a lack, all love is the want of something, all love is a seeking, Narcissus sought what he lacked in his reflected image; the very place, the only place, where what he lacked could not be. When we lack something we go looking for it in others and not in ourselves, who are in want of it. The future of every Narcissus is death, since he seeks himself in himself, beyond the surface of the water; love is the reflection of the other, not of ourselves.

Snow White's stepmother sought confirmation of her beauty in the mirror, self-affirmation. She wished to be the fairest of them all and the mirror always told her that she was. Till one day, it said she wasn't. The stepmother broke the mirror.

The mirror is human, it has a soul, emotions, feelings, imagination, memory, and only human beings know how to use it: only human beings are able to see themselves. A cow looking at itself in a mirror will never have the misfortune of discovering that it is a cow. It will never see itself, when it sees itself. A cat plays with its own mirror image as if it was playing with another cat, but since this second cat – its mirror image – does nothing more than repeat its own movements, the cat soon tires of it and abandons the game, without discovering itself in its image.

Only the human being is human, since to be human is to be able to see oneself. And Elizete was afraid of looking at herself, of seeing herself: afraid of knowing herself. Always used to seeing herself in the mirror and, on sight of herself, seeing her dream, Elizete, now deprived of her dream, no longer saw herself, she was not herself any more, and she wanted to see herself as she had been, in Bonsucesso, with the dream of the house, the husband and the children, she wanted to see herself as she had once been, not as she was now. Not as she appeared in front of us, defeated, the image of lost hope, of surrender. She knew that when a person gives up mirrors, she gives up her dream, she gives up being. Human being.

Tonight – who knows? – or tomorrow morning, for sure, all of us will have an encounter with our mirrors, we will see our faces reflected. And so too will the mayor and his assistants. As long as the problem of the swamp-dwellers of Pedra de Guaratiba remains unsolved, the Linha Vermelha will not have been finished, and we will all be doomed, those of us who still have any shame in our hearts, when we see our image reflected, we will be doomed to see Elizete's dream – not our faces! – the dream of having what she once had – a house – the dream of having a dream.

5 The Devil as muse of inspiration

The mayor had accused the PT (Workers' Party) of having made a pact with the Devil. Dema, an assistant to one of the Vereadors, dressed up as the Devil and interrupted the proceedings in the Chamber for a few minutes, provoking a major scandal. This speech was made the day after.

DEMONOLOGY is the science which, with all seriousness, studies the diverse and multiple forms of demon, including the Devil, *primus inter pares*, the Prince of Darkness. Known by the name of Beelzebub or Lucifer, Satan or Shaitan, Father of Falsehood or Genius of Evil, the ugly one – Abaddon, Adversary, Appolyon, archfiend, bastard, beast, Belial, black cat, bogeyman, brute, bugger, Clootie, cloven feet, creature, deil, demon, diable, diabo, dog, Evil One, fiend, goat, Hornie, imp, incubus, infernal, jumpy, Mahoun, man of sin, mouldy, Mephisto, Mephistopheles, monkey, monster, ogre, Old Harry, Old Nick, Old Scratch, ragman, rascal, rogue, rotter, savage, scamp, scabby dog, scoundrel, slanderer, succubus, swine, terror, villain, wirricow, worricow, wretch – the Devil, whose name was taken in vain, last week, in this House, quite openly, by Dema, the exorcist – our beloved councillor, brother and friend. Dema exorcises the Devil!

Demonology, I repeat, is the science which studies demons. Demonomania is a manic depressive sickness which causes the afflicted to see demons, devils and evil spirits everywhere, especially in the angelic hosts ranked against him. I am a demonologue; the mayor is a demonomaniac. Under the spell and power of Fata Morgana, the mythical Celtic character who deformed images – he sees mirages, he sees demons in the PT, where there are in fact only men and women, workers dedicated to their nation's good; by contrast, I am engaged in a scientific study of the demons of the prefecture, especially the Prince of Darkness, who presides over that king-less kingdom.

And, the better to understand the elegant black cat, I have studied various authors I admire, men of letters, scientists, theologians, historians and story-tellers. And I have come across a number of intelligent texts which, in a spirit of generosity, I propose to share with everyone.

I will start with Samuel Butler, an English writer of the last century. In one of his fine books, *Higgledy-Piggledy: An Apology for the Devil*, he wrote that, in matters pertaining to the Devil, we have only a partial vision, we know only one side of the story, the version of events contained in the Scriptures, which are sacred. There are no diabolic scriptures which could act as a vehicle for the Satanic thought – no autobiography of Satan; whatever we know about the Devil is from works written about and against him, rather than by him; he has always been denied his legitimate right to free expression of thought.

There are those who claim that the Devil does not exist and there are those who concur with Baudelaire, the French *poète maudit*, when he says, in one of his poems: 'the greatest malice of the devil, and the strongest proof of his existence, resides precisely in his making us believe that he does not exist.'

There are some who say they know how the Devil dresses, the cut of his Florentine robes, the quality of his tailor and his blacksmith – since he carries a trident and is shod in horse-shoes – they will tell you how he comes and goes, how he runs and flies, how he can transubstantiate himself, how he disappears into thin air and how he re-materialises, how he can sub-divide and multiply himself; they tell of his metamorphoses, his forms and apparitions; there are some who speak of his advanced age, of his quarrels with his spouse over the many extra-conjugal children which he has made with blows of his hammer, using, as it were, his own rhythm method.

On his millennarian knowledge, the well-known Argentinian poem, *Martin Fierro*, by José Hernandez, states that the Devil knows a lot for two main reasons; firstly, because he is the Devil; secondly because he is old. How many centuries, how many millennia old is he? No-one ventures to specify his dates. When was Evil born, before or after the creation of Good? And who made it?

There are some who display profound knowledge of the minutiae of his labours and intimate details of our hero's private life, and there are others who say that the Devil does not exist; only diabolism exists.

It was our companion, Dema, the demoniac, who, with his beautiful theatrical concretion of this philosophical-religious

abstraction – an admirably high-speed, yet still protagonic appari-
tion – showed and demonstrated to us, in aesthetic and ecstatic
form how ridiculous it would be to think the Devil incarnated in
human physical form. As ridiculous as God would be in the figure
of any man, excepting that of his own son, in all things an
exception.

Being spirit and not flesh, the Devil can be anyone, that is, he can
inhabit any person, as remarked by Rabelais, the famous French
writer – a medieval man, like our mayor, but much more talented
– in *Gargantua*: 'The sick Devil can be a healthy monk, the healthy
Devil a sick monk.' Rabelais knew what he was talking about: he
himself was a monk and did not enjoy good health.

Dostoevsky, the wonderful Russian writer, another tormented
genius, goes into greater detail: 'The Devil does not exist: it was
man who created him in his own image and semblance.'[1] Then he
exists, if he was created: he exists in man, his creator. Within us, all of
us, inside each and every one of us.

As he is not a physical being, but pure intense desire, the Devil is
omnipresent – though less omnipresent than God, who is truly everywhere and in everything – the repulsive Pó-de-Traque[2] (Fart Powder)
only penetrates living beings, who have the capacity to desire, and
takes possession of them, convulsively. Stones suffer no temptation,
Zarolho[3] does not incarnate himself in them; and the celebrated apple
of the Bible is object and not subject; it does not eat, it is eaten.

Though the dominions of the Devil may be ample, Daniel Defoe
(1662–1731) who wrote *Robinson Crusoe* – the story of a man who
lived alone on a desert island, in the company of his friendly goats –
wrote in another book: 'Wherever God erects a house of prayer, the
Devil always builds a chapel there;' and, 'twill be found, upon
examination, the latter hast the largest congregation.'[4]

Being the subversive that he is, the Devil turns everything on its
head. In stanzas of verse, Rudyard Kipling wrote that wherever Old
Nick goes, 'the tail must wag the dog, for the horse is drawn by the
cart';[5] an anonymous writer of the ninth century adds, with charming
inspiration: 'as the pupil teaches the teacher, the patient cures the
doctor, the sacristan celebrates mass assisted by the priest, the soldier
orders battles in which the generals die, the rich man goes hungry
and the pauper gets fat, and the obstinate wife beats up her husband.'

The mayor would do better not to meddle with this devil business,
because, as an Italian proverb says: 'You can't eat the Devil without
swallowing his horns'. The mayor would do better not to talk on

1. *Brothers Karamazov*, Pt.1, bk II, v.4]

2. Brazilian epithet for the Devil.

3. As above.

4. *The True-born Englishman*, 1701, pt. 1, 1.1–4.

5. *The Conundrum of the Workshops*, 1892.

subjects which he has not mastered, lest his boat be lost in the storm, since, as a Serbian proverb has it, 'God gives the sailor the helm, but the Devil blows the wind into his sails.'

Frightened by the polls, which show him to be in last place out of the ten worst mayors of the ten big cities, the clumsy mayor is putting himself in the place of his accusers, us – and having accused us, the moment he sees us, he takes fright, intimidated and confused. Milton, the great English poet, in a premonition, speaks of this confusion, when he writes in some stanzas from the famous *Paradise Lost*: 'Foolish, the Devil watches, impotent, and feels how horrible is Goodness.' The roles are swapped. As with the mayor.

When our alcaide, emeritus hunter of witches, shows such confidence in defining who is a devil and who is not, and struts and flatters himself and boasts of knowledge that he does not possess, of ideas he does not profess and gods he does not adore, he makes me think of Shakespeare, when he wrote that 'the Devil can cite scriptures for his purpose./An evil soul producing holy witness/Is like a villain with a smiling cheek/A goodly apple rotten at the heart.'[6] The same idea is contained in a fourteenth-century manuscript kept in the Bibliothèque Nationale in Paris: 'The Devil always speaks about our Gospels, it is his best means of self-protection, hidden and hypocritical.' Exactly like the mayor.

And a precursor of the Bard, Christopher Marlowe, wrote a play about Faustus, the man who sold his soul to the Devil in return for returning his youth. When the Cloven-footed One came to collect on the contract, the young Faustus lamented and wept: 'See, see where Christ's blood streams in the firmament,/ One drop would save my soul, half a drop, ah my Christ.'[7] Faustus is damned, he damns himself, because he assumes the powers of the Creator, by deciding of his own accord to set himself against the divine will, refusing to grow old. In the same way our mayor usurps the right which God alone has to decide who is an angel and who a devil, he substitutes himself for God and takes it upon himself to decide who is who. For this political crime and religious sin, he will pay dear: the Devil will come and he and Faustus will be condemned, damned for eternity.

6. *The Merchant of Venice*, Act 1, sc.3, 1.97–100.

7. *Doctor Faustus*, c.1592, Act 5, sc.2.

6 Resignation

Virtuous crime or criminal virtue?

Rio de Janeiro, besides its natural beauties, is also renowned for its 'waters of March': every year, it rains in abundance in that month. Everyone knows this, but no government ever takes measures to protect the slums on the edge of the mountains' abysses, measures to drain water from streets and squares which are always flooded. Three months after I took office, a dreadful tempest inundated the city causing many deaths and destroying many houses and shacks in the poorer parts of Rio. As has happened many times before . . .

IMAGINE the scene: it takes place in small villages in Africa, centuries ago, in what are now Angola and Senegal, where poverty meant that men were locked in a life-and-death struggle for survival, where populations slaughtered each other in tribal wars – imagine the arrival of well-armed white soldiers, using, among other things, bacteriological weapons – a tactic now deployed in the lands of the Yanomanis[1] by the *garimpeiros*[2], who infect the native people with smallpox and tuberculosis – imagine the number of women raped and old men struck down, and the selection of the youngest and fittest to suffer the fate of slavery. Imagine the rest of the world staying silent, seeing nothing, hearing no cries of horror, feeling nothing: it was not their problem!

Imagine the young people transported in slave ships, squatting in airless holds. Imagine the disease, the mortal longings – imagine those who died of homesickness, malaria and starvation, over half of every cargo.

Imagine how, on their arrival here, those recovering from the crossing were legally sold, as merchandise. Not even the wildest, most unbridled imagination, could have conjured up the slightest hope or envisioned even the possibility of escape. The negro, once sold, resigned himself to his fate.

1. An Indian nation in the Amazon region.
2. *Garimpeiros* – gold prospectors, usually acting illegally.

When Abolition was proclaimed, many slaves preferred to stay in their masters' houses – they preferred captivity. Resigned to their fate. It is not for us to condemn resignation, which can sometimes be a virtue.

We have to resign ourselves to death, for instance, for it comes to us all sooner or later, and each day creeps closer. Resignation in itself is neither vice nor virtue. I am resigned to not being the person I would like to have been: I am the person I am able to be, I have done what I have been able to do.

But to resign oneself in the face of possibility, to accept the avoidable disaster, to do nothing in the face of dangers which can be skirted, to be apathetic or fatalistic in the face of so many deaths foretold – resignation in these circumstances is criminal! We are not slaves and there are steps we can take – steps which must be taken. We must do something!

On Friday last, people died. We saw a young man on television bewailing the death of his father and two brothers, killed by the storm, in front of his very eyes, a man now bereft of family. We saw 30 cars swept away in one go, we saw families in anguish at the loss of all they possessed, we saw houses overrun by the waters, we saw the Praça Bandeira[3] transformed into a pestilential lake. We saw it with our own eyes: I was there, in the middle of the deluge, on my way back from the intended commemoration of the Metal Workers' Union's Women's Day in São Cristóvão.

3. This square is flooded every year during summer storms.

Like the Passion of Jesus Christ which is presented every year, at Easter time, in the arches at Lapa – this tragedy, this unholy tragedy, this profanity, is also repeated every year in Praça Bandeira, in São Cristóvão – in Maracana, in the slums, on the hillside shanty towns – and it too has fixed dates: the rains of February and the waters of March.

If this was part of God's design – sent down to punish our carnivalesque sins! – then resignation would be a virtuous acceptance of a deserved punishment. But those who are punished are those who have sinned least. They are the wretched, the poor. They are people who deserve our help, they have the right to demand it, and it is our duty to come to their aid. How? I don't know yet. My parliamentary experience is short, I don't know what resources we have at our disposal, but I know that we could do something. And I know that the mayor could do more, more than us and at greater speed.

I know that other floods will come – in this storm and the next – and other deaths will happen, predictable deaths, cars and houses will be destroyed and the Praça Bandeira will be flooded. Because that is what always happens. But just because it always happens does not mean it necessarily has to happen. Nowadays engineering achieves great things. The Castelo hill has been razed and the Flamengo Gardens were built on land reclaimed from the sea; mountains have been pierced and roads cut through them and you can go to Niteroi and cross the Guanabara Bay on foot.

I do not condemn the mayor. It is clear that he is not to blame for what happened on Friday: he has been in his post for only three months now.

But if this tragedy which happens year in, year out at the same time, accompanied by the same well-meaning words, the same images on the TV, the same anguish and the same horror, if this tragedy happens again, then yes, this mayor and his administration – and each and every one of us, with our own share of the blame – he and all of us will be responsible for the crime of resignation!

7 Memory and the torture chamber

This speech was made when the Chamber was voting on whether to allow the demolition of the Tijuca police headquarters, where many patriots had been tortured and murdered. The prefecture wanted to sell the site to a fast-food business. My allies and I won the vote and the building is still there. I am really very proud of it. I am sure – and many of my colleagues told me this was the case – that my speech turned the vote of more than one. We were sure to lose, and we won!

HOWEVER hard I might try – and I confess that I have never made the slightest effort to do so – I have never managed to make believe that I do not exist. I have never managed to pass through the world unnoticed or make myself invisible. What I am going to say might seem threatening, but when anyone looks in my direction they always see a man. A man who exists.

I am. But what does it mean, to be? I am what I do, I am what I want, I am my desire. As are we all; we are what we desire, now, in the present. But, if we desire, we are our future, we are what we wish to become. And this sets us apart from animals: we are capable of inventing our future and not merely awaiting it. This desire to become is nature's most beautiful creation. A tree, a stone, an animal – none of these are capable of wanting to be what they are not, of transforming mere potential into action.

Thus, my identity is formed from that which I am and that which I want to be. But it is also formed from that which I have been: I am the person I have been – my identity is also formed from my past.

A while back, the paper *O Globo* wanted to tell its readers of my origins, my childhood. I have been a baker, I've baked a lot of bread; many people have eaten bread I made with my own hands. *O Globo* took me back to my father's bakery, in Penha, where in times gone by I used to bake bread and sometimes serve at the counter, and they took my photo there. When I saw myself in front of that oven, my friend for a good 10 years of my life, a wonderful part of my life came flooding back to me – to remember is to live, as the song has it. I remembered, I re-lived, I lived.

But I am not made of happy bread-baking memories alone. Sometimes I remember when I was a guerrilla. This is also part of me. It is my past, what I have been, what I am. Today I think it was a mistake. An honest mistake made by honest people, decent people like myself.

I have always been a believer in the rule of law and I am proud to belong today to this House, in which laws are made, which I promise to respect. As a believer in the rule of law, I never accepted the dictatorship. If I fought against it, I fought against subversion. The subversives were those who subverted the law and overthrew a perfectly legitimate regime. It was they who initiated the wave of kidnappings, the invasions of people's homes – they taught the wrongdoers who proliferate today. In my own case, for instance, I was never arrested; I was kidnapped by the São Paulo police. Me, whose only crime was to defend the law. The law which had been violated.

I was picked up in São Paulo and, like everyone else, I was tortured. But, as happens in the great Shakespearian tragedies, the most painful scenes are juxtaposed sometimes with scenes of ridiculous farce. A scene of torture is a scene of inhuman tragedy. But the infinite bestiality of the seven orang-utans who tortured me – their incomparable ignorance – created an absurd dialogue of the deaf.

Among these seven mastodons, there was one who tried to justify everything with bureaucratic arguments. While he was giving me electric shocks on the *pau-de-arara*,[1] from which I hung naked, upside down, he said:

'You will forgive me, yeah? But I am torturing you because it's on my schedule, see? I don't have anything personal against you, honest. I'm even a fan of your plays. I haven't seen any, but I like them all, see? You know how it is, yeah? Here you do what you're told to, see? Now, you know, it's a funny old world, things change, one day it might be you who's on top and me underneath, yeah? Now if it came to that, right, you're obviously not about to forget that I tortured you, fair enough, but it was just the luck of the draw, see? I tortured you because it was on my schedule.'

This was one of the mental defectives who punished me. There

1. Literally, the 'macaw's rod': an instrument of torture on which the victim is hung by a rod under the knees – thus resembling the *arara,* the macaw which can hang upside down.

were others, of all kinds, of all races and pedigrees. The leader of the team, for instance, did not know why I was there, as the team which did the torturing was not the same as the team which did the kidnapping. There were specialised: each knew how to carry out his own particular crafts. Some made instruments of torture; others paid our country's foreign debt. All were acting in concert against a single victim – the Brazilian people.

It was then, when the pain was most intense, that I tried to engineer a break in the torment and I asked – 'What is it that you want me to confess?' I wanted a break but I had decided never to confess anything – and I never did. But I wanted to buy time, so I asked him: 'What is it you want me to confess?'

At first the dinosaur did not know what to answer. He didn't know why he was torturing me – just that it was on his schedule. But the leader of the kidnap team had given him a list of accusations, written on a scrap of paper. He scanned the piece of paper and read out the first accusation: 'Boal, when you go abroad, you defame Brazil!' Me, defame Brazil! When I never tire of extolling the natural beauties of Baia da Guanabara. 'In what way do I defame Brazil?' I asked, hanging naked on the *pau-da-arara*. Reading on, the boor answered: 'You defame it because, when you travel, you tell people abroad that there is torture in Brazil.'

It did not register with the blockhead that he was doing just that, he was torturing me. The situation was so unreal, so funambulatory, that I laughed. When he saw me laughing, at first, he could not believe it – no-one laughs when they are hanging from a *pau-da-arara*! Then he became indignant, and turned the crank to increase the electric charge and asked why I was laughing. I answered that his present activity justified my past statements: in Brazil people are tortured, methodically and cruelly, and I was the living proof of it, strung up by my ankles, there, at that very moment. In one of the few moments of lucidity of his entire life, he thought, he thought very hard and ended up agreeing:

'You're right. I am torturing you. But since you are an artist, since you are well-known and you appear on television from time to time, I am torturing you, I give you that, but I am torturing you with respect.'

This episode in my life is part of me. I would like to go back to that cellar, where my only companion was a mouse, who was even more frightened than I was – I would like to see those instruments of torture again, those deadly but efficient tools. To revisit that building.

I would like to re-see my past, to re-feel it, to re-live it. But the building, where episodes such as this took place, has been destroyed. In its place, in São Paulo, they have constructed a supermarket. They have destroyed the memory. And without memory, imagination is impossible – without remembering, one does not imagine! Without the past, the future would not exist and we would live like animals, ruminating on the present like cows. Let us not be cows. In São Paulo, because the memory of past atrocities has been destroyed, 111 prisoners were cruelly and premeditatedly cut down in Carandiru. The prisoners launched a revolt, the chief of police gave them an ultimatum, and then ordered the raid on the prison and the slaughter which resulted, coldly, conscious of the crime he was committing. On a lovely Sunday evening, the horrors of the dictatorship came back to haunt us.

I appeal to my colleagues who are, like me, involved in the business of making laws, just as I used to make bread. I appeal to them to allow me to continue existing, so that a part of my self survives my death. The Vila Isabel house holds the memories of hundreds of men and women, it holds many stories, it holds History. Living History. Many of the men and women who were imprisoned there are today in these galleries watching us, just as I am on this platform looking at you. Those who are here today, they and I, we remember, and the past lives in our memory, which is part of our being.

Do not destroy the Tijuca house. I beg you, I appeal to you.

I appeal especially to those who do not think like me, to those of you not of my party, I appeal especially to those who think the opposite of what I think, I appeal to you, I beg you: let me exist.

Sometimes we do not share the same ideas, we do not think the same thoughts, for that very reason, I beg for my sake, for our sake, and I beg also for your sake. For you to continue being who you are it is necessary that we be who we are. For you to be you, I need to be me.

Allow me to exist. And for me to exist, that portion of our past which is made of stone, must remain standing. Do not destroy the Tijuca house, do not destroy our past, do not destroy me. Vote no to the mayor's veto.

Allow that part of me, of each of us, to survive, allow me to live. And I will say thank you for that.

Many thanks.[2]

2. The mayor's veto was thrown out and the torture chamber in Tijuca will soon be a museum. This was my first victory at the Chamber, and I was very proud. *AB.*

8 One hideous crime hides the hideousness of another

In July 1993, seven children were murdered by off-duty policemen, as they slept in the porch of the Candelária church, a well-known building right in the centre of Rio. At the time, a festival of the Theatre of the Oppressed, attended by over 200 people from all over the world, was taking place in a building almost next door. The familiarity of the landmark church coupled with the presence of a number of foreigners may have contributed to media coverage and public outrage at what, in Brazil, was not that unusual an incident. Three days later, our own group of 'Street Children', who had some of their friends killed at Candelária, performed their play about their lives, 200 metres away from the site of the carnage.

THE city, the country, the whole world has heard or read with dismay the account of the most nefarious of all the nefarious crimes already committed with impunity in this country. A group of monsters, paid by the taxpayer – our taxes, our money! – men who should be the very model of valour, have given the most infamous demonstration of cowardice; in the dead of night, having first made sure that the defenceless children were sleeping – they were children, they were defenceless, they were sleeping! – these men crucified seven martyrs between the ages of 10 and 15.

This hideous crime has made us forget, for a moment, the hideousness of a first crime, a prior crime, which was one of the causes leading to this effect: the children who were murdered while they slept in the street, were sleeping in the street.

These murders, like those in Acari, Nova Jerusalém, Mandala, Carandiru, Canapi, and infinite others in many places, were committed by criminals in uniform. Who was responsible for the selection of these demoniacs? Who are the chiefs who did not spot the dangerousness of these Rottweilers?

It is not irresponsible of us to blame the executive office for these executions. The executive office is neither the criminal nor the criminal's boss. We respect its innocence of this crime, but not of the crime which preceded it, since this massacre could have been avoided. The state and the municipality have spent considerable sums on the beautification of this city, which would be cause for applause, were it not for the fact that this would deflect our attention from what should be our first national priority: the care of poor children, of the hungry. The federal government continues to pay interest on an external debt which was contracted by the dictatorship and which grows without cease. The foreign banks are happy with the punctuality of our repayments. And the children lie there vulnerable, sleeping in the open, in the porch of a church which is famous as a symbol of faith and as the setting for happy and expensive marriages.

A lesson has been taught and, let us hope, learnt. Till the last remaining street child has been given shelter, and is safely protected from the rage and fury of Nazis, till everyone has the constitutional right to education, to health, to a roof over their head, none of us has the right to sleep. Our eyes must stay open and our hands must be working.

And even then, neither we nor the government will be absolved of the blame for such inhuman misery. A single child, in the porch of Candelária, reveals the hideousness of a crime! None of us is innocent.

9 The Devil and the canny man

During my mandate, the mayor of Rio was not a person to be trusted. He would promise the Chamber one thing, and do the opposite. It was useless to engage in dialogue with him, because we never knew what he was really up to. After one of his several betrayals of agreements which had been made, I felt I had to say a few words on the subject, knowing of course that he would not change in the slightest.

WE can disagree about everything, but once we agree how things will be, having given our word, having made a pledge, we must honour our commitments. Just as, in times gone by, a hair of one's beard was worth more than a signature in a registry.

Politically we can be friends or foes, but 'yes' must always mean 'yes' and 'no' must never mean 'maybe'. If one agreement is broken, with it breaks the possibility of any agreement. Dialogue breaks down, parliament breaks down; all we are left with is simple arithmetic: who is on one side, who is on the other, who is sitting on the fence, and which way are they leaning, and why and to what extent. We know that some of our *vereadors* are always on the fence, assessing which way they will jump, according to the benefits they will gain.

But it is my opinion that, having made an agreement, only the two parties to it, together, can break it, if they both agree. That is, if they make a new agreement. The breach of an agreement by one party alone is betrayal. Even the Devil knows this. Since, as the story goes, even the Devil, in times gone by, was a respecter of agreements and contracts. Even when defeated, the Devil, a good goat,[1] shut up and paid up.

However long-lived and diabolical the Evil One may be, he can always be vanquished by the just man. Especially if the just man is a crafty man.

1. Brazilian saying: 'A good goat doesn't shout'. I think the opposite: the best goat should shout the loudest! *AB*.

155

Which is what happened when Satan met a canny peasant, a capable man who, with only a small patch of land, managed to grow a crop sufficient to feed his family, his neighbours and his friends. The Devil, lazy layabout that he was, owned immense tracts of unproductive land, which he had inherited from forgotten relatives, land-grabbing uncles who had 'acquired' it, or stolen from the indians, its first owners. Seeing the wise man's lands positively blooming with colourful crops of legumes, vegetables, trees and fruits, the envious Devil proposed they go into partnership.

'Together we will plant this enormous territory of mine. And come harvest-time, we will make a fraternal division of the fruits of our labours. Half each.'

In view of who this proposition was coming from, the canny peasant was suspicious, but he could not refuse such a tempting offer. He asked for details: 'What will each person's half be?'

The devil had already got it all worked out.

'The half which grows above ground will be mine, and mine alone; the half which grows below ground will be all yours!'

'The part which grows above ground will be yours, the part which grows below will be mine?' murmured the peasant, understanding the trick.

As this offer had been made by the powerful Devil, it was tantamount to an order. The canny man only asked, modestly, that it should be he alone who was responsible for the choice of seeds, with which the Evil One concurred, out of idleness: less work for him. They set to work. They worked hard and, to give him his due, the Devil did not spare his energies, having visions of luscious growth. Months passed, harvest-time came. And the man's cunning was revealed: he had planted potatoes. And they had all grown, as nature dictates, below ground, in the half which belonged exclusively to him.

The Devil was furious, and hungry – but he kept his word: words must always be kept, even by the Devil. He demanded: 'Let's plant again. But, this time, my share will be everything that remains below ground!'

'Whatever you say, boss. Let's get down to it.'

And again the canny man chose the seeds, this time wheat. Come harvest time, only the canny man could make bread: a deal is a deal. At least, it was in those days.

The Devil, accepting the division of spoils which he himself had proposed, but seeing the canny man tucking in with gusto, could not hold back and laid aside courtesy, chivalry, manners and finesse: 'Let's fight it out. A duel with sticks!'

'If that's how it has to be. Your Excellency is absolutely right. It seems to me that as the two-time loser, it should be you who gets to choose from these two sticks, whichever one suits you better. Here they are: this long baton, which is taller than a man and has a long reach, and this other smaller one, which is shorter than an arm's length. Which would you prefer?'

Naturally, the fearless Devil chose the long heavy stick. But the canny man reserved the right to choose the location of the fight, a narrow, dark alley. And there, the long stick was of little use to the hot-headed Devil, as it crashed into doors and windows and got stuck on steps, while the clever peasant's short stick rained a shower of blows down onto the cramped Devil's back.

This fable proves, if proof were needed, that he who chooses last laughs longest.

At the same time it proves that, even in devilry, there is a modicum of honour, without which no deal is possible, no honest parliament can exist.

Something has changed in the way relations are conducted between the executive office, the mayor's office, and this House. I no longer wish to speak of broken agreements, I am talking about disagreements.

Up to now, the executive has often tried to legalise immorality, and it has sometimes succeeded. This has happened over the last few years, for instance, in relation to the salaries of workers in the health and education sectors. Pitiably low workers' wages of 100 or 200 measly reals are paid by the prefecture, legally. Immoral salaries, though legal. The same has happened with tax exemptions: hotels have been exempted from paying their debts, health insurers have had their taxes reduced, and so it goes on. It is questionable from a moral perspective, but from a legal perspective perfectly above board. Legalised immorality!

If formerly the mayor legalised this immorality, today he is seeking to corrupt and demoralise legality. Legal decree makes it crystal clear that the State Bank, BANERJ, is the only bank authorised to pay the salaries of municipal employees. However, the mayor does not bother with this legal nicety and has the effrontery to publish in the *D.O.* (the official journal) a list of banks authorised by him to pay these salaries. If before now the mayor used to attack us, these days he ignores us, places himself above the law and writes his own.

The mayor cannot delegate powers, just as I cannot choose one of my assistants to talk on my behalf in the Chamber or to vote in my place. And yet there in his office are officers and managers, deputy mayors, mayorettes and many more, people who have no legal power but are powerful enough to order fines, sackings, food for pigeons, the removal of beggars, of street vendors, etc. The mayor allows them to do as they please, and they do it without regard for the law.

The overweening prepotency of the mayor's office forces us into a decision: either, we must energetically oppose the mayor's continuing single-handed exercise of power, or, if we continue to accept whatever he does, we would do better to convert this plenary into a bingo hall, a symbol of the times we live in in our city, where immorality is legalised and law is made immoral.

10 'Human rights' are human

The most important law that I was able to promulgate was, I believe, the 'Law of Protection of Witnesses of Crimes'. In many of our groups' plays, the fact that people are afraid to serve as witnesses, for fear of retaliation, frequently came up. We decided to form a group of specialists, including lawyers, prosecutors and even chiefs of police, to study this and to propose a law to protect witnesses from the criminal's revenge. This law included a new provisional identity card, a new home for the witness far away from the areas where s/he might be in danger, finding the witnesses new jobs similar to what they had done before, agreements with other cities and states, etc. This was the first law of this kind to be promulgated in Brazil. Later, the federal government took some hints from it. This speech was made the day I presented the law to the people, after approval by the Chamber.

ANYONE who has had the opportunity to watch the Discovery Channel will have seen the bloody struggles for survival which animals engage in, from the bottom of the sea to the top of mountains, in African deserts and glacial regions. Beautiful programmes to watch in the comfort of one's home; cruel in reality for their Protagonists.

Animals are programmed to survive. At all costs. No moral principle separates the tiger from the gazelle, only the speed of their legs. Nothing can stop the wolf from devouring the lamb, since 'if it wasn't you, it would be your father'.[1]

Civilisation is only made possible by the invention of Ethics. In the law of the jungle, brute force wins. Animals have tendencies to behave in particular ways, but these are genetically programmed. Only the human being invents the way it should behave, determining

1. As the wolf says in La Fontaine's fable.

159

rights and responsibilities, only the human being is capable of developing what goes by the generic term of 'Human Rights'. Rights for all, simply by virtue of belonging to the human species, and *not* to one particular nationality, race, group, class, caste or party.

Human Rights are fundamental rights which protect any and every citizen against the whim of the powerful and against the conduct of a state which violates international norms.

Amongst the crimes against Human Rights are extra-judicial or summary execution, kidnapping, 'disappearance', arbitrary detention and torture, slavery and slave labour, exile, ethnic, religious, racial or sexual discrimination, the curtailment of the right to a fair trial, or to freedom of expression, of association, of movement, of assembly.

The advent of humanity comes about by the invention of Ethics: the individual judged by the norms of society. In far-off times, the subjective will of the king, who was the strongest and the most powerful – nothing to do with the pallid kings of today – the royal will, the power of the king, was the reality of the law.

It was Hammurabi of Babylon, in 1750 BC, who was the first king to transfer to the judgement of society the determination of what should be the norms of behaviour for the citizen. Up till then it was reasonable to assume that the king's will would, *per se*, be just. In order to institute the Code of Hammurabi, the king had to invoke a god, Shamah, in his religion the God of Justice. The Citizen Law was thus distinguished from the person of Hammurabi by the intervention of Shamah, the Just, the God of Reason.

This was the first known penal code in history. Written in stone, it is in the Louvre museum, where we can see that civilisation's pre-occupation with a notion of Right already existed in that epoch.

Other codes came. More and more these endorsed the predominance of a superior social order or system of values intended to govern the conduct of each individual within society.

Some of the recent 'codes' became famous, such as the Constitution of the United States, in 1789, when Thomas Jefferson, its principal author, defended the 'Right to Happiness', and above all the 'Universal Declaration of the Rights of Man and the Citizen', promulgated two years after the beginning of the French Revolution, in 1791. These codes attribute the function of justice to the State, at the same time warning of the necessity to limit the power of the State, which is made up of individuals.

But how could its power be limited if it fell to the State to apply the very law limiting it? Firstly, by setting one state against other states. Secondly, by dividing the State into three parts.

From the last century to the present day, people have spoken of the right to 'humanitarian intervention', giving other states a duty to intervene in the affairs of a state which violates Human Rights. And recently, with the Gulf War, the 'Duty to Intervene' was instituted, at the heart of the UN policy, to be applied in cases where atrocities are committed by the state against its own citizens. (This duty has only been applied when dealing with one oil-rich country trying to annex another even richer country, and was never contemplated during the bloody regimes which strangled so many countries in Latin America. Or in Free Timor, today, in the stranglehold of Indonesia, under the nose of a greedy Australia.)

The 'Universal Declaration of Human Rights', promulgated by the General Assembly of the UN in 1948, stated that 'Men are born and remain equal in rights. The objective of all political association is the conservation of the natural and imprescriptible Human Rights, including the freedom of property, of security and of resistance to oppression.'

By means of the struggle between barbarism and civilisation, Humanity has been able to progress to a certain point. Barbarism, like some governments, extols the law of the jungle, the survival of the fittest. Civilisation, by contrast, seeks to create models of behaviour and, as the French Revolution taught us, extols the tripartite State, the executive, the legislature and the judiciary. The French Revolution came to reiterate what we already knew: that government cannot be simultaneously the body responsible both for legislation and judgement – which is what happens with animals in the forest and at the bottom of the ocean, as seen on the Discovery Channel.

Anyone who turns against Human Rights, is turning against civilisation and revealing their primitive side. The troglodytes had no morality – for them, Right was measured by the weight of the cudgel they carried. This is the outcome desired by those who attack the chief of police, Hèlio Luz, with the immoral argument that he is a person who respects human rights. For once, we have a humanised chief of police.

None of us is asking for clemency for criminals, kidnappers, drug-traffickers. We are asking for the law, for justice. As civilised people, we know that a man in uniform who carries a weapon is the arm of justice, but not the judge. And those who plead the case for the assassination of assassins, the kidnapping of kidnappers, without the mediation of the judiciary power – an eye for an eye, a tooth for a tooth, the automatically applied punishment, the Old Testament punishment of Talion – these people are placing themselves on the same moral plane as those who they wish to accuse, they commit the same crime they are trying to punish.

Those who speak against Human Rights speak against the humanisation of man. To declare that such Rights must protect only such and such a category of person is a crime against humanity. They wish to divide us into castes, relegating the majority to the condition of untouchables and keeping for themselves the privileges of the Brahmin.

The division of powers detailed above represents the greatest victory for humanity of the last few hundred years; we cannot stay silent, listening to imbecilities which would put punishment before sentence and have the sentence carried out by one of the parties in dispute.

However, in order for Human Rights to be exercised to the full, we must observe that, in the practice of crime, there is always a triad present. All crime involves a criminal, since the criminal act does not commit itself, it requires an agent; all crime is carried out against a victim – without an object, the criminal intention is not yet a crime; and every crime is witnessed, from close by or far off, before, during or after its execution: someone always knows something – if only the victim.

In crimes of violence, the victim is silenced by death and the witness by fear. Even in non-fatal cases, frequently a victim who is also the principal witness, stays silent out of fear, becoming doubly a victim.

In the triad of crime – criminal, victim, witness – for the first of these to be punished, the last must be protected; the witness is restorer of the truth and truth must shine before Justice can be done.

If this is to happen, the witness cannot live in fear of being the victim of a second crime; the job of protecting him or her falls to the State, since, by protecting the witness, we are defending Human Rights, civilisation against savagery.

We must seek the truth at all levels, at all times, whenever there is doubt. Knowledge humanises: we need to know. We need to know not just about recent crimes, but also about crimes of the past. Not only the ordinary crimes, but the political crimes too.

In these times of calamity, when moral values are bought and sold on the great globalised market, some proclaim disrespect for the law and would have everyone make their own. Others, exempting themselves from past crimes, invoke amnesty to make a travesty of it, turning it into a law of forgetting.

Amnesty precludes punishment, but not the uncovering of truth; though both words possess the same Greek root, the Law of Amnesty is not the Law of Amnesia. We have to find out who gave the orders and who took them – see, there are witnesses! – and not accept as valid the excuse that some of these criminals were merely obeying orders. What kind of torturer would obey the order to torture his own mother?

His mother, not someone else's.

The future is invented by the contemplation of the past. Those who are today supporting the non-observance of the law must crave the lobotomisation of memory. It is sad that many of those who are siding with authoritarianism, the persecutors of today, have been the persecuted of yesterday.

We have come here to protect the truth, which will always be threatened while the witness is in danger. The crime is prolonged in time and space, while the criminal remains a threat.

Threat is the prologue to the perpetrated crime. If it is offered to the witness, it is the prolonging of the crime. Protection is its antidote. Today, we have come here to put forward a programme of witness protection, to propose the rehabilitation of the truth. We are sure that together, as long as we do not allow ourselves to be separated by ideological differences, which we may have, or party loyalties, which we certainly have, together, for civilisation and against barbarism, we can and must initiate a huge movement which will offer a little bit of terra firma in the midst of all the moral turbulence of the new international order.

And our goal is so modest! We just want the truth. That's all.

Many thanks.

11 *Romeo and Juliet*

A story of hatred and betrayal

In September 1990, I took part in a gathering at the Federal University of Florianopolis, convened to discuss the subject of love. A subject as all-embracing as life and death, being and nothingness, zero and infinity.

When I applied my mind to the task, I thought it might be a good idea to look for proverbs or proverbial phrases which, whilst not defining the word 'love', might at least throw some light on the subject. And, on looking, I came across disparity, contrast and controversy. When we speak of love, we can be talking about anything under the sun. Especially hate.

1. Contemporary Brazilian writer.
2. *Pororoca*, is the name given to the meeting of the waters of the Amazon with the ocean; the explosion can be heard dozens of kilometres away.
3. This article was written when the greatest hit on Brazilian tv was 'Pantanal', which was stuffed full of snakes and lizards and, above all, crocodiles.

ACROSS the centuries and throughout the peoples of the world, many proverbs present love as pain or suffering. Or as a ferocious enemy which lurks in the shadows only to ambush us. Love is dangerous. Guimarães Rosa[1] says that living is very dangerous; and love, which is life in all its plenitude, is even more dangerous than life. Though, of course, less monotonous.

One of the oldest proverbs I found, written in the first century AD in Sanskrit – one of India's oldest languages – said: *love is a crocodile swimming in the river of desire.* According to this proverb, desire is a necessity, loving is a risk. It swims in the river, the river swirls, carrying it along, the river of desire transports us, the waters of the river seek out and explore channels, pressing forward, opening their way in front of them; the river of desire has a future: its meeting with the sea, *pororoca*,[2] the crocodile, by contrast, bites and kills; it can serve as an actor in an exotic television soap,[3] but is of no service in the pursuit of greater pleasures. No-one strokes a crocodile.

Plautus, the Roman playwright, wrote that *love is a mixture of honey and bile*. He wrote this two centuries before Jesus Christ, who asked for water when he was on the cross, and the centurions gave him vinegar. Plautus mixes Iracema,[4] the virgin with lips of honey, with the sacrifice of Christ.

An English proverb states: *love is a servile dog that would rather be beaten by its master than stroked by a stranger*; this English proverb treats masochistic love, though Leopold Sacher Masoch, the man who gave his name to this type of sexual perversion, was an Austrian writer. Obviously there are shameless dogs of every nationality who like being stroked and petted, every which way, by anyone available; but the proverb only applies to dogs enamoured of their master. Without love, they all bite.

Staying with the English, they say that *love is like measles or chicken-pox; the later you catch it, the greater the danger*. That is to say, old people are weaker and more vulnerable to love, which is presented here as a sickness and not a cure.

François Villon, the French poet, the author of ballads, wrote in 1473: *a thousand sufferings for a single pleasure*. Back to the idea that there is no honey without bile.

Sometimes the proverb is ambiguous; this one from the Bible – *love is as strong as death*! Stalemate? Who wins? Some optimists adapt the biblical text, making it more heroic: love is *stronger* than death. There are those who believe this, but they die all the same, even in love.

There are other proverbs which are provocative, carnal, sensual or ironic. Publius Syrus, a Roman writer of the first century AD declared in his book *Maxims* that *it is impossible to be well-behaved when one is in love, and it is impossible to love when one is well-behaved*. On the same lines, Cervantes, author of *Don Quixote*, thought thus: *love is an enemy which cannot be defeated by hand to hand combat: only by flight!* For this reason, in the past, smart rich families sent their love-smitten girls to Europe, to forget their poor lovers; today, with the economic crisis, the same families still send their girls to Europe, only these days it is to seek out a rich husband.

A fine French proverb from the Middle Ages says: *love is a sauce which makes any kind of meat tasty!* In deference to the French cuisine, we can forgive this gastronomic proverb – but let it be noted that the text speaks of meat, as if loving was tantamount to eating, devouring, chewing up the loved one. The Middle Ages were cruel times. Happily, times have changed. Have they?

Sometimes the proverbs express generalities, like this English one,

4. Iracema, a famous naive Indian girl, a character in a novel by José de Alencar.

165

which says: *A person who loves, loves at first sight!* Like Romeo and Juliet, who already love each other before they are aware that they are a Montague and a Capulet, that they are Romeo and Juliet. First sight was enough. Another English example says the reverse: *friendship can end in love, but never love in friendship!* And a melancholic Spanish version suggests *offering friendship to someone who loves you is like offering bread to someone dying of thirst!*

Aristotle, the fourth-century BC Greek philosopher, thought that *to love is to enjoy, but it is a joy just to be loved!* Especially when we do not love the person who loves us. And an Italian proverb pontificates: *the hurt is great when the love is small.* Which means that, if the love is great, anything goes, and everything is forgivable. Is it?

There is a German proverb which says something I do not understand: *love is cross-eyed and hate is blind.* Where does this leave justice? Perhaps Voltaire explains what this proverb is trying to say: *whoever you are, love rules you. It is, was, or will one day be your master.* Another Spanish maxim concurs: *in the face of love or death, the strong can do nothing.*

Almost always, these proverbs about love speak about men and women. For or against.

Bonaventure, French fifteenth-century writer: *men die of love, and women live on it.* And another French author, Mme de Staël, wrote in 1796:[5] *love is the story of a woman's life and a mere episode in the life of a man.*

Françoise Xenakis, a modern French author, wrote a book entitled: *Zut! on a encore oublié Mme Freud!* (Damn, we forgot Madame Freud again!) And what about Mme Einstein and Mme Eisenstein – who were they? Nobody knows; but we all know that behind every great man there is always a great woman; it's just she doesn't appear: she is in the kitchen preparing the food, or in bed, bearing men-children or awaiting her husband. The same Mme de Staël also said: *l'amour est l'égoisme à deux.* And an anonymous Pole thinks that: *love enters a man through the eyes and women through the ears* – which gives us men licence to be ugly and authorises women to be stupid.

Another Spaniard, muy macho, offers: *man is the fire, woman the match, and the devil comes to fan the flames.*

There are proverbs which lean towards the vulgar, such as, for instance this French one, which is also medieval: *two cocks lived in peace, till one day up jumped a hen.*

Enough proverbs.

When people talk of love, in truth, they can be talking about

5. *L'amour est l'histoire de la vie des femmes, c'est un épisode dans celle des hommes.* (De l'influence des passious 1796).

anything. But to ascertain which love we are talking about, we need to know in what voice we are conjugating the verb 'to love'.

The active voice? Amo, amas, amat – I love, you love, he/she/it loves etc.? The passive voice? I am loved, you are loved etc.? Or the reflexive voice? I love myself, you love yourself, he loves himself, and so on? Or, as some people would have it, a voice adapted to suit our interests: I love myself, you, he and she, we, you plural, they love me?

A question: is love a thing which exists between two people, a bolt of lightning flashing between two poles, or a thing contained in a single person? Is it one person's condition or a meeting between two people? I love – this is a verb; but for the love-noun to exist, do I need to be loved or is my desire to love sufficient, just as my desire to hate can be enough, when I hate without the acquiescence of the person I hate? I hate Pinochet and he doesn't even know me. I can flee from the lie that I hate, but I must search for the truth that I love – I must meet it, if I truly love it. The person one loves, does one love that person in oneself or in the other? Or does one love oneself in the other, as suggested by the Portuguese poet Fernando Pessoa? *No-one loves another, if he does not love that of himself which is in that other, or is presumed so to be.*

Romeo illustrates an extreme case of love; when he loves Rosaline (before he gets to know Juliet), he declares: *I have lost myself, I am not here. This is not Romeo, he is some other where.*[6] And where is this 'other where'? In Rosaline. And she is – or possesses – that which he wants (in the sense of lacks) to be Romeo. The he that remains, is that pure want or lack, a body without a soul and without life; for this reason, he is not there, he is in her. And, thus, he loses himself and destroys himself, he makes a paradox of himself, and weeps: *O brawling love, O loving hate/... O heavy lightness, serious vanity,/... feather of lead, bright smoke, cold fire, sick health .../ This love feel I, that feel no love in this ...*[7]

So, it is impossible to talk about love without talking about power. Though it may be within my capacity, it is not in my power to love, still less to be loved. Having the faculty to love, for my love (in its verbal form) to become a noun, I must also be loved. For love to exist, the active voice must be conjugated with the passive voice; I love and am loved. And I think that, for this to count, the reflexive voice is also necessary: I love myself. Since unless I love myself, I do not know what love is, I cannot love, nor can I recognise love, when someone loves me.

When we speak of love between woman and man, are we speaking of two equals? Clearly not. Man and woman are completely different,

6. *Romeo and Juliet (RJ)*; I. 1, 196–197.

7. *RJ*, I. 1, 178–182.

in body and soul, in what they want and what they can do, in act and in potential. Their relations are complicated, complex, cruel – relations which are more akin to the operations of war than the strategies of peace. And, in this combat, however much we, the men, feel ourselves often to be victims – and we are! – the greater victims have been women, throughout the ages and in all places.

Today, in the modern world, the inequalities of women's struggles, here and abroad, in every continent, are abysmal. It is a fact that in many countries women are winning victories and affirming their rights. And in others they are still slaves.

In Switzerland and France, for instance, women are fighting to earn the same wages as men. In the United States, they go to the extreme of affirming in the courts their right to marry one another, to adopt children or have them by artificial insemination. Meanwhile, in many African countries, infibulation – the surgical removal of a girl's clitoris at puberty – is still practised and the vagina is sown up after each birth. In China, many fathers suffocate female babies straight after birth, since women are more expendable and less productive – women, who produce men. Recently, the papers reported the case of five young Chinese girls who killed themselves because they had understood that their parents would not be able to support them or marry them off. In India, many widows are buried alive with their dead husbands. This still happens today, on the verge of the twenty-first century.

In Brazil, the non-governmental organisation IBASE[8] and Amnesty International, and even *Time* magazine, have condemned the existence of thousands of prostitutes aged 12 or under. Staying with Brazil, at the end of the Second World War, women did not have the right to vote here. And, still more absurd, in a canton of ultra-'civilised' Switzerland, Appenzell-Rhodes Extérieures, only people who own a sword may vote, and women do not have the right to own a sword; though they have the right to vote, since they don't own swords, they are deprived of that right, not because they are women, of course, but because they have no sword![9]

Following the same strand of paradoxes, Benazir Bhutto, the ex-Prime Minister of Pakistan, a Muslim country, was considered capable of leading her country but not of choosing her spouse, and, after being elected as Prime Minister, she got married to a man chosen by her family. She could choose her Ministers, with whom she would sit round a table and govern, but not her own husband, with whom she would go to bed and make love.

8. Instituto Brasileiro de Análises Sociais e Econômicas (The Brazilian Institute of Social and Economic Analyses).

9. This has changed since I wrote this: now women can vote without swords, pistols, or even Swiss Army penknives.

So, when people speak of what happens in this modern world – which we are so close to – in reality we don't know what world we are talking about. And it follows that when we talk about the Middle Ages, a far-off time, the imprecision will be even greater. When did the Middle Ages begin, when did it end? We don't know for sure. Has it even ended now? In many countries, not yet. A large part of the world still lives in pre-history. Or lives without history.

In spite of such a lack of precision, if we want to speak about the Middle Ages, some things can be taken as fact. The feudal system, for instance, is an established fact; the absolute power of the feudal lord, legislative, judicial and executive. Endowed with a sense of solitude and distance, men would build a church for the Eternal God, who was in no hurry – in contrast to hurried man – and, for that reason, cathedrals in these times, in the Romanesque style, took centuries to be built, in contrast to the Gothic style, which developed with the beginnings of the bourgeoisie. One was for Eternal God, the other for mortal men.

The rapid growth of the bourgeoisie and of commerce, at the end of the Middle Ages, resulted in the infliction of a legal homogeneity on vast territories, which was incompatible both with the absolutist tendencies of the regional nobility and with a diversity of laws and customs. It required unification.

Today, we are witnessing a similar phenomenon which has appeared in a dozen countries of the European Community, and resulted in the formation of other huge North American and Asian markets, necessitating the destruction of frontiers, customs posts and protectionist laws. There is talk of increasing the power of the European Parliament and creating supra-national laws. In France, a piece of government propaganda shows a child proclaiming: 'My country is France, my future is Europe!' – which implicitly suggests that 'my country is not Europe and my future will no longer be France'! And what is happening today is not only localised unification but world globalisation: the imposition of a single culture on all other cultures, under the auspices of the god Market.

If this is how it is today, at the end of the Middle Ages, with greater reason, a centralising power was called for. A leader. A king. A prince who would reunite the three estates, with determination and certainty – who would make the law and judge the best manner of executing it. Who would be, above all, paramount in the exercise of the sovereign power, Justice.

The Elizabethan theatre, in England – like that of the Golden Age in Spain – reflected this historical centralising imperative to dispossess the minor feudal lords of their discretionary powers and hand them over to a central power which would wield discipline over larger territories. To apply this dictum to modern-day Brazil – if we really wanted to evolve beyond the Middle Ages we currently live in – we would have to take away the power of the land-owning 'colonels' who murdered Chico Mendes, or of those who destroy Amazon rainforests, putting the blame on termites (as did the governor of the Amazon region) – and we would have to create a federal republic, which already exists on paper according to the law, but not in our daily reality.

As princes are not always capable of assuming the duties of high office or carrying them out, Machiavelli developed his own concept of *virtù*: the right of might against the rights of birth. The bourgeois right: I have a right to do anything I can do. All power is justified, because it is power: it justifies itself by imposing itself.

Many Shakespearean plays deal with heroes endowed with Machiavellian *virtù*; in these, there is a power to be conquered or preserved, by any means, as long as they are effective; the plays tell the story of the struggle to usurp political power.

Richard III and Iago are usurpers who, though brought down at the end of the play – in the England of the time the monarch reigned, and to this day still holds the constitutional, if not the political power! – demonstrate in symbolic fashion the emergence of the new bourgeois power: I have the right to do anything that I am able to do; if I can do it, then I have a right to do it. Bourgeois morality.

Other Shakepearean tragedies have another kind of hero, the indecisive usurper, the weak man, induced to act by a wife or an accomplice – Macbeth plotting against Duncan, Brutus against Julius Caesar.

In *Romeo and Juliet* there is a supreme judge, Prince Escalus. He is like the King in Lope da Vega's *The King is the Best Justice*. He is neither usurper nor usurped. He retains the power. But he is a mild man, moderate, compliant. At the opening of the play, the Capulets and the Montagues are on the verge of civil war. Escalus intervenes, stating that this has already happened three times, and only now does Escalus make a threat – this time I really mean it, enough is enough, really! If the families fight a fourth time, the guilty parties will pay with their lives.

Three pardons is at least a couple of pardons too many! These three previous pardons have already destroyed all confidence in justice and all fear of retribution. The people no longer believe in justice, the people no longer fear punishment. Where justice is weak, disobedience is possible.

By his weakness, Prince Escalus stimulates disorder. His indecision excites his misguided subjects and the morality of physical force comes to dominate, the morality of cunning, the law of the jungle. With no prince, everybody thinks they are princes; with no justice, everyone thinks they are just; and everybody hates each other – since the absence of justice allows many possible objects for hatred. A society of hatred becomes entrenched (as in Brazil today, where no-one obeys the law).

Everybody hates everybody else. Let us see . . . the servants hate each other and make their masters' hatreds their own: in the very first scene, violence explodes. They also hate women and speak of them as quarry to be hunted, animals, rather than companions, human beings. A dialogue between two of them, Gregory and Sampson, includes the following lines:

SAMPSON: Women, being the weaker vessels, are ever thrust to the wall.

GREGORY: . . . I will be civil with the maids – I will cut off their heads . . . the heads of the maids or their maidenheads.[10]

10. *RJ*, I. 1, 20–23.

Cutting their heads off or perforating their hymens: the phallus is a sword, cold steel, lethal; just as, even today, it is customary for men to refer to sexual activity by expressions far removed from making love, expressions such as 'having', 'mounting', 'possessing' – which have more to do with pursuit than love. How happy humanity will be when the terms 'macho' or 'macho man' designate not a hunter of women but a man capable of making a woman happy.

Romeo's friends, Mercutio and Benvolio, hate the old Nurse and when they are making fun of her, reach a point of actual physical aggression; her companion, Peter, who should protect her, makes no effort to defend her and only speaks of bravery when all the aggressors have already departed.

Lady Capulet hates her husband and, in the very first scene, when the latter asks his servants for a sword to intervene in the fight, she ironically suggests that he should rather ask for a crutch, which would be more compatible with his advanced age and minimal bravery, his impotence: 'A crutch, a crutch, why call you for a sword?'[11]

11. *RJ*, I. 1, 75.

171

Sword as weapon or sword as symbol? There is no sex between the two of them any more; is there something sexual between her and Tybalt? There are signs which point to the two of them being very close: it is she who manages to calm him down in the party which Romeo gatecrashes; it is she who cries for vengeance when Tybalt dies, like someone seeking vengeance on the death of their lover.

Capulet hates Lady Capulet, and when Count Paris, seeking Juliet's hand in marriage, says that many girls under the age of 14 have already become happy mothers – 'Younger than she are happy mothers made' – he answers: 'And too soon marred are those so early made',[12] referring to his own young, and now aged, spouse. Capulet even hates Juliet and tears into her when she refuses to marry the Count.

Tybalt hates Capulet; when he finds Romeo secreted into the ball, he wants to kill him. Capulet asks who gives the orders there, but gets no reply, because Tybalt does not recognise his authority.

The Nurse hates Lady Capulet (and vice versa) and argues with her over Juliet's maternity (she who lost her own daughter, Susanna); the Nurse encourages Juliet in her love, in her sexuality; Lady Capulet, by contrast, intends that the girl whom she undoubtedly hates should follow the same path as herself, that she should follow her example, that she should marry Count Paris, the Prince's cousin. Lady Capulet's thoughts are all focussed on the material advantages of such a union, her concern is that her daughter should hold a social status, that Juliet should ennoble and enrich herself, and in the process ennoble and enrich her mother still further, even at the price of Juliet hating her husband, just as she hates hers; completely without shame, when she talks about Paris, she talks of the material advantages for mother and daughter.

Mercutio hates 'both your houses'[13] and when he dies he curses them all, since he was not defending anyone; in fact, he was defending himself.

In the absence of justice or higher values, all other values are corrupted. When the Prince gives no orders, everyone is a prince, everyone decides everything for themselves; infidelity and treachery become the norm. *Romeo and Juliet* is the tragedy of hate and also the tragedy of betrayal. Everyone betrays everyone else and nobody has any respect for anyone.

There are the conjugal betrayals – certainly between the Capulets – and also the betrayals enacted by the Nurse and Friar Laurence, the most serious deceptions, which unleash the tragic outcome. The

12. *RJ*, I. 2, 12.

13. *RJ*, III. 1, 106.

Nurse betrays her masters' trust, serving as intermediary between the secret loves of Juliet and Romeo, encouraging their meetings in the church, where they feign confession; Friar Laurence also betrays them, celebrating the marriage in secret and – even worse – taking dangerous decisions on his own initiative, without consultation, without democratic debate, administering false poison to Juliet, accompanying the false burial and falsely preaching sincere-sounding sermons. And finally, unleashing the tragedy. Where the Prince does not rule, all are princes.

In this tragedy of lying and hatred, only two characters love each other: two pure people meet each other in a corrupt and corrupting world. Faithful to her spouse, Juliet accepts him and still loves him, even after the death of Tybalt, her kinsman. 'He is my husband' – this is reason enough. They are the only two characters who possess a morality.

And where did they find this morality? In the repudiation of all that is around them, in nakedness, in bed, in love, since everything in Verona is putrid! Juliet asks if Montague is a hand or foot; she asks if Romeo is a name; no: it is a man! She beseeches him to give up his name or she will give up her own: a rose by any other name would smell as sweet – a rose is a rose is a rose, always.

Romeo asks himself in what part of his anatomy his name is located and declares himself ready to rip that part out of himself, since he does not recognise it.

The struggle for political power, for land, for position, the struggle to the death with sword and dagger, the struggle for dominance, for wealth, for all forms of power – this struggle demands ornament; all the bodies are ornamented; with silks, cloaks, hats, rags, daggers, swords, crosses, crowns and sceptres; all the characters are bedecked with baubles, ornaments, distinctive marks, symbols and signals.

Only at one moment in the plot does the naked body of a man meet with the naked body of a woman. Romeo and Juliet strip themselves of everything, of all their robes, all their titles, they even divest themselves of their names, of all ideas and preconceptions: they are two people, a man and a woman. They are ready to divest themselves even of those parts of the body which represent a name, to strip away their own flesh. They are ready to divest themselves of their lives.

In this single moment – when there is nothing else between them – love is realised. Romeo and Juliet want each other, seek and find each other, in each other, each is the other. In this moment, the two of them,

173

without name, without past or future, in that instant, there and then, before the lark sings, before they doubt the nightingale, at that moment, he and she love each other. In the rest of the play, hatred triumphs. *Romeo and Juliet* is a tragedy of hate.

In the end, what is love? Hate is easy to know and easy to recognise – the desire to destroy something or someone, to make it or them disappear, the desire to be subject, to speak without audible response, to determine, the desire to be absolute. The desire to destroy that which is outside me, that which is not me.

And love? If hate is the desire to destroy, is love the desire to construct? What is the object of this desire's craving? What does the lover want?

Hate wishes to destroy that which exists, that which I do not recognise as mine, as being me. Love always wants something that it does not have. Love, in any of its forms, is a search intended to supply a lack. If I am self-sufficient, I do not love. If I love, I am seeking that which will complete me. But, what is it that I lack?

To know what love is, it is necessary to identify this lack, the thing that I seek, the thing I am wanting, the thing I do not possess. And what we lack is always the other or is in the other.

If my lack is actually the other, I need to identify this other, to recognise it as different from myself, in all its plenitude, its totality. We are two. We are dialogue. Different. Subjects. We decide. Here the verb to love can be conjugated in all its voices. I love! I am loved! We love ourselves!

But if that which I seek is not the other, and is merely in the other – it is not him or her I am looking for, it is something which is within him or her! – I must identify myself in this other, even though I do not recognise the other in his or her full individuality, since I do not seek it in him- or her-self in his or her entirety, as whole people. In them, I only seek myself.

Proust's Swann, when he encounters Odette again, once the object of his love, hardly recognises her and thinks, downhearted: 'How could I have loved this woman? She is not even my type!' He had not identified her; within her, he had identified himself. He was seeking something she possessed, but which was not her, not her in her entirety – not the other, but a piece of the other. A piece of Swann, which Swann discovered and loved in Odette.

In this sense, we cannot speak of 'a crime of love', only of 'a crime of desire'. This criminal kills, he rends the body of the victim, who possessed something which the criminal lacked, as if to reclaim from this alien body a thing he believes belongs to him.

When Fernando Pessoa writes 'No-one loves another unless he loves that of himself which is in the other, or is presumed so to be', he is precisely talking about this. If I love, it is because I encounter myself or believe I am encountering and completing myself in the loved person. She possesses that which I lack and that which makes me whole. I love myself as myself; however I love myself in the other and not in myself. I seek myself and always encounter myself in the other.

Narcissus is the exception. For that reason, he is suicidal. Because he does not seek himself in the other, he seeks himself in his own image – an image which can only reveal his lack. The image reveals not what it is, but what he is and, thus, reveals what he lacks. His image in the waters reveals his emptiness, without being able to show him what he seeks, since he seeks, in himself, that which he does not possess.

All image is surface, without being it. And all surface reflects that which is foreign to it, reveals what it is not and hides what it is, since it reflects the light that falls upon it. The mirror mirrors that which it is not, since we are before an inaccessible object: we will never be able to see a mirror, to see the mirror which mirrors us. The image of Narcissus, in the mirror, is neither the mirror nor Narcissus. Narcissus, however, is confounded and thinks that, on seeing it, he is seeing himself. Looking for himself in it, penetrating into it, Narcissus crosses through the image and comes face to face with the truth of the waters. Narcissus dies, looking for himself in his own lack. His lack encounters lack and not that which could supply it and complete it.

Narcissus searches for himself in the one place where he cannot be: in himself, in his reflected image. So Narcissus is not Narcissus, he is that which he lacks. Narcissus is the search which seeks that which does not exist. His image so barely exists, it is surface. And the mirror, the surface, is invisible, it merely reflects the light. Thus, Narcissus is not Narcissus, his image is but does not exist, the mirror is there, yet is invisible. In this confusion, in this glass labyrinth, looking for himself, Narcissus loses himself. Since love is a quest which requires an object. And the object of Narcissus's love is emptiness, non-existence.

His need seeks, in the reflected Narcissus, need itself. And searching for himself in himself, he will have to search more and more deeply, never to find himself. For this reason, he must go beyond the reflected image in the waters, he must penetrate into the image, see within it, see beyond it, seeking himself and not finding himself – and penetrating into the image, into his own image – he penetrates into the waters, he penetrates into death. Death is the truth of Narcissus. Narcissus, the man who does not know how to love.

12 The suicide of the wind

Every now and then in Brazil, there is a big discussion about the meaning of culture and the place culture would have in the advent of a popular coalition government.This article was written for one of those debates.

ACCORDING to legend, tradition or folklore – and I am far from certain whether the story I am about to tell is true or not, whether it actually happens or is the fruit of imagination – but I am sure as sure can be that imagination exists, and so imagination is real! – anyway, the story has it that there is not a bird in the world, in the universe even, which sings as beautifully as the most beautiful song of the uirapuru bird.

In the Amazon forests where it lives, when it breaks into song, all the other birds are struck dumb. At first in astonishment, then in an admiration which rapidly translates into infatuation. And it is not only the birds that are so affected. All the animals, from the most reclusive and intimidated to the most savage and intimidating, fall silent, all the animals of the Amazon delta: the painted panther and the jacou bird, the cobra, the alligator – and the elephants, if there were any! – even the snakes, with or without rattle – right down to the humble earthworms, who live underground, blind but not deaf, and rise to the surface to listen in silent ecstasy to the marvellous recital of the uirapuru.

Legend has it that even the wind, the very wind, performs an act of folly: the wind commits suicide, it stops, and listens, in stillness – a silent audience. And even the *pororoca*, the tidal bore, which, as we know, is a fight to the death between river and sea, with no quarter given, the *pororoca* which on normal days thunders tens of kilometres in all directions, even the turbulent and unruly *pororoca* is becalmed, as the revolutionary waters of the Amazon river sign a brief peace treaty with the conservative waters of the ocean, and the foaming and rebellious river mouth becomes a placid and obedient lagoon. And the waters listen to the voice of the uirapuru. Even the leaves are afraid to fall from the trees, men and animals are afraid to blink – the noise they would make by blinking would be unforgivable during the uirapuru's concert.

According to legend, the symphony and song of this bird surpasses – leaves light-years behind! – the cantatory beauty of Maria Callas and Pavarotti, Elis Regina and Mayza[1] – to name but a few voices distant in time or space.

1. Famous Brazilian popular singers.

And when does the uirapuru sing? It sings from the precise and precious moment when the female finishes building her nest up to the exact instant when she lays her first egg. This period of time lasts between 10 and 15 minutes – 10–15 minutes of rapturous music. Once the egg has been laid, the bird shuts up and will not break into song again until the following year, when the next nest is ready.

The carnivorous animals resume their blood-thirsty routine, the wind picks up again, the snakes hiss, the buffaloes moo, the pigs grunt, the frogs croak, the asses bray, the hens cluck and all are ashamed of the cacophonous sound of their voices: oh for the song of the uirapuru again!

But, happily, next year it will return to sing the same song, the same musical notes, the same rhythm, the same melody, the same musical *chef d'oeuvre*. And the uirapuru born from its egg will sing the same song – it is genetically programmed. Nature's *chef d'oeuvre*: the song of the uirapuru.

But, of all the masterpieces of nature, this, as great and as beautiful as it is, is not the greatest. The greatest is us, we, man- and woman-kind, who have the capacity to dream.

Birds, however beautiful their song may be, always sing the same tune, without novelty, without invention. Beavers, however ingenious their architecture, always build the same dams. The bee, however illustrious its royalty, always produces the same honey.

We, humans, are capable of invention. Birds sing, but are not composers; as for us, we sing and compose, we produce culture. This is nature's greatest creation: culture. And it is we who produce it. And, in the act of producing it, in the act of creating it, we recreate the nature which created us. To make culture is to invent the world so that it responds to our needs, our desires, our dream.

Without dreaming, there is no culture, since it is our dream that offers the first glimpse of it, foresees, prepares, nurtures it. But take care: there are dreams and there are nightmares. And here things become confused, since our dream can be real, it can come to be, and our reality can turn into dream.

Culture is not the superfluous, it is not decoration. It is the doing. The manner of doing. And our ways of doing the same thing are not the same, since we do not all dream the same dream, we are not all of the same heart, we are not born in the same land, we do not grow up in the same district, city or state, we do not all eat from the same dish. For this reason, culture is diverse. Culture is everything that exists, truth and lies, everything created by us, in response to our needs, desires, abilities.

As we know, there are two forms of lying: one is lying itself, telling bare-faced or less blatant lies. The other, which is more insidious, is manipulating the truth.

Today, for instance, we have witnessed a truthful lie published by the media, a mendacious truth. This says that the majority of the people consulted were in favour of the 'Plano Real'.[2] It is true that the majority said 'yes'; it is a lie that they backed the Plano Real. The truth within the media's lie is that the people do not understand this plan, to approve or reject it. They know that inflation is falling and they applaud this, but they do not know the irrational reasons which maintain an unreal and symbolic parity between the real and the dollar, which is sustained at the cost of, amongst other things, the retention of health budgets and wage levels. The people are in favour of stability of prices, but not the level at which prices have been stabilised; they approve of the strong currency, but would prefer it if this strong currency would visit their own purse with greater frequency, rather than appearing only at the stock exchange.

2. The Plano Real was the economic strategy put in place by the government of Fernando Henrique Cardoso, intended to put a stop to inflation: it had the desired effect, but the poor paid a high price as they were disproportionately affected by the savage rise in interest rates – the rich do not buy on hire-purchase.

This bad dream is also culture. We live in a culture of lying, of enticement, of falsehood, of makeshift, *ersatz*. A culture propagated by the media. A media which divides the Brazilian people into two halves: one half, the people's body, living with its feet on the ground; the other half, its mind, living with its head in the clouds, in an imaginary heaven. In their houses, the people do not have running water, but their TV screens overflow with swimming pools full of lukewarm water. On their tables they have neither bread nor beans,[3] but they feast with hungry eyes on their TV screens, goggling at splendid banquets of all kinds of delicacy.

3. *Feijoada*, a bean and pork stew, is the Brazilian national dish.

This is the same media which yesterday vanquished us and today sharpens its weapons. Let us, at least, sharpen our claws.

We have no desire to destroy the media; razed earth is not the option we wish to pursue. But we believe that we must democratise

179

it. Reform the land and reform the video, the land and the image of that land. We must regionalise it, divide *terra* (land) and *tela* (screen). We must make it accessible to the mouths of the people, to their voice as producers, rather than merely their eyes and ears, as consumers.

This is our primary aim, to democratise that which already exists – TV, cinema, video, theatre, music and dance, the arts – whether fine or not – and science. And to democratise still means today what it used to mean in Greece: *demos* – people.

But we also have to create something which does not exist; the means of developing something which intensely wants to exist, someting which we want to come into being: popular culture. For this reason we believe that a cultural plan under a Lula government – a popular government! – should have right at the centre of its concerns, as its very heart, a centre which can generate centres, a nucleus which produces nuclei, which does not commit the errors of the past, which is not centralising, authoritarian and normative in tendency, but which democratically assists the formation of other organs, baptised with whatever name we want to give them – Units, Centres of Art and Culture, Houses of Culture – but which would have the democratic goal of allowing dialogue between the different regions of the country, between different countries, between arts, between all the various activities of culture in its Brazilian manifestations, with culture considered as the primary, the principal human vocation. Culture as art and as erudition, as body and mind, and, above all, culture as invention of the future.

Today, in the present, as we think on our past, we have a duty to invent the future. This duty will be the task of these centres, units, or nuclei: to invent the future, rather than to await it.

13 The laws of the market, the law of the lion

In the gathering of intellectuals which took place in Rio de Janeiro, during the year of 1995, the theme of 'cultural identity' was proposed for discussion – the most complex and all-embracing subject to be discussed at this gathering, because, first and foremost, it asks us to consider our own identity: who are we? Following on from this, it requires us to identify the object of our concerns, of our study: culture – what we do. Finally, it forces us to identify the destination and the intended recipients of that which we produce: for whom are we doing it? Our task was to identify the cultural producers, the production and the product.

BY the broadest definition of 'culture', we are all cultural producers, because the thing which we cultivate first, the primary object of our cultivation, is life, our own life. We cultivate biological life, affective life, social life, work and play, war and peace. We all produce culture: the people of a single street or city, of a region, a religion, a race or country. The existence and continuation of life makes certain demands. It is in the responses we make to the exigencies of life that culture is born. Culture is the 'doing', the way of doing; the 'how', the 'why' and the 'for whom' it is done. Not what is done, but the way it is done.

We cultivate everything that we need: we supply needs. Nature is cruel. In order to live, we have to transform it, satisfying our necessities. We invent the wheel so that we can travel further than our legs would carry us; we make bridges to cross rivers; we build houses to shelter us, we make clothes to protect our bodies from sun and rain. Culture is all the activities which satisfy necessities, whatever they may be, even those which are superfluous. It is the 'how' of our doing what is done, the way we do what we do.

We are all cultural producers but, even when engaged in the same activity, we do not produce the same product.

To cover a table one needs a tablecloth. Any seamstress can cut a piece of cloth and, hey presto, we have a tablecloth. A lace-maker from Ceará, however, also makes tablecloths, but she exceeds the basic requirements. She satisfies the same need, but the product she fabricates is something more, it is art. The lace-maker is answering not only the demands of objective practical necessities, but also her own aesthetic necessities. Her tablecloth serves both to cover the table and to gratify the eye. Its value is greater. So great that it can even prevent us from using her tablecloth to protect the table: we need to protect the tablecloth. So great that sometimes the lace-maker herself cannot afford the product she makes. The seamstress and the lace-maker are engaged in the same cultural activity – the fabrication of tablecloths – but the woman from Ceará goes beyond the requirements of mere necessity.

Paul Bocuse and I engage in the same cultural activity; I do it every Saturday in my house; he spends his whole life doing it in restaurants: we cook food. What I cook does for me, my family and my understanding and co-operative friends, it satisfies our hunger; his food, a work of art, becomes a precious commodity, an expensive product. Eating a dish cooked by Bocuse is more than simply eating.

And what about theatre? We all spend our whole life making theatre. The human language is the language of theatre, which is the sum of all possible languages. However, some of us write scripts or go on stage, and in this we surpass the mere quotidian use of theatrical activity. What we are doing is of greater value.

Cultural producers do not produce only for themselves. By producing for others, their product becomes a commodity. Yet the artist, a producer like any other, creates beyond immediate necessity, s/he creates pleasure. And this pleasure can become necessary and can also be transformed into commodity.

This is where the mortal danger resides. Because when artists produce art, they are responding to their necessity, their way of seeing, observing, feeling, reacting, thinking. When this art is transformed into a commodity, a new element is introduced: external demand. Art, transformed into commodity, now confronts the competition of the shelves, the rituals of the auction; the artist responds no longer to himself but to the demands of the market which, as everyone knows, is not spontaneous – it is induced, it is led by propaganda.

In the 1970s, an exhibition of indigenous art was mounted in São Paulo. One of the exhibitors confessed: 'In our village we make these same statues, but without these bright strong colours, which we add for the Paulista market! In São Paulo the buyers prefer them like this: multicoloured statues!' What happened to the identity of that Indian, who was an artist and became an artisan? Was this still indigenous art? Or indigenous art for the white man?

One often meets actors who complain about the work they are obliged to do, almost always of an extremely superficial nature, in the television soaps. Or about being forced to perform in boulevard plays, because that is what the market consumes. The markets dictate, the artists are forced to follow. Market as subject, artist as object, anti-artist.

Happily there are counter-examples. The most famous is Van Gogh: during his whole life he only sold a single picture, though he painted hundreds. He lived and died in poverty, supported by his brother Theo. Today his paintings sell for 70 million dollars or more,[1] not to be offered for the general enjoyment of the public but to be hidden deep in the vaults of a large bank in Tokyo, where financial transactions are carried out. This really happened. Van Gogh hidden away in a Tokyo bank, like a secret stash of money!

1. Even when they are suspected fakes, like the 'Sunflowers' which broke all records at auction.

When he was alive, Van Gogh preferred to be an artist and to ignore the market. To be master of his own voice, instead of being the voice of his master. Now he is dead, he can do nothing about it. The market triumphant! Viva the dollar!

The confrontation between artist and buyer often becomes a life-and-death struggle; inevitably, because every artist is, in essence, a subversive. S/he reveals, creates the new, that which did not exist, that which has no parameters. In contrast to the artisan who reproduces, ad infinitum, the same model. Mestre Vitalino, who invented popular figures made out of the earth, the sand, in Pernambuco, was an artist; those who imitated him, his followers and heirs, are only excellent artisans.

It is difficult to see the new! The market judges according to the criteria of what is available, it sees the new with the same tired eyes it saw the old. And it does not understand. It misunderstands.

In accepting the market, its laws are accepted. And the laws of the market, the laws of supply and demand, are the laws of the marketeers, just as the law of the jungle is the law of the lion.

183

In the wild there also live other animals, whose interests and necessities are not taken into account by the leonine law. Unhappily, in the wild it is impossible to institute a moral law which could help to undo injustice. In human society too, there live other beings whose principal preoccupation is neither cash nor profit; there are teachers, gardeners, scientists, ballerinas, researchers, poets and dreamers.

It would be ridiculous to imagine that all social activities should become lucrative, as the laws of commerce would order. The fire brigade, for instance, is very lucrative during the summer months, in the balloon-filled São João nights;[2] at this time of year they save incommensurable patrimonies. In winter, however, the firemen hibernate. For them to be profitable, they would have to create a special Brigade of Pyromaniac Firemen which would set out to set fire to everything, so that their more aquatic colleagues could follow behind them carrying out the noble mission of extinguishing fires and bonfires. Only in this way would the money invested by the state become fully justifiable in market terms.

2. The São João festival, when hundreds of burning balloons are let loose in the sky, at great peril to the population and causing many fires.

In Vienna, at the end of 1989, the existence was revealed of a group of three nurses who were systematically killing sick old people; in their trial, they alleged that they wanted to see the hospital flourishing and that the old people no longer produced anything and consumed too much. They were a drain on the State, now they were old. Better to murder them.

When we enter into this competition, we fall into the abyss, into the seduction of the siren song. Today we are witnessing a dog-fight for the television audience, a ratings war over the 8 o'clock soap opera, the 10 o'clock soap, the 10.30 soap, and the midnight soap. Before this, all the TV stations used to be extremely moralistic and used to accuse the left of all the immorality. Recently, one of them started showing pictures of a young woman taking a bath in the nude; a hit! The supply of this unclothed body caused the demand of millions of avid TV viewers. The other channels retaliated by showing a man and a woman naked and, as sure as three follows two, a bed was added and – *ipso facto* – the sexual act. Success beyond their wildest dreams! The first channel countered with a man and a woman, still naked, making love in the water, in the midst of teeming bubbling nature: a masterstroke!

The success of this soggy saga derives from many reasons, one of which relates to the awakening of unconscious religious feelings. Where have we seen this before – a naked man and woman making love in a terrestrial paradise, with angels flying threateningly low overhead? Precisely – in the Bible, in the innocent story of Adam and Eve. Innocent? Eve who, in a kind of way, symbolically transmutes into a lynx, I mean, snake, just as Juma, the naked Protagonist of the aforementioned soap opera, becomes a snake, I mean to say, lynx. Lynx or snake, it makes no odds – dangerous animals, the both of them. Scenes which make the unconscious itself explode, since making love in warm water, whether a river or the swimming pool of a roadside motel, is in the end a version of making love inside the maternal uterus. The viewers of this TV soap are taken back to their first foetal sensations.

Against all this symbology, the other station responded with explicit sex: Sônia Braga in an old car, Sônia Braga in the undergrowth, Sônia Braga everywhere, viva breasts and thighs, viva Sônia Braga!

And now? Where are we heading, in this no-holds-barred fight for ratings? All possible forms of sexual activity have already been shown, in every possible exotic or cosmopolitan scenario. Now all we are lacking is the grand climax: a love scene between animals of the same sex but different species: steamy lesbianism between a female crocodile and a painted lynx, partly underwater in deference to the crocodile's habits, partly at the top of a tree, for the lynx's pleasure. What kind of tree? Why, a syringa, the rubber plant, since nothing works better than to set a soap in an exotic location, thus promoting tourism by means of the natural beauties of our land, at the same time as presenting undeniable social and political content: Xapuri, the city where Chico Mendes was killed, in the Territory of Acre. Ah, yes: at the moment of the sexual climax, the unsatisfied lynx, seeing Osmarino (a famous peasant leader) pass by, would murmur in an off-screen voice (which would mean that the lynx was thinking): 'I need to change my life and meet a macho like that, and not a shit like you!' The crocodile smiles, unaware of the voice-over, and morality is restored.

If this race for the market continues, soon all the drama schools in Brazil will be obliged to introduce special courses in the *Kama Sutra* onto their curricula, alongside Voice Projection, Shakespeare, Modern Drama, etc., or perhaps within the broader subject area of bodily expression, for reasons of economic expediency.

As we see – as even a blind man could not fail to see! – the market economy, in art, is corrupt and corrupting! It leads to mediocrity, to the prizing of the obvious, to pure cretinism.

185

Thinking along these lines, it was with amazement and horror that I read in the pages of the *Jornal do Brasil*, on 8 August 1992, an interview with the then Minister of Culture of the federal government and one of his assistants. In it, it was stated that the government would open a line of credit for the financing of artists' projects and that 'We are going to turn it into a professional business: the people who will decide whether a project is any good will be the bankers; it comes down to entrepreneurship'. It also talked about 'transforming art into box office' and said that 'the government will delegate to the financial sector the task of financing artistic projects'. The law of the jungle! All power to the rhinoceroses!

It is impossible to feel anything less than repugnance when confronted with these declarations which attempt to impose on the artist the bankers' criteria, which weigh the value of the artistic product in terms of dollars and cents, when we know that the function of the State, in the field of art and culture, is precisely the opposite, i.e., to stand against the laws of the marketeer and to encourage the flowering of all forms of culture, whatever their current Stock Market valuation. In the jungle, a Moral Law cannot be instituted. But where are we: living all over Brazil or hanging from the branches of Amazonian trees? Why is it always the lion's turn?

As producers of art and culture it is our duty to alert everyone to the monstrous genocidal and anti-cultural policy which will bring in this new official credit department for the financing only of those projects which do not need financing. The lucrative projects. Sure they will yield a profit. But will they be culture?

14 The show of the dream and the dream as show

This is the text of a paper I gave at a conference.

THE theme we have – 'The Show and the Dream' – is, at the very least, imprecise and ambiguous, which makes it, for that very reason, hugely rich in possibilities for development.

In the first place, the phrase contains two polysemic substantives which can be defined in a great variety of ways: what is the show? what is the dream? And we may observe that these two substantives are linked by a conjunction of little syntactic power, a particle which merely juxtaposes or stacks up the substantives, without allowing them to interact and modify each other.

Were the theme more precise, it would also be more restrictive. Let us look at a few examples:

'The Show is the Dream' – in this case, our theme would be the actual process of creation, that is, the way in which artists organise reality, according to their desires, feelings and emotions, their individual characteristics, their personality. The artist dreams his or her show before bringing it into being: with this formulation, we would be dealing with trying to unravel and reveal how the artist is able to dream the work of art – the poem, the picture, the play . . . before making it concrete. How the artist conceives – behold! – that which does not yet exist, that which has no corporeal existence, and how, following on from this, the dream is made concrete, by writing, painting, composing . . . Our task would be an analysis of how the solitary dream can be transformed into a public performance.

We would be trying to analyse how certain human beings are able to translate a thought, emotion or sensation into a thing. And how this thing – the work of art, a dream! – has the capacity to awaken in the viewer his or her own dream. The work of art – the thing – is not necessarily capable of awakening in the viewer the same dream as the artist's; the important thing is that it has this aesthetic property of unloosing dreams. The work of art is the path and the link between one dream and the other.

If, instead of substituting the verb 'is' for the conjunction 'and' we had substituted a colon – 'The Show: a Dream' – then, the theme would be exactly the opposite, that is, the impossibility of realising 'in reality' the work of art dreamed in the imagination. In this sense, the show would be a dream – i.e, utopia, a chimera! The theatre director Gordon Craig, to overcome this problem, even went as far as imagining the construction of super-marionettes, super-electronics, hyper-robotics, which were to be virtually human but without that undesirable characteristic human beings will persist in possessing – individuality! – which was apparently so irksome for Gordon Craig, since it prevented him from realising his dreams on stage, which were spoiled by the intermediation of the actors. This dream of engineering, however, remained a dream.

The conjunction can also be replaced by a preposition: 'the Show OF a Dream'. There are many writers who have made their characters dream on stage. In *A Midsummer Night's Dream*, Shakespeare showed his characters first as they were in real life – well behaved, each preparing to marry another, the person for whom they are destined, according to the most acceptable social norms; by means of a magic potion (a hallucinogen?) they then reveal all that is going on in their hearts, the prohibited becomes permissible, and everyone falls in love with everyone else, without regard for larger moral or legal considerations or matters of State. Till Titania falls in love with a donkey. Which does not stop being perfectly normal.

Continuing our variations on a theme – or rather, our search for themes hidden within the explicit theme – we could equally well invert the substantives: 'THE DREAM IS A SHOW'. And, in truth, it is, or is very like one: both have characters, ideas, passions, settings – which are sometimes multicoloured, though many people only dream in black and white – music, sound effects and, most extra-ordinary of all, all dreams have a perfect theatrical construction, they are full of suspense, they are Hitchcockian or Agatha-Christiean. The suspense lasts right up till the moment the dreamer wakes up. And, sometimes, beyond.

But when we say that the dream is a show, what kind of show are we talking about? If we examine its etymology, the Portuguese word for a show, *espetaculo*, has a Latin root: spectare, to look. And this also applies to the modern usage: a show is an event which is witnessed.

The presence of the spectator as witness transforms it from mere event into a show. If the curtains are closed, there is no show: this we call a rehearsal. We require the spectator to verify the existence of the show: in the dream, the spectator is the dreamer him- or her-self. More than 'watching' the dream, the dreamer is, at the same time his or her own dramaturg, director, lead actor, sound operator: an accumulation of functions which is every theatre artist's dream . . .

Shows differ according to the spaces they take place in and the means at their disposal. Thus, we have first of all, the theatre show: a building or a space constructed in such a way as to create a separation between auditorium and stage, the former de-activated, conducive to the act of receiving, passive; and the latter conducive to action, active. On the stage, a FICTION is produced: people create other fictitious persons called CHARACTERS. We all know – even if during the theatre show we must pretend not to – that each character cannot exist without the activation of another personality, generally dormant within the person of the actor. Character and personality are potentialities of one and the same person.

The theatrical show does not occur only in the theatre, nor only in the current form of 'show': electoral rallies are equally theatrical (where the 'persons' of the candidates present themselves as wonderful characters, all capable and possessed of good intentions, in front of a receptive audience); or the coronation of kings and queens in Europe or Central Africa; or the opening for business of banks or the inauguration of public works, etc.

There exists a third current form of show which is the cinema, similar to the theatre in terms of the space it occupies, though in it two fictions are realised; firstly, images, which are mechanically produced, create the fiction of real, present human persons; secondly, as in the theatre, these persons create characters, personae.

A third form of show, unhappily extremely current, is the television, which resembles the cinema in that it creates two fictions, yet differs from it – and also from theatre – in its relationship to stage and auditorium. As far as the latter is concerned, television does not demand its own space but rather, on the contrary, has the characteristic of invading other spaces, originally created with different ends in mind, especially the living room, a room created for more convivial ends. It should be remembered that the television set transforms the nature of the spaces it invades: when a person watches television, they do not see themselves, nor do they see the person by their side who is also watching. Intransitivity *par excellence*. Big Brother.

Happily, in spite of the extraordinary technological advance of the cinema and television, the dream continues to be as low-tech as the theatre. Imagine the contrary, imagine one of those wonderful extravagant nightmares one sometimes has, reduced to the miniaturised dimensions of a Japanese TV. We would lose our fear . . . and the dream would lose its beauty.

Thus, I believe, the show of our title is by its nature theatrical. And what about the dream? What dream are we talking about? 'The dream is the realisation of a desire' (Freud). What desire and what form does it take?

On this I can only offer personal testimonies; I can talk about my own dreams and the shows they have occasionally given rise to. These are of three kinds; the titles I will give them do not in any way reflect any scientific reality, but they go some way to explaining my own thoughts and feelings.

THE DREAM OF REASON: Martin Luther King became famous for many reasons, including the opening line of one of his finest speeches: 'I have a dream . . .' What dream was he talking about? His strong desire to see a world without racial prejudice, a world at peace, full of prosperity and love. A dream. A thing which is possible, but not probable.

There was a whole period of my life when I wrote plays or put on shows which were waking dreams, my dreams of reason, since I wanted the same things as Martin Luther King, and even a few others: I wanted Bolivar's independent Latin America and other things of that kind. One of the plays I wrote and mounted in this category was *The Little Moon and the Dangerous Journey*,[1] a title taken from the last words that Che Guevara wrote in his Bolivian diary; he died the following day.

I have written many pieces like this, which talk about dreams – mine and those of the oppressed classes. Of all my plays, these have been the best-intentioned, though not necessarily the best.

THE HYPNOGOGIC DREAM: the hypnogogic state is that indeterminate supposed frontier between sleep and waking, and the dreams we dream there are the kind where everything is mixed together, desire and reality. Desire becomes real (it is enough to want); people divide and sub-divide, get larger or are condensed; time is telescopic – it goes forwards and backwards – and all this happens in a state in which the dreamer maintains a degree of control over what he or she dreams and wants to dream. Reason, though confused, remains in suspense, but does not completely

1. *A Lua Pequena e A Caminhada Perigosa.*

abandon its hold. And it can re-assume its full power in case of oneiric necessity, or greater risk.

In France, there are two words for dream: *rêve* and *songe*. Today, the two words mean the same thing, but they have very different etymologies. The hypnogogic dream is the *rêve* which comes from the old French word *esver*, which comes from the Gallo-Roman *esvo* and *esvagus*, all of which have to do with wandering, and *desver*, to lose one's way. *Rêver*, to dream, is to allow the wandering of the mind. A Swiss proverb has it that the dream (*rêve*) is the Sunday of thought.

I have dreamt some hypnogogic plays. The one I like best is called *Murro em Ponta de Faca*.[2] It contains a mixture of facts and events, countries and languages, I condense and divide people into characters who are all me myself, and who I am none of. One of the characters, a teacher-poet, is at least two people: one I met in Buenos Aires and he taught me to make *carne de ferrugem*,[3] the other taught me to make *vatapá*.[4] The only thing they didn't teach me was how to make verses which the Protagonist of *Murro*, who is also me, though different, had to learn alone and at his own risk. There is a character called Maria who commits suicide and who, naturally, is also me, and I continue to be alive. There are men and women in it, from the past and the present – and I wander in and out of all this, around and about it.

Besides these two first modes of dreaming, there is a third, the dream which is pure dream, the dream which goes deeper, which penetrates unseen zones, from which one returns with no memories, a place to which one goes and from which one can only depart with a promise not to look back (and, even when one does look, one sees nothing, except on the odd occasion when lying back on the couch). This dream is called *songe* in French, which comes from the Latin *somnium*, which means sleep. The barriers are lifted, anything is possible. Across this frontier lies the great unknown, so unknown that people say contradictory things about it. According to a French proverb, *'tous songes sont mensonges'* (all dreams are lies). Aeschylus, the Greek tragedian, prefers to think that 'in the dream, the mind has the clearest visions' (*Eumenides*).

In this DREAM-SLEEP, DEEP DREAM, UNCONSCIOUS DREAM, the dramatist allows the thousands of characters we have buried within us to surface, personae who inhabit certain inaccessible regions, where they perpetrate unacceptable acts and practise all our unrevealed desires.

From their descents into these turbulent oneiric regions, dramatists

2. Literally, 'A Stroke at Knifepoint' – but there is a Brazilian expression, *dar murro em ponta de faca*, which means to insist on the practically impossible.
3. A Brazilian meat dish with a rust-coloured sauce.
4. A Brazilian dish made of manioc flour, oil, pepper, fish and meat.

bring back deformed characters, who are repainted, reshaped, cut into pieces, so that they eventually become acceptable, though they retain their strangeness. I have done two experiments of this kind as a director. Two surrealist plays. The first was Julio Cortazar's *Nada Mais a Calingasta* (No More Goes To Calingasta), that writer's only play. The setting was a mixture of restaurant, post office and the entrance hall at a convention of police officers. Every day an impartial Judge came and ate there, a man who made a habit of never eating on days when anyone he had condemned to death was due to be executed. His repast was always the same; a few grams of carrot, weighed out on his own scales, which he always carried with him. One day, inadvertently, he eats carrot on an execution day. Repenting of this folly, he wants to flee the restaurant-delegation-post office, but is held back by his fascination for the Maître d'hotel. The latter, at the end of the play, rolls up his sleeve to reveal a star tatooed on his arm: the star of death. The Maître d'hotel is none other than the dead man. Alive. For someone like myself who was used to doing *mise-en-scènes* of a more or less rational nature, in which the actors' movements always had a certain 'logic', the 'choreography' of this piece was not easy to organise. It was so difficult, and so agonising, that I only managed to resolve the problem one night, late one night . . . dreaming. In my sleep, in dreams, Cortazar's characters began to move with a perfect logic . . . an oneiric logic. This was in 1984, at the Schauspielhaus in Graz, in Austria.

In Wüppertal, in Germany, in 1985, I had my second surrealist experience with an unfinished and never-performed play of Garcia Lorca's, *El Publico* (The Public). German actors, as a rule, want to understand why they do something. Causes and effects. And in this Lorca play it was difficult to explain why the Protagonist, the Director, orders the public to enter and four white horses come in; why Julieta rebuffs the warm love offered by the heroic Black Horse and prefers to be violated by the spiritless White Chargers; why each time the Director tears off one of his garments, the clothes pass through a screen and come back on stage alive, with new characters occupying them: Harlequin, Ballerina, Worker, etc. Why the King eats a small child alive behind a Roman ruin. It was difficult to explain even though, for me at least, it was very easy to feel.

In theatre, symbols or mere images are polysemic and are perceived as such by the spectators. There is always another meaning behind every meaning, which in turn hides a third and a fourth. An onion of meanings. In surrealist theatre, it seems to me more important to work on the signifier than the signified, since the former contains many of the latter. 'This' means 'that', but also 'the other' and many more things. If the actors feel the need for clear and simple explanation, and if we give it them, we are reducing the polysemy of the image. 'This' means 'that', and nothing more. 'The other' and the many more are lost, everything is lost.

In *El Publico* there was a scene in which the Emperor wanted to know which of the two prisoners he had was 'the one' and which was 'the other'. And the two prisoners agonised over it because not even they knew who was the one and who was the other. And I thought it right that the scene should be exactly like it was. However, a few actors wanted to know the meaning, the signified, of the one and the other. I found it painful to reduce Lorca's images to 'this' and 'that'. But I did not have to go on stage, and they did; I had to give them some certainty to hold onto. To this end, at one side of the stage I arranged a lavish banquet table, and on the left, another table, piled high with instruments of torture. And I said to the two prisoners: you are Jews in a Nazi concentration camp; the Colonel comes in and wants to know which is the one who will come and dine with him at the banqueting table and which is the other who will be handed over to the Centurion to be tortured. This meaning was undoubtedly contained, among thousands of others, within Lorca's text. However, by reducing the polysemy of the text to one of its valences, obviously we are reducing – Lorca miniaturised.

The show and the dream – both are theatre. Theatre and life – both are life. Fiction and reality – both are real. The only fiction which exists is the word fiction. The image of the real is real as an image. Image is also a reality besides being the image of a reality.

When I directed Racine's *Phèdre*, with Fernanda Montenegro, in the Arena theatre, on the floor we had a bamboo square delineating the stage. And I used to tell the actors: 'Once you step over the bamboo, you are forbidden to do theatre. We do theatre all our lives, everywhere. Save on stage; there, the dignity of our art obliges us to live'. Conclusion: there is life in theatre and theatre in life. Dream in the show and show in the dream. Reality in fiction and fiction in reality.

On the subject of this interdependence, I have always been taken with the Chinese story of the two drowned men: two completely different men, one magnificently decked out in garments of silk, the other in rags; one a general, the other a peasant; one was descended from an illustrious family whose family tree had branches stretching back five or six centuries, the other could not remember who his father was; one was a millionaire, the other a beggar. Two men who could not be more different. There were real and concrete differences between them, social differences, economic differences, etc. But both were on board the same boat. Along came an enormous wave and capsized the boat. And the waters of the sea did not recognise any differences between them at all, either in economic or social terms. Both drowned.

The differences were as real as the waves of the sea. However, there are degrees of reality . . .

15 *Family*

A playscript used during the mandate as a basis for Forum Sessions

CHARACTERS (IN ORDER OF ENTRY)

MARIA DA GRAÇA (the younger daughter)
MARIA DA GLORIA (the elder daughter)
SEBASTIANA (the mother)
BETO (the brother of Gloria and Graça)
ORLANDO (the father)
GRANDPA (the grandfather of Gloria and Graça)

Setting:

The scene takes place in a lower-middle-class household. A single set contains a dining table and, close to it, a television; a bedroom adjoins this room. Everything very simple, decorated with family pictures. Sunday, lunch time. Seated at table, Gloria is doing her homework and Graça is watching TV.

GRAÇA: Wow, Fernanda's managed to escape from the clinic. She doped up the nurse with a whole heap of drugs and ran for it. She's the best! Did you see the way she cried?

GLORIA: (*Without taking her eyes off the book*) Who?

GRAÇA: Fernanda. Yesterday she had this amazing wedding dress, all embroidered, she looked like a saint.

(*Silence*)

GRAÇA: Gloria, I need to talk to you about something – I'm in a bit of mess, see? I've got problems and I don't know what to do.

GLORIA: (*Without taking her eyes off her book*) What?

GRAÇA: I've got problems. I thought you might be able to help.

GLORIA: (*Looking at her sister*) I've got an exam tomorrow, I've got loads of revision to do. And if I was you, I'd get down to some homework too. They failed you last year and if you carry on like this you're going to fail again this year.

GRAÇA: I haven't got the brains for that stuff.

(*Gloria goes back to reading her book*)

GRAÇA: I wrote something this week, but then I tore it up 'cos I knew they wouldn't like it. I like writing, but I can never find the right words. I reckon writing is a way of getting stuff of your chest. I write things I can't say. In school everyone says that my writing is awful – what I'd really like to do is write a TV soap.

GLORIA: Graça my love, you're distracting me.

GRAÇA: Distracting you, distracting you from your precious work . . . you never think of anyone but yourself.

GLORIA: Don't be a brat. Stick to your soap and leave me in peace.

GRAÇA: (*Laughing*) If you only knew how true to life my soap is . . .

GLORIA: (*Looking seriously at her sister*) I know more than you think, madam. (*She returns to her book*)

(*Enter Sebastiana*)

SEBASTIANA: Girls, come and help me finish the food and lay the table.

GLORIA: Mum, I can't, I'm studying. Get Graça to help.

GRAÇA: Why me? I'm watching TV. It's always me who helps.

GLORIA: I do more than you. Who ironed the sheets today?

GRAÇA: Oh sure – today. What about all the rest of the week? You spend your whole life studying. You're always inventing exams.

GLORIA: I don't invent them. I am studying. You iron the sheets once and it's like you've done a whole day's work. All you care about is going clubbing, you go from the beach to the cinema, from the cinema to a club, and then you get home late and spin some yarn to Mum.

GRAÇA: You're jealous!

GLORIA: Jealous? Me? Get a life!

SEBASTIANA: Enough bickering! Gloria, lay the table. Graça, come and help me in the kitchen.

GLORIA: Yes, maam!

GRAÇA: Oh shit!

(*Graça goes into the kitchen with her mother. Gloria lays the table and gets back to her homework*)

GRAÇA: (*Shouting from the kitchen*) Hey! Lunch's ready, come and eat.

(*Enter Beto*)

BETO: What's happening? I'm starving. What's for supper?

GLORIA: Beto, don't sit down at table covered in sand!

BETO: Sunday's old macaroni? I can't handle any more macaroni.

GLORIA: You should thank God you've got food on your plate.

BETO: I bet you even the Italians don't eat as much macaroni as we do.

(*Beto changes the TV channel*)

GLORIA: Don't turn over, I was watching that!

(*Beto blows a raspberry at his sister. Enter Sebastiana carrying the plates.*)

BETO: (*Chanting*) Mum, mum, mum!

SEBASTIANA: Take those grubby hands out of here. Go and wash, the food's ready.

(*Enter Grandpa*)

GRANDPA: Where's the food?

(*He sits*)

GRANDPA: (*To Gloria*) Are you going to read and eat at the same time, child? You can't whistle and suck sugar cane at the same time.

GLORIA: I'm just finishing this book, Grandpa – I've got an exam tomorrow.

GRANDPA: What about you, Beto? When are you going to do something useful with your life?

BETO: Do something useful? I'd rather have another beer. And while we're on the subject, what about you? When are you going to make an honest woman of Dona Ofélia?

GRANDPA: What are you on about, lad? What's the big joke?

BETO: Eh? She's a widow, you're a widower – put two and two together. And she's still in good nick, considering how many miles she's got on the clock. They say that she was a cover girl on the first Bible . . .

GLORIA: You really are the king of the blockheads, aren't you, Beto?

BETO: And you're my favourite subject, darling.

   (*Enter Orlando*)

ORLANDO: Tiana!

   (*Mother runs and gets her husband's slippers*)

SEBASTIANA: Lunch's ready, Orlando.

   (*While her mother goes into the kitchen, Graça sits at table*)

ORLANDO: Get a move on, I'm starving, Tiana.

GRANDPA: So, Orlando, did you talk to Mr Manuel about the sale, about the notebook business?

ORLANDO: It's all sorted, I've already fixed it up with him, old man.

AVO: I didn't much care for the airs he was putting on, yesterday. (*To Beto*) Oi half-pint! Go and put a shirt on, don't you know it's bad manners to sit at table half-naked?

BETO: Half-naked! Honestly, Grandpa! (*He makes a face and gets his shirt*)

   (*Sebastiana starts serving the food*)

GRAÇA: I'm not hungry, Mum.

SEBASTIANA: What's this, Graça? Have a few mouthfuls at least.

GRAÇA: I'm not hungry!

SEBASTIANA: Don't use that tone with me, my girl. You don't know what hunger is. If you don't want to eat, say that you've got no appetite, don't say you're not hungry.

ORLANDO: Stop pampering the girl, Tiana. If you don't want to eat, don't eat. If she had any idea how much food costs. So many people in the world desperate for a plate of food, begging for the love of God . . .

GLORIA: Her mind's on other things, folks!

GRAÇA: Leave me alone, Gloria!

BETO: (*To Gloria*) Stop getting at her, girl! What a poisonous little cow you are!

GLORIA: She spent the whole night crying her eyes out.

ORLANDO: Come and sit down, Tiana!

SEBASTIANA: What's up with you, my girl?

GRAÇA: Nothing Mum, I'm just not feeling well.

(*They all silently make the sign of the cross*)

GRANDPA: Praise be to God, and our Lord Jesus Christ – and don't forget to let me into heaven when I'm done with all this.

(*They all laugh*)

SEBASTIANA: If only it was as easy as that.

(*They eat*)

SEBASTIANA: I got up at three in the morning to buy milk today. When I got to the grocery, there were already people queuing.

ORLANDO: Where's it all going to end? I don't know.

GLORIA: I don't know why you bother, no-one in this house ever drinks milk.

SEBASTIANA: Your brother drinks milk. Remember, Orlando? Beto was on the breast till he was 7 years old. I had so much milk that it started leaking out of me. Little Graça and Gloria were the same; I had to put pepper on my nipples to get them to let go.

(*Graça looks ill and gets up from the table. Sebastiana follows her*)

GLORIA: What did I tell you?

(*They all go on eating. The focus moves to the living room, where Graça and Sebastiana talk*)

SEBASTIANA: What's up, child?

GRAÇA: Nothing, Mum.

SEBASTIANA: How can it be nothing? You're white as a sheet!

GRAÇA: I'm just feeling sick.

SEBASTIANA: Gloria said you were crying all night.

GRAÇA: Well she was fibbing.

(*Silence*)

SEBASTIANA: Graça, my girl, tell me. Have you got tummy-ache?

GRAÇA: No mum. There's nothing wrong with me. I just haven't been feeling well.

SEBASTIANA: Is it something to do with a boyfriend and you're ashamed to tell me?

GRAÇA: Yes it is, Mum. I'm ashamed. I'm so ashamed!

SEBASTIANA: Ashamed of what? Tell me!

GRAÇA: I think I've done something stupid, Mum!

SEBASTIANA: What sort of stupid?

GRAÇA: I haven't had my period for two months now.

SEBASTIANA: You mean . . .

GRAÇA: I think I'm pregnant!

SEBASTIANA: Why didn't you say anything? Don't you trust your mum?

GRAÇA: I didn't think you'd understand. I was frightened, Mum!

SEBASTIANA: You were frightened? What about me? What am I supposed to do? Which little wretch did this to you?

GRAÇA: You don't know him.

SEBASTIANA: You didn't bring him here to our home and show him to me? Don't you learn anything at school?

GRAÇA: Mum, Mum. You never explained anything to me. You never taught me anything about love, anything about what happens with men and women.

SEBASTIANA: When I was your age, when I was seventeen, I didn't know anything about the world, but I could never have made a mistake like this, I would never have brought this heartbreak on my mother.

GRAÇA: I am different from you, Mum.

SEBASTIANA: You don't know anything about life!

GRAÇA: You're the one who doesn't know anything about the outside world. You spend your whole life slaving away indoors, suffering – you hardly go out.

SEBASTIANA: And what do you think is going to happen now?

GRAÇA: I wanted something different from all this – I don't want to spend my whole life stuck indoors, I've got dreams, I don't want to live like this, I want to live a different kind of life.

SEBASTIANA: Why? Isn't this good enough for you, my girl? What do you lack? We've struggled to bring you up in a decent home, your father almost kills himself to bring things into the home. Why have you done this? You'll break my heart!

GRAÇA: I knew it, Mum, I'm so sorry. It felt right at the time . . .

SEBASTIANA: Gloria was right, she's the only one with any brains in this place. Your father will kill you, and me.

GRAÇA: I knew it, I knew it.

SEBASTIANA: Now I want to see you talk to him, because I haven't got the guts.

GRAÇA: But Mum, help me, for the love of God, help me!

(*The focus moves to the dining room*)

ORLANDO: Tiana! Graça!

(*Enter Sebastiana*)

GLORIA: Graça, Daddy is calling you!

ORLANDO: See that, old man! You work your fingers to the bone to make sure no-one goes short at home and that's what you get – waste! (*Pointing at the plate*) What's up with Graça?

SEBASTIANA: Nothing. She's poorly.

(*They eat in silence*)

BETO: What did the earthworm shout when he fell into the plate of macaroni?

GLORIA: What?

BETO: Whoopee – an orgy!

(*They all laugh, except Sebastiana*)

GRANDPA: I once had a cup of coffee that was so weak, it was so weak, that it wasn't strong enough to flow out of the pot.

(*They all laugh, except Sebastiana*)

ORLANDO: That one's so old it's got grey hairs.

BETO: Good one, Dad!

(*They all laugh. Sebastiana gets up nervously and starts clearing the plates quickly*)

GLORIA: I haven't finished yet, Mum.

(*Sebastiana agitatedly gets the other plates*)

GLORIA: I was taught that you were supposed to chew each mouthful three times if you don't want to get indigestion.

(*Grandpa turns on the TV. Sebastiana brings the coffee. They watch TV. Gloria takes her plate out and comes back. Graça appears in the doorway and calls Beto*)

GRAÇA: Beto!

BETO: What?

GRAÇA: Come here a minute.

BETO: You come here.

ORLANDO: Go and see what your sister wants.

GRANDPA: He's bone idle, that boy!

(*Beto goes to Graça. Focus on the living room*)

BETO: What is it?

GRAÇA: Did anything happen in there?

BETO: Like what?

GRAÇA: What's the atmosphere like? Did Mum say anything?

BETO: No. She looked like she'd seen a ghost, but she didn't say anything, Lord knows what's up with her. Was she supposed to say something?

GRAÇA: No, nothing. What about Dad?

BETO: Dad complained that you didn't eat anything, but it's OK, it looks like he's had a drop to drink.

GRAÇA: What's everyone doing?

BETO: (*Laughs*) Our Maria da Gloria has got her face stuck in a book, as part of her efforts to become an intellectual housewife. Gramps is drooling over the babes on the TV. Mum is working away like there's no tomorrow. Dad (*making a gesture of drinking*) is relaxing after a hard day at work. Is that all you wanted?

(*Beto is on the brink of going*)

GRAÇA: No, Beto . . . I wanted to ask you something . . .

BETO: Hey, Graça, you know I'm broke, and Dad hasn't got a sou. Now if I have a decent run of luck, we'll all be laughing.

GRAÇA; Beto, I'm serious.

BETO: Me too – so pray for me to have a winner on the Lotto and you'll be the first to hear about it – you know I'll see you right.

(*Beto starts to go*)

GRAÇA: Wait, Beto, stay here with me for a moment.

BETO: Oh, for Christ's sake, I'm missing this great film, give us a break.

(*Beto leaves. Focus on the dining room*)

ORLANDO: What did she want?

BETO: Nothing!

GLORIA: Nothing? I doubt it!

ORLANDO: Tiana! What are you doing?

SEBASTIANA: I'm doing the dishes!

ORLANDO: Oh Tiana! It's Sunday, why don't you call one of these girls to help you, poor soul?

SEBASTIANA: I'm alright, leave the children be.

ORLANDO: Leave them be? No way! There you are working yourself to death while one of them is lying down and the other is watching TV.

GLORIA: I am studying.

ORLANDO: Graça! Graça!

(*Graça comes in, looking terrified, and Sebastiana also appears*)

ORLANDO: Graça, go and help your mother.

SEBASTIANA: She can't.

ORLANDO: What do you mean she can't? She was just lying down.

SEBASTIANA: Leave the girl, she's not well today.

ORLANDO: I can see that she's not well, she hasn't eaten a thing.

GLORIA: Um, Dad, she's not been well for a while, she's got a problem and it's not going to go away . . .

ORLANDO: What sort of problem? How long has this child not been eating, Tiana?

GLORIA: It's not that, Dad . . .

SEBASTIANA: Shut your mouth, child, don't make things worse!

ORLANDO: Make what worse, Tiana? What on earth is happening in this house?

(*Graça bursts into tears and hugs her mother*)

SEBASTIANA: Orlando, Maria da Graça is expecting a child.

ORLANDO: You what?

GRANDPA: A child?

BETO: Christ alive!

ORLANDO: What on earth? Tiana?

SEBASTIANA: It's not my fault, Orlando. I didn't know anything about it, I've only just heard myself.

GLORIA: Didn't I say that it wasn't right to keep lying to Mum????

GRAÇA: Shut your mouth, you idiot!

ORLANDO: You shut your mouth! How could you do this to me? Did you give a single thought to me? Or your mother?

GRAÇA: Sorry, Dad!

ORLANDO: Sorry my arse!

SEBASTIANA: I don't know what to say, I am just as shocked as you, Orlando!

ORLANDO: You're her mother, you're to blame!

SEBASTIANA: I know, Orlando, but I thought that everything was fine with the kids. She made a mistake, the poor thing!

GRANDPA: Made a mistake – how? No-one falls into bed with some-one else by mistake . . . How can you fall into bed with someone by mistake . . .!

GLORIA: What now? I'll die of shame in school. What am I going to say to people?

BETO: What people? It happened, it's not the end of the world, is it!

ORLANDO: Shut your mouth, you wretch! I am going to kill that little bugger!

GRANDPA: The only thing to do is get them married!

GRAÇA: But he is already married!

ORLANDO: You little tart!

(*He advances on Graça, slapping her. Sebastiana and Beto rescue her*)

ALL: Calm down, calm down!

SEBASTIANA: Ai, Mary Mother of God!

(*Orlando sits, in shock*)

GRANDPA: Calm down, Orlando, calm down. Violence won't solve anything.

ORLANDO: Oh give it a rest, old man. Think about it. One more mouth to feed, fucking hell!

GRANDPA: My girl, how could you do this? You of all people, the youngest, the apple of your mother's eye, of all people. This has never happened in our family, never! We are poor, yes, but we are decent people. Our name has never been dragged through the mud. What happened to all the education you had? All the morality, Christian values we taught you? This is an act of complete irresponsibility. Give an inch and you take a bloody mile! I said to your mother, 'watch that girl', 'that girl goes out a lot'. Just the other day, a car hooted here in front of the house, none of you took any notice; she was just waiting for that car and she jumps in, just like that. Didn't we always say that a girl should never get into a car with a man . . .

BETO: What a sermon! What a load of rubbish! She had her own life to live. It happened – what's done's done. We should be thinking about what she is going to do now. Whether she wants to have this child or not!

ORLANDO: Maria da Graça! You are no longer my daughter! From this day on, you do not live here. You can go and walk the streets for all I care!

SEBASTIANA: For the love of God, Orlando, don't throw her out! Poor child, don't be so hard on her. I know that the little fool has done wrong, but that is going too far!

BETO: Can I inject a little sense into this conversation?

GLORIA: Sense? You?

GRANDPA: The boy is right –

ORLANDO: No, I'm not listening – I will not have her stay in this house a moment longer.

GRANDPA: Hold on, hold on – we can't throw the child out into the street. But from now on things are going to have to change round here – she will no longer be free to come and go as she pleases! Enough is enough!

SEBASTIANA: That's right, Dad.

GRANDPA: Otherwise, her name will be dirt. From now on her life changes. If you learn how to behave yourself, you never know, you might be lucky, someone might still come along, an honest, clean-living man, a worker; then you get married and sort your life out.

GLORIA: There is always Dona Inẽs's Octavio – he's mad enough to marry her.

GRANDPA: Well?

GRAÇA: But I don't like him!

SEBASTIANA: What does it matter if you like him or not? Men who want to marry a fallen woman don't grow on trees. Still less one with a nipper hanging onto her apron-strings . . .

GLORIA: Well, who knows? Octavio is stupid enough – he'll probably think he's the father!

BETO: What are you on about? She can abort. Take out the baby and that's that!

SEBASTIANA: What – abort the child? It's a mortal sin!

BETO: What sin? It's perfectly normal in these situations. Loads of girls do it.

ORLANDO: That's enough! Enough of this foolishness! From now on, Graça stays locked in her room.

GRAÇA: Oh, my God!

SEBASTIANA: But . . . Orlando!

ORLANDO: We will say no more about it! (*At the door*) Tiana, don't expect me for dinner.

(*Orlando leaves, Graça goes to her room in tears, Sebastiana goes into the kitchen, Grandpa falls prostrate on the chair, Gloria goes on studying*)

BETO: Families are shit.

(*He leaves the stage with the TV under his arm*)

THE END

Categories
of
Popular
Theatre

Prologue

This text was written in 1971, when everything in Brazil was black or white; this explains the simplicity of the analysis – it was written for publication in 1973. *AB.*

In order to arrive at an accurate definition of the categories of popular theatre, we must first establish the fundamental difference between 'the population' and 'the people'.

'The population' is the totality of inhabitants of a country or region. The concept of 'the people' is more restricted: it includes only those who sell their labour power. 'The people' is a generic designation which encompasses workers and peasants, and all who are temporarily or occasionally associated with either group, as happens with students and other sectors in some countries.

Those who constitute part of 'the population' but do not fall within this definition of 'the people' are the bosses, the landowners, the bourgeoisie and their associates (their executives and managers) and, generally speaking, all those who think like them – we might call them 'the anti-people'. Workers are 'the people'. 'The population' also encompasses the masters.

If these definitions are correct, we then have three categories of theatre which pertain to the people. In the first two, any piece of theatre presented comes from the perspective of the people. In the third, the perspective which informs the show is that of the bosses. Two perspectives: the first reveals a world in permanent transformation, complete with contradictions and movements, such as the workers' campaigns for liberation. It shows that men enslaved by work, by habits and traditions, can change their situation. Everything is in a state of perpetual transformation, and this change has to be driven forward all the time.

The second perspective seeks to demonstrate, by contrast, that after a long history mankind has arrived at the best of all possible worlds, i.e., the present system, in which the masters have gained possession of the land, the means of production, while the workers work with God's consent. Two different ways of seeing life and the world!

There is, in fact, a fourth category of theatre, in which theatre is made by and for the people. That will be covered separately (see p. 213f).

1 The first category of popular theatre

By the people and for the people

THIS category is eminently popular: the show presented conforms to the transformation-oriented perspective of the people, who are also its intended audience. Performances usually take place in front of large concentrations of workers, in union meetings, in the streets, in the squares, in residents' associations and other such places. Here at least three kinds of popular theatre can be presented: Propaganda Theatre, Didactic Theatre and Cultural Theatre.

PROPAGANDA THEATRE

This is used in various countries, including the US, where the expression 'agit-prop', meaning agitation and propaganda, was first coined. In Brazil it has been practised for many years, especially prior to 1964 – the date of the first *coup d'état* by the dictatorship – by the so-called Popular Centres of Culture, which taught the people so much in the way of culinary art and choral song, dance, theatrical performance, cinema, painting, etc. The theatre shows organised by these centres were concerned with whatever problems were of greatest urgency and importance for the communities at the time. In some cases, the workers themselves would write the plays or supply subject-matter and accounts of the events which would then in turn be dramatised and written up by others.

Many centres were led by students, and they frequently took part in election rallies. Often, theatrical scenes would be shown as a preface to the carrying out of political actions: the scenes dealt with the subjects which the speakers would debate moments later. This kind of Propaganda Theatre might involve, for instance, an extract of a show entitled: *Only Jânio gives Esso the most*. This title parodied a very well-known advertisement; 'Only Esso gives your car the most'. The Jânio in question was Jânio Quadros, a reactionary candidate for the Presidency of the Republic: the piece showed the links between Quadros and imperialism. Indeed, imperialism was the main theme of this type of theatre.

The José da Silva and the guardian angel episode taken from my own play *Revolution in South America* was also often performed before political discussions of candidates of the left. The scene showed a day in the life of a Brazilian worker, forced to pay royalties to the America businesses from the moment he turns on the light (LIGHT AND POWER), through cleaning his teeth (PALMOLIVE) and washing his hands (LEVER S.A.), having his coffee (AMERICAN COFFEE COMPANY), going off to work, whether by (MERCEDES BENZ) bus or on foot (with GOODYEAR soles on his shoes), till he tucks into his tinned feijoada (SWIFT, ARMOUR or ANGLO); then, he goes to the cinema to see a cowboy film (HOLLYWOOD produces more than half of the films shown in Brazil), and the process goes on, encompassing the very air he breathes in the cinema (WESTINGHOUSE air conditioning) and his journey up in the (OTIS or ATLAS) lift; until finally, despairing of such continual levies and royalties, he tries to kill himself – but even in the hour of his death, as always, along comes the guardian angel of capitalist interests: an angel with an English accent, who takes a percentage from poor José on behalf of SMITH AND WESSON, famous gunsmiths.

This scene, in spite of its obviousness, and sometimes for that very reason, revealed in stark clarity to its audiences of peasants and workers the omnipresence of imperialism, bringing home to them the true meaning and relevance of that word. The actors would go around in each city or province collecting the typical local details and characteristics most suited to the purpose of the play. The scene, which originally used to last five minutes, ended up being presented as a whole hour-long play, once it had taken on board all the demands and suggestions which came directly from the people's audience.

In Brazil, whenever an important political fact or event came up, the Popular Centres of Culture immediately mobilised to write and present a piece of theatre on this subject. On the same night that President Kennedy ordered the naval blockade of Cuba, a group of writers gathered together to write a play in the National Students Union in the State of Guanabara; they finished it the same night. The actors rehearsed it the following afternoon and that evening it was presented in the open air on the steps of the Municipal Theatre. It bore the title *The Morality Play of the Broken Blockade*. The blockade had been authorised the previous day and the Russian ships were continuing to sail towards the island, and at that point the outcome of the problem was far from certain. The text showed the causes of the conflict and its possible ramifications. The piece was a great help to the popular movement in defence of the Cuban Revolution, and to the general raising of the people's consciousness, who could see it every night (with additional elements according to the events of the day) right up until the total suspension of the blockade. Similar pieces with the same goal played continuously. It will suffice to cite a few titles: *Land or death we will win, Cuba yes, Yankees no*, etc. The Centres of Popular Culture were so important that the dictatorship's first decree was to close them down!

The Propaganda Theatre did not limit itself to international themes. It also dealt with problems of lesser import, designed for more specific audiences. For instance, the students of São Paulo Polytechnic presented a piece on the difficulties presented by the lifelong tenure of professorial chairs, the problems of 'over-academic' teachers and antiquated teaching methods. Clearly, the techniques employed corresponded to the objectives; there was no place for theatrical niceties when playing on top of lorries, nor for subtle symbolism in a 2,000-seat amphitheatre or in a square with a standing, moving audience, where the traffic noise and the shouts of street-sellers competed with the actors' voices. This aesthetic is neither superior nor inferior, no better or worse than any other. It is what it is! The Polytechnic students, in the latter case, had no hesitation in using the crudest means to evidence their point of view; the assistant woke the 'cathedratic professor' in his coffin to give a lesson on the colour of Dom Pedro the First's underpants when he proclaimed Brazil's independence. This was an insolent theatre, aggressive, rough, aesthetic. Theatre is a form of knowledge, ergo it is political; its means are sensory, ergo it is aesthetic. In street theatre, there is no time for the psychological subtleties surrounding such and such a figurehead of imperialism, or landowner or gorilla[1]: once it had been decided that a particular character would be easily recognised by an obvious symbol, it was used, however obvious it was; so an actor would come on riding a broomstick (the symbol of Jânio Quadros) or with enormous eyes and crows' wings (Carlos Lacerda[2]), or with a blue and red top hat (Uncle Sam), etc. When

1. The term 'gorilla' was generally used at that time to designate people associated with repressive Latin American regimes.
2. Another right-wing leader.

there was no rapidly identifiable symbol to hand, often people would resort to a placard bearing the character's name.

Were the masks of the *commedia dell'arte* any more subtle? The tattered rags in which Arlecchino was clad were transformed into diamond colours, but only when that popular character was reduced to a gentle divertissement for the elites. The same softening process eventually happened to all the other masks and the crude situations on which this popular theatre form thrived; the original Brighellas and doctors and the like could not have been conceived in a cruder or more caricatured and grotesque form.

Clearly, the point of these *commedia* devices was to present a caricature which maintained and amplified the essence of the person being caricatured; and the same applied in Brazil – Lacerda was a bird of prey, uncle Sam the super-villain.

The objectives of the Propaganda Theatre were very clear and well-defined. There was a need to explain to the people an event which had occurred. And there was an urgency: this work of explaining and enlightening included as one of its goals political imperatives such as persuading the spectator to vote for such and such a candidate or to take part in a particular strike or confront a particular act of political repression.

DIDACTIC THEATRE

While Propaganda Theatre always tackled the most immediate subjects, Didactic Theatre – also practised by the Popular Centres of Culture and by professional groups, such as the Arena Theatre of São Paulo – focused on more general problems. The intention of this type of theatre was not to mobilise the public to face a particular event which was looming – such as voting, going on strike or demonstrating – without first offering it a theoretical and practical teaching. It would choose a theme say, justice. We knew that the dominant classes always seek to impose their ideas, their moral values, on the dominated classes. Thus they try to make everyone believe that justice is a single universal thing, concealing the fact that it is they, the dominant classes, who are entrusted with the prescription and execution of this justice – which they intend should be the only justice available.

However, if the hypothesis of a God-given justice is done away with, and if it is admitted that men are divided into classes, it becomes evident that there will be as many justices as there are classes into which men are divided, and that the strongest will impose their justice as unique and universal in application.

An abstract explanation such as we have just given will not reach the consciousness of the masses. For this reason, didactic theatre tries to expose it in a concrete and sensory manner. Lope da Vega's *El Mejor Alcalde El Rey*[3] (The King is the Best Justice) played for three months in street theatres – on lorries, in churches etc. – for a popular audience made up of manual workers, peasants, domestic servants, students etc.

In the play, Sancho is a young peasant in love with the beautiful Elvira, who reciprocates this love. Elvira tells him to ask her father Dom Nuno's consent; the latter agrees, but in his turn asks him to seek the consent of the master of all those lands, who was, of course, also the master of justice, which he exercised in person. The master in question, Senhor Dom Tello – a good-hearted man – feels proud to possess such loyal vassals, so respectful of the laws and the holy medieval customs. He turns out to be so big-hearted that he decides to give the couple 20 sheep and 40-odd cows, by way of wedding present. Furthermore, he decides to preside in person as patron of the marriage, to honour such exemplary vassals. On the wedding night, Dom Tello visits the bridal pair's hut and, as was to be expected, when faced with the beauty of Elvira, he also falls in love. He puts back the wedding, saying that he wishes to honour the bridegroom still further, since he finds the future bride so beautiful. The bridegroom protests, but the senhor, Dom Tello, is the master of the law, and his desires are always just.

During the night, the noble gentleman orders his servants to kidnap Elvira and bring her to his castle. The young woman resists, but Dom Tello demands his right. Justice disposes that on the first night the bride belongs to the owner of the lands; Dom Tello, assisted by justice, seeks to collect his due entitlement. Sancho, inflamed, goes to the king for help. In our adaptation of Lope's work, the king is busy with his wars (and on account of this, needs the support of Tello's forces), and in the greater scheme of things, he is not going to concern himself with the loss of a single virginity – one virgin more or less, who cares. The serf returns downhearted; and then his friend Pelayo comes up with a stratagem: he disguises himself as the king and, assisted by various peasants, arrests Dom Tello, sets up a trial and dispenses justice. But he argues: there are two justices here; one is the bridegroom's justice (and by extension

3. Lope Félix de Vega Carpio (Lope de Vega), 1562–1635, prolific Spanish dramatist, poet and novelist. This play dates from 1620.

217

that of the peasant class in general) and the other is the senhor's justice (and that of the nobility in general). How can total justice be done? By doing both.

The judgment begins. While Sancho was on his way to see the king, his bride had been raped and, therefore, according to the Spanish code of honour of the time, could no longer marry Sancho. Pelayo judges Dom Tello according to the standards of justice a noble would expect, and consequently condemns him to marry Elvira, the plebeian, with whom he is in love. The act of sexual violence is punished with the marriage of the noble to the plebeian (at this point the audience used to groan in protest and almost bring the judgement to a halt, because they were in such complete dis-agreement with it). After this – and before the audience physically interrupted the play – Pelayo went on to the second judgement. In accordance with the peasant's justice Sancho was entitled to, the noble was condemned to the scaffold for having unilaterally exercised a right which the peasants did not recognise. At the same time, Elvira, having been widowed, would inherit half of his property, recover her honour – by having married the person who had taken her innocence – and obtain an unlooked-for dowry. The play ended with the marriage of Elvira and Sancho, and everyone understood that, while there continue to be differences between men, while there are still exploiters and exploited, while social classes exist, there will always be one justice to which some are entitled and another justice for everyone else.

Often at the end of the show, the peasants who had seen it, sometimes perched on trees or standing on the roofs of neighbouring houses, would discuss its content with the performers. When they were asked about Dom Tello, they would answer: 'Who? You mean Colonel[4] Firmino?'; they understood that Dom Tello, albeit in the guise of a distant epoch, and with a language of verse, was actually their enemy of there and then. When we were talking about Sancho, they immediately identified him with any simple, unsuspecting peasant.

This Didactic Theatre often presented works of this type, in which a particular ethical problem was discussed and analysed. On other occasions, its content was not of a moral character, but objective and material; Didactic Theatre was applied even to subjects such as agriculture. In the north-east of Brazil, a warm reception was given to short plays in the style of fables, which taught how to use a certain insecticide to combat a specific blight or plague; for instance, the

4. Brazilian landowners adopt spurious military titles, just as industrialists give themselves spurious academic qualifications.

damsel in distress would be the carrot, the abominable villain the disease-bearing insect and the young hero who saved her the insecticide; the play explained the process of the struggle between them, and how the villain could be destroyed. The story was designed to enable the peasants to learn and refine particular agricultural techniques.

In São Paulo, the Department of Transport tried to use these methods to teach pedestrians to cross the road safely, but apparently they did not succeed ... In the end, Didactic Theatre is not infallible.

CULTURE THEATRE

To be popular, theatre must always tackle issues from the people's perspective, that is, the perspective of permanent transformation, of anti-alienation, of struggle against exploitation etc. This does not mean that it can only treat subject-matter which is usually designated 'political'; all human life is relevant to the people, and consequently of interest to the workers.

Though we may accept that no subject-matter is necessarily alien to popular theatre – that the word 'popular' when attached to theatre relates to its focus and not its subject-matter – there are still questions of priorities. And it is in response to this matter of prioritisation that more relevance is given to recognisably political subject areas; though the popular theatre may often be accused of monothematism, it is entirely appropriate that the combating of imperialism should be considered to be the most important theme, the theme which informs all other subject-matters.

The political theatre in Brazil is always centred on very radicalised content, and strenuously resists subjects of more limited scope – an attitude which some might justifiably consider erroneous. But we must take into account that the bourgeoisie, for its part, offers *only* lesser and secondary themes, in order to distract the audiences' attention from questions of real importance. I have never seen a single TV series which dealt with the problems of the penetration of yankee capital into this country and the rest of Latin America, or the importance of the rise of popular governments in relation to the liberation of the peoples of our continent; by contrast, I have seen numerous plays dealing with individual neuroses and isolation. Of course the bourgeois canon often occupies itself with minor 'social'

219

themes, such as the relations between classes. In Brazil, at this very moment, under the most terrible and murderous of the dictatorships that we have experienced, there is a television series about the lives of working people. What is the nature of this drama? One of the workers falls in love with the boss's daughter, and after many psychological struggles to convince the old man, they get married, produce many baby workers (or baby bourgeois?) and live happily ever after. Censorship prohibits the play from containing any references to 'strikes', 'wages', 'the cost of living' and other subject areas which might 'threaten' national security.

The classics of the past – Shakespeare, Molière, Aristophanes, Goldoni and others – can also serve the agendas of the popular theatre and, equally, the folkloric can be good entertainment for the people. But it should be borne in mind that when the content of a play is not sufficiently clear or is open to diverse interpretations, the bourgeoisie can and will always manage to come up with the version which coincides with its interests, by means of particular actors' performances or particular directors' readings. Similarly, with respect to folklore, the bourgeois interpretation will attempt to show the people 'faithful to its origins', rather than fighting since its origins for a future which it must construct; just as – as Angela Davis has remarked – in its reading of the Bible, it dwells on scenes of obedience and respect for the established order, hiding those passages which show change and revolt against the established violence.

The fact that the bourgeoisie have made appropriations from folklore does not diminish its importance in its own right; it is perfectly valid to offer shows of song and dance in which the people can develop and practise their own rhythms and movements. However, it is necessary to be alert to manoeuvres by which the dominant classes attempt to use folklore and the folkloric for their own ends. In Brazil, for instance, Carnival has always been employed as an escape valve, a form of catharsis to eliminate any latent anti-establishment tendencies: individuals transgress the laws and customs for three days, only to return afterwards to the authority of law and order. The Brazilian government has started to give subsidies to the famous schools of samba. And the people who participate in them believe that such 'generosity' has no strings attached; in reality the authorities demand in return that the schools censor the stories, the fables they use, to bend them to suit the dominant ideology. For this reason the schools of samba perform the history of Brazil from the *descobrimento* (discovery) up to establishment of the Bolsa de Valores do

Rio de Janeiro (Rio Stock Exchange). Those who sing of this 'progress' are the same exploited and starving people who made it possible, thanks to the inhuman exploitation of labour of which they are victims and which made the stock markets more lucrative.

The political theatre before 1964 also used folklore: it used to present songs and dances, sometimes in conventional form and sometimes introducing original changes; for instance, the well-known dance *'Bumba meu boi'*,[5] during which a symbolic bullock is quartered and its parts offered to the people present, according to their just desserts; the heart is given to someone you wish well, the shit to someone you wish evil, the horns to an unhappy husband, and so on with all the rest of the bullock's body parts. At the end of the dance, the bullock is once again reassembled and comes back to life. In the province of Bahia, a Popular Centre of Culture presented a version of *'Bumba meu boi'*, in which the bull was Brazil and its quartered parts were stolen by foreign companies – the mineral companies, the coffee exporters, the oil companies, etc. In accordance with tradition, at the end the bullock was reassembled (as revolutionary Brazil) and counter-attacked its butcher who, suffice to say, was dressed in blue and red, with a star-spangled top hat.

So we can acknowledge that it is true that the popular theatre does not deal with neuroses or love triangles, just as the bourgeois theatre does not denounce the interference of the US in the internal affairs of Central America, or Standard Oil's interference in countries throughout the world.

5. Roughly, 'Bang went my bullock'!

2 The second category of popular theatre

From the popular perspective but aimed at another audience

IN countries like Brazil there is also a professional theatre, subject to the vagaries of success or failure, which is dependent on the consumption of the bourgeois or petit-bourgeois audience – on how many of these people buy what the theatre has to sell, i.e., tickets – and on the support of the constituted governments – which are almost always anti-popular – in the form of subsidies. Is this theatre condemned to be a bourgeois theatre, to serve the interests of the dominant classes? The proof that this need not be the case can be found in the period of the Nazi occupation of France: Sartre wrote *The Flies*, Picasso *Desire Caught by the Tail* etc., carefully disguised works which, far from pandering to the desires of the pro-Nazi government, actually revealed the necessity of struggle against that government. A theatre whose meaning was disguised but perceptible to the audience it was aimed at.

We must make this fundamental point absolutely clear: a show is 'popular' as long as it assumes the perspective of the people in the analysis of the social microcosm which appears in it – the social relations of the characters, etc. – even if it is performed in front of a single spectator, even if that single spectator is only present at a rehearsal, or even if the rehearsal takes place in front of an empty auditorium – and even when its destined audience is not the people. The mere presence of the people does not *per se* determine the popular character of the show; often the people are present as victim of a theatre show.

It could be objected: if the destined audience is not the people, why do this type of theatre? That is the question, more often that not the accusation, directed at groups of the left who try to make popular theatre for paying publics in conventional auditoria. Such accusers say that popular theatre made for the bourgeoisie is useless.

If we let ourselves be guided by language alone, this reasoning might appear correct, but once we take reality into account we can ascertain that this is not the case. In reality, the so-called 'bourgeois' public is not made up exclusively or even predominantly of bourgeois people. In Brazil at least, it also includes petit-bourgeois, bank clerks, students and teachers, liberal professionals, etc. who, as a consequence of their alienation, often accept bourgeois ideology, without enjoying the advantages of the bourgeoisie; they think like the bourgeois, but do not eat like them. They are middle-class people. They have the same ideology because they are subjected to the broadcast and printed media and other means of diffusion of information, which are the property of the bourgeoisie and consequently transmit the bourgeoisie's ideas and opinions – newspapers, TV, radio, advertising, universities, etc. But as they are for the most part hybrid people – thinking like bourgeois people without reaping bourgeois benefits – their political convictions are open to modification or substitution. If this public is able to see a play which presents a social problem from the people's perspective rather than from a class perspective (which is invariably the case) – it is very probable that its social thought will be enriched and that this richness will qualitatively change the audience. Let us not delude ourselves: the bourgeois audience actually contains a mere 10 per cent of bourgeois people: the rest are aspiring. Let us not forget that in capitalist societies, or societies that are tributaries of capitalism, the bourgeoisie is actually made up of a very small number of people – this being the principal reason why we must fight against the injustices of the inequitable division of wealth. In Latin America at least, we cannot abandon the public which habitually goes to the theatre, just because we label them as 'bourgeois'.

The fact that shows from the popular perspective are presented for this kind of public serves, in the main, to sharpen the contradictions of the bourgeois. This type of theatre sets itself against the means of information controlled by the bourgeoisie and the official media, offering the middle class, in exchange, the people's information.

Nixon spoke of 'the silent majority': who are they? Those people who by virtue of their social condition are actually nearer to the people but, as a result of the deformation they suffer, feel closer to the 'status quo'. It is a fact that reactionary governments, and the right in general, fight for the hearts and minds of this great mass of people, and for this very reason the theatre of the left must also struggle to win it over; the majority becomes silent when it does not know what it wants to say, when it does not possess the necessary information to decide. It would be an artistic crime not to try to offer them that data so that they can break their silence. This majority is taught love of country, obedience for laws, respect for supreme heroes and, it follows, that if the laws of the country order aviation heroes to drop napalm bombs on women and children in Vietnam, one of the poorest peoples in the world, they do so. It is no wonder that this majority remain silent, its moral values destroyed, its convictions enfeebled, while the Nixons of this world continue to bellow hypnotic words (law and order and the like) in their ears. Our duty is to proclaim our truths as well.

To enable people to speak is to enable them to become part of the struggle of this century, to become involved in the highest human objectives of this historic moment: the humanisation of mankind.

The bourgeoisie is very clever; in Brazil – and throughout Latin America – it prescribes the theatre to be dispensed to the public, though it abstains from consuming it. The sponsors of the most successful TV programmes charge their executives with the task of monitoring the social index of the audience. They prescribe the poison, whilst cleverly taking care not to ingest it themselves.

THEATRE WHOSE CONTENT IS IMPLICIT

There are shows and plays which do not immediately reveal their true significance; in this genre we might include the previously cited play by Lope de Vega, *The King is the Best Justice*, played to a paying audience. When the need for agrarian reform was being discussed in Brazil, various theatres showed Brecht's *The Caucasian Chalk Circle*, to show, by means of a fable, that the land belongs to the people who work it. Evidently, after so many centuries of fighting over the ownership of land, in which it seemed perfectly just and natural that a particular person should be lord and master of kilometres and kilometres of land, and lord and master of the people who lived in that land – after so many centuries in which inhumanity passed for the Law of God – it was difficult to convince even the peasant himself of the fact that the land belongs to everyone, as does the air and the water. Confronted with the idea of agrarian reform the peasant, himself the principal victim of this established injustice, felt like a usurper (just as the victims of the slave trade, when given freedom, continued to think of themselves as slaves). For centuries, the peasants have been on the receiving end of endless sermons on theft and sin: the world is changing and today sin and theft are the province of the *latifundia* (the concentrations of huge land-ownership in the hands of a few families). Brecht's play shows that the son belongs to Grusha and not to the person who gave birth to him; he belongs to the person who watched him grow, the person who educated him and taught him all that he knew, and not to the princess who abandoned him; the land, like the son, belongs to the person who makes it productive and not the person who may be able to show legal title to it.

In Europe, during the Nazi occupation, many texts were performed from the perspective of the resistance, including Sartre's *The Flies*, which has already been cited; the audience may have included people who did not resist. In São Paulo some political people demonstrated in the street with the slogan 'With God, for the Family and Freedom'. In a Tartuffian way they were affirming that only they knew how to interpret the word of God. For this reason we presented Molière's *Tartuffe* for mixed audiences, heterogeneous audiences, which also included many people who had marched in the streets and who, in the show, saw themselves demystified.

When the government of the dictatorship harped on about the corruption of the governments prior to the *coup* of 1964, we mounted Gogol's *The Government Inspector*, giving greater prominence to ideas the text already contained: the conceit that the primary corruption in underdeveloped and dependent countries like our own resides in accepting the exercise of power, even if this power is already a subordinated power. The governments of Brazil seek to proclaim its political independence while every day falling deeper and deeper into more ignominious dependence on imperialism. This was the 'original sin' of corruption in this country.

THEATRE WHOSE CONTENT IS EXPLICIT

This type of theatre has few means of subsistence. When the popular perspective is openly shown for an audience which is not the people, censorship usually makes an appearance. In São Paulo we did a 'Paulista Fair of Opinion' in which we invited six playwrights, six composers and an infinity of plastic artists to give their views of the dictatorship. The show became a veritable trial of the local government. Each artist used his work (10- or 20-minute theatre scenes, songs and plastic works) to give his opinion on Brazil 1968. One told the story of a fisherman who was arrested because he was the only one on that beach who knew how to read and write, for which reason the authorities suspected him. Another scene showed various gorillas censoring a theatre text. A third told of the misery of the interior of the province. Another was about how the mass media worked as a mechanism for conditioning public opinion and another was a collage of texts by Fidel Castro and Che Guevara on guerrilla warfare. As may be imagined, this type of theatre is only possible at special moments of liberalism. Soon after this the second fascist military *coup* took place, in December 1968.

3 The third category of popular theatre

From an anti-people perspective and aimed at the people – populist theatre!

THIS third category is the only one abundantly patronised by the dominant classes, which have always made use of art in general and the theatre in particular as an efficient instrument for the formation of popular opinion. It is, at the same time, the single category which really has nothing of the popular (in the true sense of the word) about it, except its appearance. Theatre includes the vast majority – if not the totality – of TV series, cinema films ('made in the USA') and most of the plays presented 'on Broadway', 'on Calle Corrientes', 'on Avenida Copacabana' and all the other 'ons'.

The dominant classes employ two main tactics to inject their own ideology into the people:

- They avoid subject matter of any real importance to society, any all-embracing social discussions, by restricting the story and the characters to the minute microcosm of the spectator. By means of an empathy which subjugates the spectator, reducing him to impotence, society is shown through the perspectives of individuals whose problems can be resolved exclusively within the realm of the individual. All problems are individual and consequently so are all the solutions. All the characters accept the prevailing morality – when they don't, they are punished. Vice and sin, i.e, the rejection of established rules, are always punished.

- They give prominence to, and thus reinforce, actual or fictional characteristics or ideas which perpetuate the current situation, such as the 'docility' of slaves, women's ability to cook and keep house, the 'goodness' of the peasants, the 'aversion to violence' of factory workers, etc. This process is laid out in stark relief when we analyse characters of such works as *The Teahouse of the August Moon*, *Gunga Din*, and others (see pages 230 and 231).

This category can also be presented either in an explicit manner (much less dangerous for being so manifest) or an implicit manner. We must always be aware that the mere presence of the people is not sufficient to verify the classification of a show as 'popular'. In this category the people are the victim, whether the shows are mounted in circus rings, stadia, public squares or wherever. Any real judgement of the quality of the popular involves the content of the work, the way in which the subject-matter is focused.

THE EXPLICITLY ANTI-POPULAR CATEGORY

This category does not tend to produce very efficient results because its anti-popular propositions are too obvious. Moral Rearmament, a rightist organisation, practises this type of theatre, informed by a general notion that it is a matter of urgent priority 'to purify our souls', so that mankind may healthily transform society. In Brazil they have come up with various shows bearing the names of animals – *The Condor*, *The Tiger* and I don't know what other animals. *The Tiger* dealt with a Japanese bourgeois family, very rich but at the same time very unfortunate; the father was adulterous, the mother was depressed, the son smoked marijuana, the daughter hung out with a bad crowd (and evidently had lost her virginity at a tender age). The author – my own opinion is that the play was written by a computer, but let us admit the existence of an author – with a curious analysis of cause and effect, blames the situations exposed for the fact that the workers – having been shown such bad examples by their bosses – are becoming ever more impatient and recalcitrant, till they reach the point of striking and, even worse, of demanding salary increases, an absolutely absurd presumption (according to the author of the play).

The theoretical philosopher of the 'Rearmament' is Doctor Frank Buchman, author of *The Magnificent Experiment*. According to the members of the organisation, a reading of 40-odd pages of the book was sufficient immediately to set in motion a change in the reader's soul. In *The Tiger*, a friend of the bourgeois character gives him a copy of the book, which he reads, and suddenly the miracle takes place; he feels that a purification of his soul is the only solution likely to resolve his differences with his workers. He dismisses his lover – who loses her job without having any recourse to an employment tribunal – and returns to his nice house where he blurts out to his wife and his sons the noble propositions that now guide him. Even though they have not read the book, the poor wife's health improves, the son lays off the drugs (here is a splendid suggestion for detoxification units in hospitals which use more complicated and expensive procedures than a simple reading of Buchman's book) and the daughter, finally, resolves to marry one of her lovers.

When the workers are informed of these spectacular changes, they decide to send a deputation to the boss to tell him that they have now withdrawn all their demands – including the wage rise – since they have now understood the innumerable difficulties involved in doing business and absorbing so much profit.

When I tell it like this, it sounds unbelievable; but take my word for it, no-one told me this story, I saw it with my own eyes at the Municipal Theatre of São Paulo with free entry for the general public. The only time the people can get into the Municipal Theatre here in Brazil is to see things like this.

After the play, there followed a pot-pourri of personal testimonies. When all is said and done, the play was a fiction and ran a serious risk of not convincing the spectators. For this reason, it became necessary to have live witnesses, *théâtre-vérité*. The witnesses – people who had read the famous book – came on and told their experiences 'before and after'. A certain Dutch millionaire, who was part of this group, was apparently a racist prior to his reading of the book, whereupon he immediately started loving everyone. Another used to hate poor people and, afterwards, began to give charitable donations; there was also a dangerous urban guerrilla who, having read the book, was revealing himself as an extremely open-minded man with great love for the authorities in his country.

The procession of witnesses playing this tune culminated in the grand finale, the appearance of a very aged red-skinned man – he was over 90 and toothless – who made his entry singing and dancing in true Hollywood Indian style. After his choreographic exhibition, the facilitator asked him about his experience of the book; the old man answered in all seriousness that he had once been a cannibal, but since his reading of the book, he hadn't even been able to eat a hamburger. I swear that I saw this.

Clearly, such shows – however strongly they may offer their

advice to their patrons – are far from effective in changing hearts and minds. Audiences will not let themselves be taken in so easily. For this reason, in Brazil at least, such manifestations have now ceased, though we still continue to be inundated with texts whose ideology is implicitly anti-popular.

IMPLICITLY ANTI-POPULAR IDEOLOGY

It is now some years since the State Department of the USA mounted a tour of Latin America by a Mexican company of John Patrick's work *The Teahouse of the August Moon*. Some innocent – or interested – critics heaped praise of this demonstration of liberalism by the State Department, interpreting the event as a further proof of its beneficence with respect to the arts. The piece introduced us to Sakini, a lively and quick-witted native of Okinawa, who ran the whole gamut of practical jokes and mockery at the expense of the North American colonel who was head of the occupation forces on the island. The colonel, at first with great reluctance and then increasing pleasure, began to assimilate the customs of the natives. In actual fact, the colonel was the butt of continual ridicule, but only in respect of his habitual incompetence and his fear in the face of new situations. At no time did the play debate the fundamental problem, the fact that Okinawa was occupied and that the colonel was the chief of these occupying forces. Unconsciously, the play sought to convince its audience of the possibility of peaceful cohabitation with the North American invaders. As long as we allow the occupation of our countries, we may be permitted to take the mickey out of them from time to time. These Yankee occupiers are such good guys that these things hardly bother them at all. *The Teahouse* might appear to be an example of liberalism but, in reality, it is a piece of propaganda which acts on the unconscious, a political weapon.

To criticise appearances whilst avoiding the truly fundamental themes – this is the most dangerous technique. Plays of this kind, whose reactionary content is often difficult to spot, abound on TV and in the official stage media. An example is *O Demonio Familiar* (The Devil You Know) by the Brazilian writer José de Alencar, whose Protagonist is a slave who arouses the spectator's sympathy with his never-ending trickery, his cunning, his crafty intelligence. At the same time it shows the great affection he feels for his masters and the tenderness with which they treat him; when he is administered a punishment, it is only to try to 'correct him'. But hand in hand with the punishment, what affection the masters display! The punishment serves to make him better. How better? A better slave . . . Ah yes, the play avoids any debate about the rights and wrongs of slavery.

The North Americans are masters of this type of political theatre, and they flood us with works like *Born Yesterday*, which features a single corrupt senator (amongst the hundreds who are not!) and *The Best Man*, whose story deals with two candidates for the Presidency of the Republic who start a defamatory campaign against each other, laying bare all the corruption at the heart of the system of nomination for candidature; the author takes care, of course, to signal that neither of the two cheats will be elected. The 'best man' of the title is a third candidate, and sure enough, he is of impeccable reputation.

During my childhood, I saw a film which infuriated me, though it was very well made: *Gunga Din*. It was the story of a Hindu 'native' who dreamed of being a bugler for Her Majesty, the Queen (of England, that is, not India). The forces of liberation appear in the film as 'hordes of fanatics and barbarians . . . with a thirst for blood'. Driven by his dream and by his dedication to the foreign country, Gunga Din denounces the presence of soldiers of the liberation forces, blowing his bugle and alerting the English soldiers to the imminent mortal danger facing them. Gunga Din is killed and decorated with a posthumous medal. A more blatant example of cynicism would be difficult to find in any cinema anywhere; to decorate a traitor and to offer him as an example. I was young when I saw this film and I still remember it today with rage.

The cinema is even fuller than the theatre of examples of 'natives' depicted with great 'charm', with great gusto, especially in respect of any of their characteristics which relate to their 'underdevelopment'. Zorba the Greek, so comical and so stupid, tries to solve the problem of the transport of wood, but he fails. By happy chance, along comes some imperialist 'know-how' to teach him how it should be done (and how to pay them royalties). The fact that subliminal ideological propaganda is more intensely disseminated in the cinema is easily understandable, since the production of films – as it requires large capital resources – is a much more industrialised process than the theatre; in the theatre, producers with comparatively little capital can still produce shows at low cost. The more expensive the production, the greater the imposition of capitalist ideology.

231

Georges Sadoul wrote in one of his books that at a certain point the Hollywood industry made a decision to recommend and indeed demand from its writers only three basic types of film.

- **The 'self-made man' genus**: this genre is based on a notion of individual initiative, according to which everyone can reach the highest position even if they start from the most lowly condition. For example, Abraham Lincoln, woodcutter, gets to be President of the Republic. Of course, this example actually constitutes the exception to the rule, though it seeks to affirm that all woodcutters can be presidents; a unique case is presented as an example. The unique is reconfigured into the universal.

- **The 'salt of the earth' genus**: in this genre, we are sold the idea that not all woodcutters would in fact enjoy becoming president – that the fact of attainment is not the most important thing, since true happiness can be found in simpler things. The 'salt of the earth' characters of the title are, as a rule, poor but happy people, happy in spite of hunger and poverty, always willing to give what they have to those who have even less. 'The best things in life are free', according to the North American song; its advice, on similar lines, is that one should not desire wealth, given that it does not bring happiness.

  Also within this genre is the story of the peasant who lived close to a river and worked from dawn to dusk, feeding himself only a single apple which the river brought him every day, by the grace of God. One day he protested and God sent an angel to him as an emissary. The angel transported him down the river and showed him another peasant who, like him, worked the land from dawn to dusk and, in return, ate only the peel that the first peasant threw away, which the river washed up every evening. Maybe, the angel explained to him, we should not bemoan our lot or protest, because there is always someone worse off than ourselves. Having imparted this great lesson, the angel flew back, high above the river (this time on his own) and – though the story doesn't usually include this passage, it needs telling – joined all the other angels and *latifundiários* from whose table, groaning with delicacies, each morning a single apple fell down into the river; still higher in the sky than the angels was God, from whose table fell banquets.

- **The 'highlife' genus**: for all those who were still doubters, Hollywood commissioned films about 'highlife', crammed to the gills with swimming pools, beautiful women and tedium. The richer the character the unhappier! So no-one in their right mind would want to be rich.

4 The fourth category of popular theatre

Newspaper Theatre

THE growing fascist repression which followed the second dictatorship coup of 13 December 1968 led to military and political intervention in almost all the unions, schools and faculties, with tactics which included the infiltration of spies amongst the workers and the students. The mounting of popular shows which might command a 'mass' presence by the people became almost impossible. From 1968 onwards, the production of 'popular' shows became impracticable, apart from those which were clearly identifiable as 'anti-popular', such as a smattering of musicals mounted directly by the government. At the same time, there were frequent occasions when festivals, which had no political content but were sponsored by unions, resulted in the mass imprisonment of the workers present. Unions and universities turned into dangerous meeting places. Such events signalled the necessity to create a new category of popular theatre, in which the people – the people themselves – would make the theatre rather than simply receiving it as consumers.

As we have seen, in the first category of popular theatre, the show is presented with the people's perspective and for the people themselves; in the second, with the people's perspective but for a different target audience; and in the third category, though the people may be considered its target audience, the work presents a perspective contrary to the people's interests, reflecting the ideology of the dominant classes. In Newspaper Theatre – the fourth category of popular theatre – the theatre is made by the people and for the people. In the first three categories, the people receive, consume, are passive; in Newspaper Theatre, for the first time, the people are creative agents, and not merely the inspiration for or the consumers of the show. The people are active; they make the theatre. In the first three categories the mediating presence of 'the artist' is interposed, while in Newspaper Theatre the people themselves are the artist, eliminating the 'artist–spectator' duality.

Newspaper Theatre seeks to popularise the 'means of making theatre' so that the people themselves can use them and make their own theatre. To use the analogy present in the title of this method – though we have our own presses, we don't try to print our own paper and make it popular; our endeavour is to hand over our presses to the people, so they can print their own paper. For this reason the means utilised are very simple: the first show which we produced with this form of Newspaper Theatre was called *First Edition*, and it was a demonstration of theatrical techniques.

The primary objective of Newspaper Theatre is to devolve theatre to the people. The secondary objective is to attempt to demystify the pretended 'objectivity' of most journalism, to show that all news published in the paper is a work of fiction at the service of the dominant class. Even accurate news, where the facts are not mis-represented (a very rare thing), becomes fiction when published in a newspaper at the service of this class.

The importance of a piece of news and the significance we attribute to it depends on its relationship with the rest of the paper. If, on the front page of a newspaper, we read a story about a young woman miraculously saved after having set fire to her clothes as a result of a disappointment in love, the fact that this tragedy is front-page news reduces events like the criminal massacres of Song My in the Vietnam war to the status of mere *faits divers*, just another story. These crimes of imperialism appear as natural, acceptable, quotidian, alongside the sensational suicide attempt. What is more important: the fate of the Brazilian team in the World Cup or the government's lack of concern for the fate of millions of peasants dying of hunger in north-east Brazil? The headlines of the papers are plastered with the national team's goals, rather than with photos of infant mortality, an area in which Brazil leads the world. In *Citizen Kane*, Orson Welles stated with good reason: 'No news is important enough to merit a newspaper headline; but if any news is printed as a headline in any paper, then it becomes an important piece of news.' Thus, public opinion is manipulated; the process is simple and painless. The presence of 'accurate' news, devalued by its dispersal throughout the paper, and by the layout of the paper as a whole, seeks to give the impression of 'impartiality'; when in actual fact, the placing of each piece of news gives it a very particular weight. An important element

235

of Newspaper Theatre – and one of its principal objectives – is to teach people to 'read' newspapers correctly.

Newspaper Theatre constitutes something closer to the 'reality' of the facts, because it presents the news item directly to the spectator without the mediating influence of placing and layout. Some of its techniques, such as 'improvisation', are reality itself; here the idea is not simply to show a scene but to live it each time – and on each occasion, it is unique; like each fact, each instant, each emotion. The event or fact is presented without adjectivisation; the spectator looks straight at it from his own perspective, informed by his own political position. There is no deforming mediation. 'Reality' emerges right in front of the observer. In other techniques, however, Newspaper Theatre is also fiction, as is the case with 'rhythmical reading'.

The third objective of the Newspaper Theatre is to demonstrate that theatre can be practised by anyone (even though they may not be an 'artist'), just as anyone can play football, even though they may not be an athlete, in any place, even though it may not be a regulation football pitch. Of course, to play in the national squad it is necessary to be an athlete, and a good one at that, but anyone can play in their own back garden. Just as the pleasure of a hard-fought game between amateurs does not depend on the refined execution of a shot, the pleasure of making theatre in a room, in the hall of a union or in a tenants' hall or wherever, does not depend on the exquisite perfection of the Berliner Ensemble; anyone and everyone, whoever they may be, can defend their ideas by various means, and theatre is one of them. We can defend our ideas in a meeting without recourse to oratorical skill. We can also show and defend our ideas in the theatre without it being necessary for us to have refined our dramatic art. And in the same way as all people are potentially 'theatre artists', so also all spaces are potentially 'dramatic spaces' and all subjects are potentially 'dramatic subjects'. Everything can be theatricalised: items in the papers, political discourses, jingles, didactic books – one of the 40 or 50 existing Newspaper Theatre groups in Brazil specialises in showing 'corrected' versions of books used in history lessons in Brazil; others use the Bible, documentary films, statistics etc.

NEWSPAPER THEATRE: THE FIRST 11 TECHNIQUES

Newspaper Theatre owes its name to the nucleus group of the Arena Theatre of São Paulo, because when it first started investigating these techniques this group used news items from newspapers. However, the application of these techniques is not limited to news stories from the papers; it is equally efficacious if used with the minutes of discussions, acts of assemblies, chapters of books – when it comes down to it, it can work with any written texts.

The name 'newspaper' is also valid in the sense that the majority of these techniques are born out of the demystification and decon-struction of the habitual techniques of journalism. Every form of fiction has its own specific techniques and this applies equally to 'journalism-fiction'. The novel utilises fable, the realist theatre uses the conflict of free wills, lyric poetry uses the poet's subjective vision of the external reality which stimulates him or her. Journalism utilises the techniques of organising the layout of the articles: in this resides its fictional character. As a weapon, it is used on behalf of some and against others. And, like private property, it is used by its proprietors on behalf of the dominant classes.

1 The simple reading

Those who defend the idea that journalism is 'objective' assert that a news story can relate a particular event exactly as it happened. And this is true. But the reader of a newspaper does not read 'the news'; he reads 'the paper'. Which is to say: he has in front of him a front page, a middle page, a last page. Will a piece of news have the same 'objective' value regardless of whether it is published on the front page or the final page? Newspapers use various typefaces, ranging from the very large, which is visible at a distance, to the very small, which is lost in the body of the newspaper. Sometimes, the overall look of the newspaper orients the 'translation' that the reader must make of the news. In Buenos Aires there is a newspaper, which usually publishes more photos of cows, bullocks, calves and bovine livestock in general, than of human beings. And in the latter category, they often have pictures of Nixon and Kissinger, and local person-alities of the same ideology. An 'objective' news item published by the aforementioned paper, even if it had been edited by Marx, in close collaboration with Lenin, Mao and Fidel, would most certainly acquire an anti-popular meaning. The news of the struggles of workers in Córdova does not have the same meaning when read in isolation as it does if it is printed beside a photo of a cow fraternising with Nixon. The meaning changes, obviously.

Thus, the first technique of Newspaper Theatre consists of reading the news item, clearly and sincerely, without comment or commentary. It consists of extracting the news story from the layout imposed by the newspaper's proprietor and reading it out loud.

When the ex-president of Uruguay, Pacheco Areco, gave a reception in honour of the yankee ambassador, all the papers published news of the banquet. During a theatre show mounted in the Peñarol stadium, the actors of the Theatre Club of Montevideo decided to read the menu from the Areco banquet. That's all; just to read the names (which could almost be called titles) of the dishes on the menu. During the reading of the hors d'oeuvres the audience burst out laughing. The choicest delicacies were on offer. The caviar was not just any old caviar but a caviar which is produced by a particular kind of salmon in a specific part of Russia at a particular time of year; the white wine was of a particular vintage, from a particular part of Germany, etc. When they got to the pheasants, the audience stopped laughing; by means of this laying out of the news in its reality, and not in the pages of the bourgeois papers, the audience made its own connection with the fact that the same president had recently banned the eating of beef for four months across the whole country, to favour the export market: he had recently decreed the spectre of hunger! No-one felt like laughing at the fact that the president and his friends should be stuffing themselves with 'Bellavista lobsters prepared with anchovies imitating dolphins pushing the carriage of the God Neptune, stuffed with fruits de mer' or a 'Cutlet of veal Menonville à la Marsala with duchess potatoes and clusters of watercress decorated en papillote with papier glacé'.

When they started to name the desserts, the people gathered in the Peñarol stadium were no longer laughing. Here, with a simple reading of an item of news, was a graphic demonstration of the profound injustice of a class system which enslaves and reduces to hunger the majority of human beings in order to allow a few to enjoy all the pleasures. No mass discussion was necessary, no political lecture; a simple reading of Pacheco Areco's menu was enough, once it was separated from the layout of the papers which supported the same Pacheco.

2 The complementary reading

One of the techniques most used by the bourgeois press consists of highlighting a single detail to give a completely different meaning to the news. Sometimes, the lack of a word or a phrase gives a particular slant to the reality presented; in this case the news is not false, it is incomplete, and, by this means, the way the news item will be received is adulterated, and reality is deformed, paradoxically, by means of genuine information.

A newspaper published information about Paraguay in its tourism section. Everything they printed there gave the impression that Paraguay was a land where all the people were happy, friendly etc. As for Paraguayan restaurants, the paper reported that 'its beefsteaks are the best in the world, not only in terms of size but also in their quality'. The item begged to be completed: 'the steaks served in the main restaurants cost 15 dollars, while the monthly per capita income in this country is under 30 dollars. The beef may be the best in the world – this may be the truth but it is part of the truth, and therefore this partial presentation of the truth lied about reality. Paraguayan steaks are the best, but they are not the best for the Paraguayan people, who are prohibited from eating them.'

During the last election campaign, in which the life-president Stroessner tried to make believe that his country was a democracy; the dictator plastered the country with posters which read: 'If you love liberty, vote for Stroessner'. And it was the truth, but only half of the truth and therefore it was mendacious. This advertisement lacked the complementary information which would have turned it into the whole truth. And so someone supplied it on a poster at Assunção Airport, by writing underneath: 'because if you don't, the police will come looking for you in your home'. This complementary annotation restored the truth of the advertisement: 'if you love liberty, vote for the dictator, who has ways of knowing who each person votes for, and ways of incarcerating all those who do not agree.' The prisons in Paraguay are full.

A Bolivian paper criticising the transitional regime in Chile, in Allende's time, affirmed: 'In Chile there are queues for everything; in Bolivia the shop windows are crammed'. And, in part, it was true. But it was necessary to complement this news: 'Because in Chile, up until September 1973, the purchasing power of the people permitted them to eat, while in Bolivia the people, enslaved by their own oligarchy and by Brazilian sub-imperialism, are used to walking along the

1. This was written
before the bloody
fascist coups of
Pinochet and friends.
[Footnote in the
original text. A.J.]

street without being able to afford to go into the shops – whose products thus stay in the window waiting for a rich man to pass.[1] And that completes the news.

During the month of July (their Spring), and in the Summer months, the Rua Florida in Buenos Aires is packed with Brazilian tourists: these tourists are the middle and upper class of the few cities where the national wealth is concentrated. A shop in Rua Florida used to advertise the prices for Brazilians in cruzeiros. The advertisements demanded to be complemented: 'A pullover for 50 cruzeiros, plus one person tortured by the Political Police, whose officers work on a 24-hour rota, in permanent teams of torturers, to ensure that the people accept low wages. The price of a pair of shoes is 80 cruzeiros (plus the censorship of the press); the price of a week in Bariloche is only 1,000 cruzeiros all inclusive, flight, breakfast and lunch, ski-ing lessons and, for sure, a national congress where any-thing can be discussed, except politics.'

3 The crossed reading

Sometimes in the papers, they publish news items which contradict each other or give the lie to each other – or, if they are linked together in a crossed reading, one can complete the other's meaning.

In a carriage on the train line which rises from the river Tigre in Buenos Aires, the Newspaper Theatre Group Team performed a crossed reading of two news items; the first was the legal decree instituting a state of emergency in the province of San Juan, in the light of an increase in infant mortality which had reached dangerous levels as a result of demographic underdevelopment. This news item was crossed with a report about Mirtha Legrand, a very well-known actress thanks to the TV programme *Lunching with Mirtha Legrand*, in which she used to interview well-known people from artistic and political life; in the report, she was asked if, apart, from her famous TV lunches, she was also in the habit of taking dinner. This woman, who made herself famous by eating in front of the cameras, answered in the affirmative, that she liked to dine, but never invited more than 10 people a night, for fear that the conversation might become too fragmented; apart from which, she always had a few surprises in store for her guests. For instance, when everyone was expecting that the dinner would start with cooked ham, she served them fine French cheeses. And the report on the famous gastronome went on from surprise to surprise, each dish cross-read with news items on the death of children in San Juan, from malnutrition.

4 The rhythmical reading

All rhythm 'filters' the news according to the connotations usually attributed to this rhythm. It works well, for instance, 'to sing' a speech by a well-known politician, in which he laments not having won the elections, as if it were a tango. The public utterances of the self-proclaimed Brazilian government acquire their true meaning to the sound of 'Lili Marlene'.

The rhythm, in this case, does not have to be especially 'musical' — that it to say, it can use repetitions and refrains and other devices more usually identified with poetry. Or forms of poetic declamation which are already more or less ritualised. For example: Nixon defends himself against the accusation of spying on the Democrats in Watergate, declaiming like Berta Singerman. It greatly enhances his performance.

5 The reinforced reading

Advertising directs itself at the few who have money to spend to persuade them to buy more than they actually need. In countries like ours in Latin America, where the production of material goods is not sufficient for the basic needs of our peoples, the advertising of even these goods is grotesque and absurd. Close to a shanty town in Buenos Aires, there used to be an enormous billboard advising the people to drink milk, while in this slum hundreds of children were dying precisely for lack of milk.

To get good results, advertising uses the most irrational methods possible. It can never speak the truth, the truth does not suit it; for this reason, it uses simple music, easily reproducible jingles; it uses photos of pretty girls; it uses short phrases designed to make an impact, in spite of the fact that they are meaningless. Categoric statements; 'If it's Bayer, its good'. (The proof of its efficacy is that the napalm produced by Bayer is distinctly superior to any other company's.)

Advertising is not used only for the sale of material products; it is also used to sell 'images'. The international image of the self-proclaimed Brazilian government is very bloody. So it uses advertising to create a more acceptable image for itself. It uses the same techniques as the cigarette companies, with the same lack of shame. It fills the radio and TV slots with phrases devoid of real meaning. These phrases can be used as 'reinforcement' for the better understanding of certain news items.

In the same way that however beautiful the girl who advertises a cigarette, it will do nothing to reduce the number of cancers caused by smoking, however hypnotic the Brazilian government's advertising it does nothing to alleviate the problem of hunger or to reduce the number of prisons.

The bishops of the north-east of Brazil, amongst them Dom Helder Camara, published a document which the censors then banned, in which they declared: 'In contrast to government declarations, the people live in a state of hunger, epidemics and unemployment'. (REINFORCEMENT: the actors sing 'My Brazil, I love you, my Brazil, I love you', the propaganda anthem of the dictatorship.) '200 thousand inhabitants of the north-east suffer Chaga's disease; in every thousand people, 80 die of tuberculosis'. (REINFORCE-MENT: The actors chant 'Brazil – love it or leave it', a well-known slogan of the dictatorship). These slogans, used here as reinforcement, are much heard on TV, even in programmes presented by people who know full well the reality of our national situation, but feel no shame in profiting from the poverty of their people.

6 The parallel action

This consists of miming actions which contradict or complement the news item which is being read by an actor.

The Senzala group, to show the lack of serious commitment on the part of some of the intellectuals who participated in the Inconfidência Mineira, an eighteenth-century rebellion against Portugal, read texts by these intellectuals and mimed actions in opposition to the bravery proclaimed: scenes showing the 'literary guerrilla' at work, in which many fine words are spoken and much is drunk, but little is done. A text which appears to be revolutionary is read against a background of scenes of the literary salon, revealing the lack of sincerity behind the words – easier to talk than to do.

7 The historical reading

This consists of relating the news item together with facts related to the story. It can be done in various ways; for instance, a news item which deals with the low wages paid to workers today can be preceded by a scene showing the same type of relationship between a slave and his master, in times when slavery was openly practised in Brazil. Or, as happened in my play *Zumbi*,[2] the struggle for freedom of the Brazilian people of today is narrated as the struggle for the liberation of slaves in the eighteenth century. Or the comparison can be between different countries in the same epoch, a piece of news about an Argentine labour problem can be preceded by a scene which presents the same problem sucessively in Brazil, Peru and Cuba. The various different possible solutions (or absence of solution) are presented as alternatives. How did other people deal with this, when and in what conditions. This need not be about following examples, but having real historical alternatives in front of us, not to follow them, but to study them.

2. *Arena Conta Zumbi* (The Arena Tells of Zumbi), possibly Boal's most successful play with the Arena theatre of São Paulo, told the story of the famous slave leader, relating it to modern times.

8 Improvisation

This may be the most commonly used technique. The improvisation can be done starting from a basic outline or not.

In Guayaquil, the Student Theatre presented a show on a serious problem for this city in particular and for the whole country in general, which was (and still is) the problem of unemployment. With so little work and so many people unemployed, large numbers of men and women consider emigration to the US. Given the quantity of people who want to do this, the yankee consulate puts every possible obstacle in their way, demanding, amongst other things, an examination of the faeces of every applicant. As hygiene conditions in Guayaquil are not of the best, there is a lot of water pollution and this results in the majority of inhabitants' shit not being of the highest standard, from the yankee-medico point of view. But there was one man in the city who was the creator of the most perfect shit in all the land, in which no yankee could find even the smallest non-permissible microbe. His shit was a marvel. As might be expected, the gentleman ended up living off his own excrement, he ended up becoming his own factory, he industrialised his product, selling small quantities in match-boxes to all interested in emigration. The scenes, improvised within this general outline, showed the day to day problems arising from this phenomenon: the consul discovered the ruse and demanded that all future defecation should take place within the actual consul premises, and be caught in little jars sealed with the yankee eagle etc.

The whole show was based on improvisation and was open to modification according to any new tactics adopted by the consulate, and to the responses to these invented by the people.

Improvisations can be performed as shows in front of an audience, as well as being technique and development for the actors, especially when the latter are workers or students who do not wish to become actors themselves but simply to act.

Improvisation serves to get to know the enemy better: for instance, before a meeting with the management, the workers can improvise it, with some worker-actors taking the parts of the boss, the deputy, the manager, etc.

Improvisation can aspire to the level of 'illusion', with the actors really getting into character, or can be the mere enunciation of who or what a given character would say or do. The actor does not become totally involved, does not 'live the part', does not try to be anyone else, he merely comments: 'If I was him, I would say . . .' Or it can be a mixture – while some people live their parts, others enunciate theirs.

9 The concretion of abstraction

This consists of making visible, sensible, through the use of analogy, symbols or any other equivalent, particular words or facts which, through over-use, have lost their capacity to give rise to the corresponding emotions in the reader or spectator. This is a matter of discovering which live images are capable of making certain dead or worn-out words real in a way they have not been. The concretion can take a direct form (the physical and concrete illustration of an action; physically showing the death of a miner stuck in a mine because of an explosion which was badly planned in order to save explosives: showing a graphic image of the lungs of a worker after 30 years of breathing the polluted air of a mine, eight hours a day); or an indirect form: the exhibition of the innards of animals, the dead bodies of small animals like pigeons, the burning of puppets, etc. to symbolise the death of human beings. The means employed to make the abstract concrete can be as varied as possible, the important thing is to awaken the spectator's sensibility and capacity to absorb the news as something real and concrete.

10 Text out of context

This technique consists of reading the news in a different context from the one in which people are used to reading such news, finding a way of marking it so that the subject is seen afresh.

One time, in Argentina, an admiral was killed, shot down in the street; when the gossip columnist's style was applied to the description of the burial, a scene of terrible black humour was produced. These columnists like to describe details such as what each character is wearing. They concern themselves as much with the hat as with the head which bears it.

Describing the widow, it said: 'The colour black, refined, impeccable, set against the grey of winter and the smoke of the city, seemed the safest bet, a trump card played by all the leaders of fashion. To adopt this colour, rather than to adopt the "hit" of the moment, is to affirm a vivacious, luminous, dynamic personality. Her younger sister was the very image of a black swan, volatile, trousers almost as wide as skirts, of chalk white, with the finest trimmings from waist to ankles. The deceased . . .' And the black humour went on. No less black, no less tragic than the same process applied to the description of the burial of a child dead in some poor village, critically applying the gossip-column style to the clothes of the mother bought in the market, the patched trousers of the father, the bare feet of the brother, etc.

11 Insertion into the actual context

The most sensational programmes have a habit of showing the detail as the central fact, the accident as the essence, and by this means, with the weapons of 'objectivity', betraying the objective truth. There is a TV programme which specialises in showing the negative aspects of the city of Buenos Aires – but always chooses for its victims, for its sacrificial scapegoats, those who are least culpable. One day a child died because the doctor was unable to diagnose the real illness and gave him medicines for simple constipation when it was actually a

245

case of pneumonia. The indignant presenter commented on the fact, showing the doctor's face and exclaiming: 'Things like this still happen in a city which thinks itself civilised'. And he went on with his accusations, in the guise of brave campaigner, against the unworthy professional. But the 'objective' truth could only have been understood if this same scene, with the same words from the presenter, could have shown the real context in which the 'crime' occurred, showing in additional scenes the actual living conditions in the village, the number of children who die without any recourse to medical attention; in this particular case, the doctor, far from being irresponsible, was working most of the time without the slightest hope of payment, whilst among the indignant viewers of the programme, there were doubtless many doctors who dedicated their lives to helping fat women lose weight or to rejuvenating the looks of 50-year-olds ... To understand the doctor's problem, we have to look into the actual context, which includes other doctors and other patients.

Afterword:
The Metamorphoses of the Devil

The individual and the twenty-first century

WHEN I was little, I used to wear clogs. Till one day, I began to think it was ridiculous to wear clogs. It was not easy to make the change: I lived in Penha, a hot place, with lots of dust, normal shoes made one's feet sweat: athlete's foot on sight! The ascesis from clog to shoe was difficult. So then I said to myself, with due solemnity: 'from the first day of the New Year, I will never wear clogs again'. And the New Year came and I forgot my oath.

When I was an adolescent and began to get interested in the girls in my school, one day, the prettiest, whom I loved, expressed the sentiment that I was fatter than her aesthetic allowed. Once again, I swore passionately: 'From next year on, from the very first day of the New Year, I will never eat sweets again'. It so happened that I used to work in my father's confectionery shop, and gluttony had always been one of my favourite sins . . . New Year came and went and I steered clear of the scales.

I needed a date in order to believe that the change would be possible, a date some time in the coming year. Not today – too close and not too far in the future: at the very start of the first of January, the first minute, not a moment later. Till then, with an untroubled conscience, I would continue eating bonbons and madeleines, heavenly delicacies and 'monk's bellies', wearing clogs, getting fatter and dirtying my feet.

Today it is neither my feet nor my weight which most concern me: it is the future of humanity, a serious matter. We are so worried about our future – if only we could set a date and time for it, like making an appointment at the dentist, then we feel our future might be further from our fears and closer to our dreams.

I ate sweets thinking how handsome and slender I would be . . . next year. But next year was contained in the chocolate sorbet I was eating now. My feast in December would be January's pudginess. This is the way of the world: today we are digging the communal grave in which masses will be buried in the twenty-first century.

When I think of the future, I see it right now in Haiti – the twenty-first century is here. Rwanda, Zaire, Angola and Mozambique . . . how many Nazi holocausts have already been committed in that continent, in this decade? In Yugoslavia, Bosnia, in Indonesia, in Timor – half of the population murdered. In Brazil, the street children, the landless peasants, the workless workers. We may comfort ourselves with the thought that these countries are primitive, savage. But who sells the electronic or chemical weapons with which these troglodytes kill thousands and millions of people? The so-called civilised peoples, that's who.

We are all responsible.

International relations are motivated by the predatory instinct, as in animal man. Imperialism changes its name, but continues in the same way. Today, it is called 'globalisation'. We are told of the economic necessity of unifying the world, that we must all be part of this immense global village, administered by a single authority or government . . . not our government, that's for sure.

For us to become globalised – for us to be phagocyted – it is necessary to atomise, to isolate individuals, because, as Brecht said, if cows talked to each other they would not go so innocently to the slaughterhouse; globalisation demands the destruction of the unions – Thatcher in England, Reagan in the US, and in Brazil, each government does its bit! – any form of mass demonstration or popular organisation is made difficult – since these are occasions where dialogue might exist! – and individuals are glued to the TV screen, where monologue rules. People are brought together only in pursuit of hypnotic passions, such as football and boxing, never in fecund debate of ideas.

Culture is at the whim of the market and transforms the artist (the person who creates the new) into the artisan (the person who reproduces a model). The individual disappears, lost in the class or group to which he or she belongs.

The paradox of globalisation: to globalise, it is necessary to isolate the individual, not in order to strengthen his individuality, but to make his differences disappear, the things which render him unique. We cannot forget that our identity is created by what we are, but also by what others are, which allows us to be what we are, in our relationship with them. I am a father because I have children, a man because there are women. In the current globalism the individual is isolated so that he loses that essential part of his identity: difference. The individual is isolated so that he will lose his individuality. Individual without identity, nameless: a number! The individual is isolated so that he may become a recipient, a container into which the media and the technocratic discourse may pour contents. The individuality of the individual is kidnapped, the individual transformed into a thing. The individual, unique in himself, becomes the mass; the concretion becomes abstraction. The discontinuity between one individual and another is eliminated: the exemplar becomes the species.

The man/atom, a free radical, seeks a grouping: profane and religious sects prosper, financial miracles and religions proliferate. Globalisation wants formless or uniform masses, obedient, structured, not men and women; its intention is monologue not dialogue.

If it goes on like this, in the twenty-first century there will be no difference between one individual and another, just as there is no visible difference between one grain of sand and another, between the grain of sand and the beach. By way of contrast, I prefer to think – and I think that we should all think – that we should unite and affirm those things in which we resemble one another, yes, but also those which separate us, refusing to be globalised into a formless mass, without character.

If, magically, we were able to see the end of this century without being part of it, it would be good to observe the metamorphoses which the Devil has gone through. Lucifer was always the rebel, the contradictory one, the powerless one in search of power. The devil's temptation was always the offer of the impossible.

Who was Satan in the transition from feudalism to the bourgeois world? He was the Machiavellian hero, the man who was master of *virtù*, who in Shakespeare might be called Iago, Richard III, Lady Macbeth, and who in the books of Dale Carnegie came to be called *self-made man*, the person who can affirm his power whatever his origins. I do because I can, not because I must. The Devil – surprise, surprise! – was the Individual – his offer, freedom! In feudalism, birth prevailed – the son of the viscount was the baby viscount, the viscount to be! – man fulfilled his destiny; in the bourgeoisie, he invented it. The law of Man against the law of God, the perishable against the eternal, the Gothic style versus the Romance style.

The bourgeoisie affirmed the primacy of the individual and of freedom, but, lest anyone delude themselves on this point, not the freedom of all; if on the one hand, it confronted the nobility, on the other, in order to be victorious, it had to depend on slave labour, or something akin to it: once again the individual separated himself from the mass, from the chorus, and became Protagonist of History. The bourgeois individual placed himself at equal remove from the feudal structure and the ignorant people. This was the first modern Devil to show his face. The singular individual.

Today, the devil lurks in the stock exchanges and multinationals, the plural individual. Of course when one reads the list of the hundred wealthiest millionaires and billionaires, Mr Buffet and Bill Gates are at the head of it, but who are the actual owners of the big multinationals? Thousands of people. Even the person who owns one measly share without voting rights can think of himself as a master, an owner. Anonymous Society – the Devil in anonymity. The big Devil pulverised into millions of little devils, some larger, some smaller.

In order to grow, the Bourgeois-Renaissance-Devil – businessman, banker, shipbuilder, arms dealer – needed to destroy the customs borders between one principality and another, between duchy and earldom; it was necessary to create a single law, unifying nations. Today, imperialism needs to achieve the same goal on a world scale: to break down the frontiers of these nations – this is the meaning of globalisation: one law for all, the market. But make no mistake, these new little devils do not seek to mix; they may break down borders of nations, but not those between classes. And so borders rise up again, no longer between one country and another, but within each country. Divided cities. In the Northern hemisphere they are busy erecting walls against immigrants – here in the South they put electrified fences round their houses.

The neo-Imperialists say that globalisation is modern. Then long live the modern Roman Empire, for what was Pax Romana if not the globalisation of the power of Caesar? And Genghis Khan? And Attila, the Scourge of God, what did he want? And what did Hitler want with his thousand-year Reich, if not the same as the imperialists of today? Globalising is as modern as the Treaty of Tordesilhas which divided the world in two, half to Portugal, the other half to Spain. Today, the One Remaining Superpower wants to unify our world: a single language, a single fast food, a single film rewritten by computers a thousand times, complete with the same shots, the same blood and guts, the same blonde Barbies.

For this to happen it is important to hide the truth. 'The facts don't matter; what matters is our version of the facts!', according to a Brazilian politician.

The 'spin', rather than the truth. The thousand-fold repeated lie becomes more truthful than the silenced truth. We hear travestied lies, and we stay silent. It would be enough to look at them, to see them naked, but already we have our eyes closed. Recently we had the privatisation of Light, the electricity company. The main argument: it is modern to privatise – only private initiative can manage public utilities. They have sold the Light company to the EDF, the French state company. And they have sold the Rio electricity company to a group led by the Chilean state, where Pinochet is still the commanding officer of the army.[1] Is this what privatisation is to be? The handing over of the Brazilian economy to other governments? Of our state to other states? Haiti is here, the twenty-first century is already with us!

1. Now, in 1998, he is 'only' senator for life!

Modernity is not a value in itself, just as the values of yesteryear are not, by dint of their age, necessarily bad: the ideas of Christian solidarity have been around for almost 2,000 years now. Must we chuck them in the bin? And bombs – atomic bombs, napalm bombs – bombs are modern. Must we venerate them for their youth?

The young Barbosa Lima Sobrinho, a journalist who is 101 years of age this year (1998), has demonstrated in his Sunday column that the enormous and rich Vale do Rio Doce[2] was constructed with money raised in taxes and belongs to the people, not to the state. If statesmen who have been elected to manage the people's wealth, if these managers, today, want to sell it, at least they should ask the owners if they agree: that's what plebiscites were invented for. Paralysed, we are witnessing the transfer of funds belonging to all into the purses of the few. Robin Hood in reverse. These are our managers, these people are now in power.

2. Huge Brazilian steel company, a symbol of sovereignty until it was recently privatised.

Economists tell us that the economy is complex. It's true. But it's also true that astronomy is complicated. But, however complicated astronomy may be, there are simple truths which we can be sure of: I can swear that the sun will rise tomorrow morning, I can prohibit it from shining during the night and order it to go to bed in the afternoon! And my orders will not be contested: they will be obeyed. With astronomical rigour!

The economy is difficult, but it is easy to understand that, if state concerns like Vale yield up millions of dollars worth of profit every day for the State and therefore for the population – if they are sold and privatised, they will yield up the same profit into private purses. It's easy to understand, difficult to swallow.

It is elementary to state that we should not sell the goose that lays the golden eggs – just the eggs. And no princely ratiocination can convince us that it is better for us to unload the concerns which make a profit and keep those which lose money. That this is modern. It is easy to understand that, if we continue paying more than a billion dollars a month to service our external debt, as Brazil does now, we are enriching foreign banks and even further impoverishing our people. If the huge unproductive *latifundia* (estates) continue to be unproductive, our *favelas* will continue their demographic explosion, and earlier than we think, the whole thing will explode. Haiti is here, the twenty-first century is already with us.

Chomsky saw and stated the glaringly obvious: 'Imperialist countries want a free market for the under-developed nations, and protectionism for themselves.' The objective of neo-liberalism is to annihilate the decision-making power of the individual and give it over to the banks, the multi-nationals, and their supporters.' To render elections pointless since the citizen will only be able to choose between a burger from McDonald's or one from Burger King, but either way it will be the same burger stuffed with mad cow.

Arthur Miller, the playwright, wrote an article, 'Let's Privatise Congress!', in which he suggested that the deputies and senators should be obliged to wear shirts bearing their sponsors' colours: Texaco, Coca-cola, General Motors, like football players. Only then would we be able to tell why and for whom they were voting.

Haiti is here, the twenty-first century is already with us.

What should we expect then, we individuals, from the twenty-first century? Above all, we should not expect anything, we have to act, today, *now*. If we do not want the Thousand Year Empire to be installed in the world, if we do not want the end of History, if we still want to exist as individuals and not merely as statistics, grains of sand on the immense global beach, we must develop popular organisations which allow debate, plurality, diversity, transitivity of dialogue, rebuttal, the power to say no!

Because Haiti is everywhere, and the twenty-first century is here!